Henry Mancini

Music in American Life

*A list of books in the series appears
at the end of this book.*

Henry Mancini

Reinventing Film Music

John Caps

University of Illinois Press
Urbana, Chicago, and Springfield

Photos appear courtesy of the Henry Mancini Estate
unless otherwise noted.

Lyrics to "Moon River" courtesy of Famous Music Corp. Lyrics to "I'll
Give You Three Guesses" and "Whistling Away the Dark" courtesy of
Northridge Music Co. & Famous Music Corp. Lyrics to "Six Bridges to
Cross" courtesy of MCA Inc., formerly Universal Music Corp. Lyrics to
"Days of Wine and Roses" courtesy of Warner Brothers, Inc. Lyrics to
"Moment to Moment" and "Charade" courtesy of Northridge Music Co.
& Northern Music Corp. Lyrics to "Dear Heart" courtesy of Northridge
Music Co. & Warner Brothers, Inc. Lyrics to "Wait Until Dark" courtesy
of Northridge Music Co. & Warner Brothers, Inc. Lyrics to "Two for
the Road" courtesy of Northridge Music Co. and 20th Century Music
Corp. Lyrics to "Crazy World" courtesy of EMI Affiliated Music, EMI
Variety Music, Hollyweed Music, and Stage & Screen Music Ltd. Lyrics
to "Where Do You Catch the Bus for Tomorrow?" courtesy of Ale
Music, Threesome Music Co., HM Ent., 20th Century Fox Music. Lyrics
to "Suspicions" courtesy of Rockabu Songs/Arista Music, Inc. Lyrics
to "Welcome Home" courtesy of EMI Worldtrax Music, Inc., Henry
Mancini Enterprises, Inc., Spirit Two Music, Inc. Lyrics to "Life in a
Looking Glass" courtesy of EMI Music Publishing & WB Publications,
Inc. Lyrics to "Insanity" and "Do I Laugh or Do I Cry?" courtesy of
Stage & Screen Music, Ltd/Henry Mancini Music.

Library of Congress Cataloging-in-Publication Data
Caps, John.
Henry Mancini : reinventing film music / John Caps.
p.   cm. — (Music in American life)
Includes bibliographical references and index.
ISBN 978-0-252-03673-6 (hardcover : alk. paper) —
ISBN 978-0-252-09384-5 (e-book)
1. Mancini, Henry—Criticism and interpretation.
2. Motion picture music—United States—
History and criticism. I. Title.
ML410.M2715C36   2012
781.5'42092—dc23   2011027788

To the memory of my so-musical parents

Contents

Illustrations follow page 148

Acknowledgments

Thanks go out to Ginny and Monica Mancini for their cooperation and encouragement of this book, to Michelle Weis at Henry Mancini Enterprises for photo research and multiple helps, but particularly to Laurie Matheson, senior acquisitions editor at University of Illinois Press for, first, bothering to read through my monstrously long draft manuscript, then for suggesting how to better focus it and encouraging me throughout. Sure, that's the job of a good editor—to scout, acquire, shape, and finalize books that seem to have value and potential. But Laurie's strict guidance, while still cordial and inspiring, went way beyond her job description toward a real sense of partnership—the very sort of alliance that keeps book publishing vital and alive, even in this era of electronic web alternatives, which are too often impatient, impersonal, and reckless. But that's another subject. For now, let me add personal thanks to my classical music mentors Lisa S. and Justin K.; to my film music mentors Dan, Dave, Susannah, and Luc; to life mentors Deborah, Johanna, Michael, and my sister Marilyn, for their steadfast support through bad times; and to Chop and Maryanne for being life models of genuine Christian humility. And in a similar vein, one final thanks to the late Henry Mancini, who, ignoring fame and wealth, modestly and generously conversed with me on numerous occasions as though we were absolute equals. No wonder his music—whether power tracks like "Fallout!" or even those demure, obscure background ballads like "Dreamsville," "Soldier in the Rain," and "Fumiko"—still rings true.

Henry Mancini

Here Was Something Fresh

I t is no accident that Henry Mancini became the first publicly successful and personally recognizable film composer in history—practically a brand name in pop culture. He was perfectly placed, by time and temperament, to be a bridge between the traditions of the big band period of World War II and the eclectic impatience of the baby boomer generation that followed, between the big formal orchestral film scores of Hollywood's so-called Golden Years and a modern American minimalist approach. On the one hand, his respect for pre-wartime pop and movie music represented continuity, even advocacy, of tradition. On the other hand, for many young postwar families, newly empowered by the Kennedy-era optimism of the 1960s, the Mancini sound seemed to represent the bright, confident, welcoming voice of a new middle-class life: interested in pop songs and jazz, in movies and television, in outreach politics but also conventional stay-at-home comforts. Mancini's music combined it all naturally, along with color and youthfulness, wit and warmth, and, best of all, after the paranoid and anxious interim of the 1950s (characterized in movies by radiation-enraged monsters and angst-torn juvenile delinquents, and in music by raw rock 'n' roll or tortured urban jazz) it had a cosmopolitan, clear-eyed, and lyrical sense of "cool." Here was something fresh.

In a sense, Mancini was reinventing the language of film scoring. His personal sound was more than mere pop music while something less than pure jazz: a combination of pop melody and jazz inflections of the so-called

West Coast Cool school. Mancini's first reinvention, then, was to popularize that sound in Hollywood and adapt it to the dramatic, narrative needs of movie soundtrack scoring. Learning the history of traditional symphonic screen music was easy for him, as he settled in California after the war working for one of the last of the big assembly-line movie studios, turning out background music for mediocre formula films destined for double-feature drive-in theaters—dumb comedies, wooden westerns, hysterical horror flicks and UFO thrillers, and the latest fad, teen melodramas. There he could practice how to score typical movie chase sequences and gushing love themes; he could perfect the orchestral scream, the instrumental chuckle, and a "safe" corporate version of rock music (actually as mild as a sock hop). All of those voicings would find their way into his version of jazz-pop as he sought a style for himself. Why, the very idea of eclecticism was in tune with the magpie times. Certainly, film composers had been exploiting all those clichés for a long time (hear Erich Korngold's post-romantic scores in the 1930s, David Raksin's atonal modernisms in the 1940s, Elmer Bernstein's pseudo-jazz scores in the 1950s), but Mancini's particular blend was the first to capture the public's attention in a big way, first in films and then on records. He was the first multimedia music superstar precisely because he was reinventing the relationship between the soundtrack and those boomer ticket buyers, speaking in their vernacular.

Furthermore, it happened that Mancini's arrival in Hollywood coincided with two other developments in pop culture that enabled him to become famous. First was the collapse of the big movie studio system, which, soon enough, sent him out on his own as a freelance composer to be hired by television, where fate awaited him. Second was the revolution occurring over in the recording industry: the introduction of a new "high fidelity," multi-miked recording process called stereo. Major record labels like RCA Victor and Columbia hoped consumers would spend a lot of money on new stereo home listening systems that promised "life-like sound." Mancini's second reinvention, then, was to repackage soundtrack music as widely marketable discs for home listening. Best-seller charts, recording industry Grammy Awards, and even *DownBeat* magazine jazz polls all praised and promoted his early television music for the detective series *Peter Gunn* and, soon, a whole sequence of jazz-pop albums by Mancini. Suddenly he was not just a screen composer behind the scenes but a recognized recording artist. In years to come, *Billboard* magazine would list him as the nineteenth highest-selling album artist in history on the same chart that includes Elvis and Sinatra, the Rolling Stones and the Beatles. And with one mega-hit each year for the next decade, either in television and movies or on records (*Breakfast at Tiffany's* and *The Pink Panther* were film scores first, then rearranged into wildly successful albums), Mancini became a household name and a millionaire, amassing a music catalog that could only be envied by others.

By the middle of the 1960s he was world famous with three generations of fans: the war veterans who were wrestling with middle age, the young marrieds who were buying their first houses (well equipped with state-of-the-art televisions and music systems), and baby boomers lucky enough to enjoy the freedom of choice between the happy path to New Suburbia or the conscience road to the protest culture of the late 1960s. As an expression of that luxury, boomers in particular seemed willing to sample a wide range of music, all the way from jukebox rock (both black and white talent) to "social conscience" folk music à la Dylan or the Kingston Trio, to the four B's of pop (the Beatles, the Beach Boys, Burt Bacharach, John Barry's *James Bond* music). Mancini seemed to have recognition value across that whole range. He was probably best known (and still is) for three iconic musical acts that spanned the audiences just outlined—the raucous jazz-based but rock 'n' roll–driven "*Peter Gunn* Theme," the warmth and universal nostalgia of the song from *Breakfast at Tiffany's* "Moon River" with its longing lyric about "two drifters off to see the world . . . someday," and the cool humor of the "*Pink Panther* Theme" with its slinking bass line and throaty sax lead that was both hip and wry. Those also represent Mancini's three pillars of pop—jazz forms and features, melody as an expressive device (sometimes in song form, other times as orchestral miniatures), and film scoring (which we will see is another discipline all its own).

By the mid-1960s Mancini was becoming a force of influence within each of those categories. Colleagues in Hollywood talked about their own music as having "Mancini chords" and spoke of themselves as being freer to write, thanks to him. Young composer/arrangers like Quincy Jones, Burt Bacharach, and Lalo Schifrin readily acknowledged Mancini's prominence. Even veteran song writers like Irving Berlin publicly welcomed Mancini's contributions as the return of classic American lyricism after a static and pallid decade. Mancini represented loyalty to the old with the spirit of the new. With ninety films and ninety disc albums to his credit, with twenty Grammy Awards (National Academy of Recorded Arts and Sciences) out of seventy-two nominations, and with four Oscar Awards (Academy of Motion Picture Arts and Sciences) out of eighteen nominations, Mancini eventually became an industry leader. But it is important to realize that there is more to Mancini's catalog than those Kennedy-era films and recordings and to be able to explore and expose the steady evolution of his music from the early assembly-line scores for B movies of the 1950s, toward his first personal scores and his television successes, then fame as a spokesperson for the jazz-pop style he championed, and his perfection of the Mancini Touch in the 1960s. The 1970s were more experimental years working through a wide range of ethnic tonalities (Chinese, Russian, even Eskimo music) and even some theme-less avant-garde writing. Mancini's music of the 1980s, then, seems to unite all the tendencies he had shown so far, yet with a mellowing and a maturation and a personalization that transcend the commercial and utilitarian genres that he served. The 1990s promised further evolution—music for electronic instruments; a score for director Tim Burton's film about the last days of the studio system, which Mancini had known so well; and his first Broadway musical score—but it was all cut short by his unexpected death in 1994 at the age of seventy.

That Mancini's output paralleled its own times is not surprising. He meticulously studied all the trends and vogues in music and the recording industry around him so as to be prepared for any kind of film score assignment that might come along. He even heeded the big retro trend of 1970s Hollywood back to large-scale symphonic scores spearheaded by the triumphant career of his own former employee John Williams (*Jaws* and *Star Wars*). But more importantly, Mancini's music at its best precisely paralleled his *own* personal growth, and it is that progress I track here. As he and his family matured, you can hear him seeking new layered harmonies in his writing, more complex melody structures that venture beyond the conventional thirty-two-bar song format, and a more dramatically developed score architecture—even a more refined way of scoring a story on screen, not just with a series of charmed pop tunes but in a more serious orchestral language.

Mancini never intended to be a self-expressive musician just as, indeed, he usually deflected self-revealing conversation from himself. He was a reactive person who tried to reach people only through background chat or background music. But somehow he had a lot to say, and it stood out in spite of him. Of course, he gloried in the sounds he was able to produce, and he wanted to share that music with people. Even mere pop music, even cool jazz in its 1960s dialect, can be exciting today; even a yearning baby boomer ballad can give poignancy to the New Millennium. What was fresh once can still have pertinence and power if it is personal. The best of Mancini, while no longer new, is thus self-renewing.

CHAPTER 1

Allegheny River Launch

Born in Cleveland, Ohio, in 1924 as Enrico Nicola Mancini, the young Henry would grow up just over the Pennsylvania border in the steel town of West Aliquippa, where two great rivers, the Allegheny and the Monongahela, come together to become the Ohio River, not far from Pittsburgh. Mancini's father, Quinto, worked for a while at the Jones and Laughlin Steel mills there and was known in the local community as something of a loner. To Henry he was always something of a mystery. Quinto was a laborer all his life, yet he voted with management for Republican candidates; as a teenaged immigrant from the mountainous Abruzzi region near Rome, he had identified with the Italian enclave in West Aliquippa, yet, unlike those who kept close ties with their relatives in the old country or brought them over to the new world as soon as enough money had been saved, he never spoke of his family. According to Henry, Quinto had been the fifth child of his parents and was quickly farmed out to the care of an uncle. Then, while still a young teen, he made what Henry called "the maverick decision" to take off for America. In Boston by 1910 or so, Quinto moved to Cleveland, where he would meet the five-foot-tall Anna Pece, whose family had come to Ohio from the Italian province of Campobasso when she was an infant. Her English was finer than Quinto's, and her familiarity with the Italian American communities in the Northeast was always handier than his. She appreciated his ambition and sense of silent, sometimes brusque, authority—and, of course, his total independence. Along with that mystery about Quinto's past, Anna (known everywhere as Annie) found intriguing the fact that this privately opinioned laborer had taught himself, also without comment or clue, to play that most gentle and whimsical of instruments, the flute.

Mancini described his parents' marriage as based on Annie's admiration and affection for Quinto but always returning to the foundation of her strength. She was the homemaker; he the breadwinner. With equal parts of puzzlement and pouting, Mancini later admitted in his autobiography, "I never saw my father display a trace of affection for her or for me either, for that matter . . . or give her a gift, not even at Christmas or her birthday."[1] Journalist Gene Lees, who worked with Mancini in writing that life story, talked to family cousin Helen Musengo, whom Mancini always thought of as a sister, and reported her opinion that Quinto was actually a very sentimental man, proud to the point of bragging that his son had been able to escape the steel mills of Pittsburgh and become a famed musician. But he would only do his bragging away from the family. At home you did not verbalize praise or passion. Stoicism was strength. It is tempting, then, to trace Mancini's later reserved sense of yearning in his most personal music to that estrangement from his father, just as one can hear his mother's reassurances and good humor in his warm ballads and witty jazz-pop. Yet it is also clear that father and son were never completely alienated. It is to Quinto, after all, that Henry owed his first lessons on piano and soon the flute. And when there seemed to be some talent there, it was Quinto who sought out someone all the way in Pittsburgh to coach his son. The maverick ambition of the father obviously passed strength and confidence to the son, if Mancini's forthright, clearheaded, masculine early scoring style is any indication. But young Henry was developing a musical hunger of his own, too, and seems to have been encouraged by his father—or at least not discouraged—to follow it. He may have wished for a more demonstrative father, but his whole career demonstrates an essential integrity in the household where he grew.

Ninety percent of West Aliquippa in the late 1920s and early 1930s were Italian immigrants with a few Slavs and a handful of Jewish families. To the wider world, though, the Italians were still a minority and, as steel laborers, considered to be from the other side of the tracks. The backward coal-mining towns of West Virginia were not far in miles or style from the life of West Aliquippa. Whether Quinto felt that prejudice, no one can say. There were rumors that he had been cheated out of some real estate inheritance in the old country and that he had felt rejected by his family in being sent off to an uncle; perhaps that was a source of his severity as a parent. But Henry was never able to confirm any of it. As a child, Henry had been sickly, struck with rheumatic fever at age thirteen and then with a series of pediatric ailments. As a result, he more often viewed his parents' relationship, the community around him, and his grade-school activities from the sidelines (a mere reactor even then) rather than as an active participant. A perfect pastime, then, was going to the cinema in town.

The first time Mancini became aware of the music score behind a movie, the first time he thought to separate the moviegoing experience into its component parts, was during a trip to the local movie theater with his father in 1935. Something in the grandiose score to a picture called *The Crusaders*, composed by Rudolf Kopp, made him pay attention to the role that music was playing in the adventure story. "First I wondered where the orchestra was sitting, where the sound was coming from. Then I understood that music had been recorded right onto the film stock already with the actors' voices and sound effects." The very idea intrigued him. "I had thought that there was a big orchestra behind the screen but my father said this just showed what an ignorant little *cafone* [hick] I was."[2] That day Henry took into his head the idea that he wanted to compose like *that*—to somehow be involved in music for the movies. To Quinto's mind, his son should go to university, avoid the steel mills, and become a teacher of some kind. Yet, in the meantime, he still taught Henry piano lessons, and although those sessions seem to have been more about the rap on the knuckles (with a wooden canary perch stolen from the nearby birdcage) after every mistake than about the inspiring qualities of music, Henry learned his scales. It was all part of the 1930s patriarchal steel-town solidarity—a tacit agreement under which sons were raised to certain standards of discipline, taught chores and skills and maybe one area of refinement (say, music), and then turned out into the community at large.

As his own flute fluency improved, Henry learned that there was more to music than a single lead line, that with the piano one could fill in charismatic harmonies and add nuance. In private he experimented on the piano after school, even hand-sketched staff lines in a notebook to create music paper. He joined the Sons of Italy band, though he was still somewhat younger than his bandmates. They played at all the local graduations, parades, and sport games, and eventually Henry developed a quick sight-reading ability. The local high school even heard about him and recruited him for their band two years before he was of age. And at the same time, he was beginning to explore chord structures on a neighbor's piano. As though to verify his father's opinion that he was intentionally dreamy and impractical, Henry spent much of his mid teens in his room listening to distant radio stations whose late-night signals found their way down the Allegheny River bringing big band music and popular vocalists of the day to the mill fords downstream. He was drawn, not to the romantic lyrics or the posturing singers, but to the subtleties and shadings, the beats and blends of the orchestras behind the tunes. He began to memorize the names of his favorite band arrangers. He would practice writing out, on that self-lined music paper, their arrangements—how the trombones were used as a section against the trumpets, what the woodwinds were doing in support of the harmony, and, for that matter, how the arranger portioned out the individual winds—flutes, clarinets, saxes, to create the full woodwind section's sound. He was already able to distinguish the harmonic differences between the simple power swing of bands like Benny Goodman or Count Basie and the more elegant chromatic sophistication in the arrangements (called "charts" by insiders) of Duke Ellington and Artie Shaw—and he was beginning to understand what made them different.

Radio helped him reach beyond the piano lessons and marching band repertoire. A whole universe of more exciting, more challenging music was out there: life was not limited to what he experienced in the neighborhood. Even as one could still see Ku Klux Klan crosses burning in the far hills surrounding Beaver Valley and hear of African American families in jeopardy, the radio was presenting a whole range of dynamic black talent from Ellington's and Fletcher Henderson's bands to singers and soloists from faraway New York City. He only began to think about the black influence on American popular music and the whole question of race in society (as an isolated immigrant himself) when he started to come into direct contact with black musicians. The first was a particular sixteen-year-old trumpet player he encountered when they worked together in a regional ten-piece band—the boy taught Henry to play what is called a 6–9 chord, common in the big band charts of Bix Beiderbecke at that time. He spent all night exploring that chord, approaching it on the piano from different directions and seeing what it could do as a transition chord to move between different keys and how it could be manipulated. For Mancini, it was a small window on jazz language that he could exploit for years to come as well as a fast, practical appreciation of the equality of the races, starting with music as the common interest.[3]

Mancini was also trying to notate (with all the proper harmonies and rhythms and assigned instruments) the few classical recordings that his parents owned—Rossini, Tchaikovsky, Gershwin, and, more difficult because of the impressionistic washes of sound rather than straightforward theme lines, Debussy and Ravel. And so, to his father's credit, and somewhat contrary to later criticisms of what it felt like to be Quinto's son, Henry progressed in a fairly open environment. Quinto began to recognize the evidence of all that secret study when he saw Henry's music scribblings around the house. He agreed to take his son to Pittsburgh for some structured piano lessons in the classical style from a famous German maestro named Ochsenhardt and soon flute lessons at Carnegie Tech. The strict regimen of those instructions went along with Henry's new seriousness about music. He still preferred music arranging to any kind of instrumental performance, but taking apart a Chopin mazurka or a Schumann sonata in order to play it helped him see how it had been composed—how the puzzle of form, meter, melody, harmony, and counterpoint had been solved by previous composers.

To satisfy his hunger for independence on those trips to the city, after a couple of pressurized hours with the maestro, Mancini would often depressurize by wandering across the street to the Stanley Theater, where local and regional traveling vaudeville acts would perform—comics, singers, animal routines, all accompanied by a resident pit band of twenty to twenty-five players. Conductor for the Stanley band was one Max Adkins (1910–1953), whom Mancini has since called "the most important influence of my life."[4] Certainly through Adkins, Mancini gained in confidence, progressing from wannabe flutist and arranger to a productive apprentice. Adkins was also important in the early education of other Hollywood music men like Joshua Feldman, who became Jerry Fielding, known for scores like *The Wild Bunch* and *Hogan's Heroes*, and Billy Strayhorn, recognized for being Ellington's right-hand arranger and song conduit ("Take the A Train," "Lush Life"). Adkins's lessons began simply as music notation exercises and advanced to studying the best ways to orchestrate for a theater band. His consistently encouraging acceptance of Mancini's inexperience and mutual enthusiasm for the big band sound (especially when out-of-town bands would come and play the Stanley Theater) helped Henry develop quickly and deeply internalize the lessons. Thus, Mancini's natural feeling for the shape of a melody was developing alongside his fluency in orchestration.

At the same time, Adkins was becoming a personal advocate for the young Mancini as well as a sympathetic father figure, who helped him buy his first real suit of clothes and coached him in ways to present himself in the adult professional world on *this* side of the tracks: how to tip at a restaurant, how to shine his own shoes, and, later, how to prepare for an audition and for job interviews. It was a much-needed elementary education; before Adkins, under that steel-hard small-town immigrant upbringing, Mancini had begun to assume a quiet core of discouragement that could only be countered with what Mancini called a "crazy irreverent sense of humor."[5] But through

Adkins's encouragement, he found some bearings and a lifelong penchant for self-discipline. Once, Adkins even introduced him to Benny Goodman, who was coming up strong on the big band scene. Henry wrote an arrangement for Goodman, as he had begun doing for Adkins's pit bands, and sent it on to New York for review.

Meanwhile, out of high school, he applied to the music program at Pittsburgh's Canaan Institute of Technology. A grander goal, though, as with many young musicians, was the Juilliard School of Music in Manhattan. When word arrived from Goodman's office that the arrangement Mancini had sent had been well received at a band read-through and that maybe Mancini could move to New York, it was decided that he would end his lessons with Max Adkins and apply to Juilliard. Although the chance with Goodman never materialized (the second chart he submitted was considered too difficult, too self-conscious and inexperienced), Mancini auditioned at Juilliard with a Beethoven sonata and an improvised "fantasy" on Cole Porter's "Night and Day." He was accepted on scholarship at the age of seventeen; the year was 1942. The eight months of his Juilliard career Mancini later called "not an easy time for me, emotionally or financially."[6] He was forced to major in piano for the first year, because all the classes he wanted to take in orchestration and composition were not scheduled until the second year. He felt aimless and oppressed—a far cry from Adkins's enabling proactive environment. In a way, it was like his early teen years all over again, sitting at home, searching the radio dial, except that at Juilliard, for relief from piano class and music notation lessons, he would sit up in the library listening intently through headphones to their 78 rpm record collection and reading along in the printed scores of Debussy, Ravel, Bartok, Mozart—listening "as if for life" (as Charles Dickens used to say of his own youthful devotion to books).

Partly a result of that discontent with an academic regimen and partly from a feeling of urgency that the growing war in Europe was raising in everyone, Mancini used the occasion of his eighteenth birthday to circumvent the draft and enlisted. That meant he was called up to serve not from Pittsburgh but from New York City, which, in turn, meant the difference between being assigned to a regular army division and getting instead a stint in the Army Air Corps. They sent him to Atlantic City for basic training, and there he met members of the band that Glenn Miller was trying to form. Others who had seen some of Mancini's early arrangements urged him to talk with Miller to see if there was a vacancy in such a band. Miller was hand-picking musicians and arrangers who would eventually be shipped up to Yale at New Haven, Connecticut, by mid-1943 to begin rehearsals before heading "over there." Miller's hope was to find soldier/musicians who had already been with other bands before the war: Goodman arranger Mel Powell, Artie Shaw's trumpeter Bernard Privin, Tommy Dorsey's guitarist, Will Brady's sax player, each found a place with Miller. But the eighteen-year-old Mancini would not. Band historian and musician George T. Simon has written, "I recall spending several evenings walking the Atlantic City boardwalk with one quiet and rather lonely musician who must have assumed that he too would soon be going up to Yale. Perhaps Glenn didn't know enough about his talent to realize how valuable he would be. In any case, Henry Mancini was never called to New Haven."[7] Instead he was assigned first to the 28th Air Force Band on Miller's referral, and then, when in the worst months of the war the bands were broken up and raided for all the infantry soldiers they could supply, he was sent overseas to hook up with the 1306th Engineers Brigade in France. There his duties were numerous and included driving a jeep for the company chaplain and playing for services "out in the middle of a field somewhere on this silly pump organ."[8] By mid-1945 he had been through Germany and Austria following elements of Patton's Third Army and escorting prisoners in the vicinity of Mauthausen concentration camp. "The cremation ovens were still warm," he wrote years later.[9]

When on May 8 the European war was declared over, Mancini was to have been reassigned to the Pacific Theater to take on the Japanese war machine. Instead, he was taken into an infantry band that was in need of a good flute player and spent the rest of the war with them stationed in Nice for "one of the best periods of my life, ever."[10] The army's repatriation system, for a soldier's postwar release from active service, was based on points earned for months of service, time in combat, and so forth. When Henry Mancini had accumulated enough points, although he claimed to have been willing to stay in Nice forever, he was shipped home to New York, where, at least for the time being, big band music was riding high—by now no longer the sound of sentimental farewells and military absences but of civilian celebration.

CHAPTER 2

Not Quite Jazz

Once Mancini was released from active army duty in March 1946, he went home to West Aliquippa. His father was urging him to return to Juilliard and graduate. But Max Adkins was supportive of Henry's wish to strike out on his own toward a job with some big recording/touring band. Only a few nationally successful bands were still doing the travel circuit. Mancini remembered the band that had impressed him most before the war among those that had passed through the Stanley Theater in Pittsburgh: the early Fletcher Henderson group. But since Mancini's old master sergeant in the army was now one of the arrangers for what was called the Glenn Miller Orchestra with Tex Beneke, a job was found for him there, first as an occasional arranger and in the late 1940s as the band's rather underused pianist at $125 per week. Miller had been lost at sea near the end of the war, that tragedy only further freezing the sound he had invented as the archetypal big band memory. Now Miller's widow, Helen, owned the band. At first she hoisted Beneke into the postwar leadership position, since Glenn had always championed Tex not only for his easy sax style and regular-guy vocals but also for his laid-back personality.

Everyone got along with Tex. His sound never approached the absolute precision and purity of Miller's best band, and certainly not the authority of Goodman's or the artistry of Shaw's, but it had an appropriately transitional sound—enough tradition to fit into the late big band movement yet a certain awareness of the trends to attract new listeners. The Beneke group was fine for the times—a prestige gig for a young pianist and an invaluable school for a novice arranger like Mancini. At first his most urgent duty was to rehearse and supervise the new vocal quartet hired as the band singers. They were called the Mello-Larks—three untrained male studio singers and one female lead vocalist who could sight-read music well. This was Ginny O'Connor. Mancini never relished the assignment of vocal coach, but in adapting the old tunes for the new crooners he also got to arrange some of the background blends of the band. Beneke's organization had expanded to include a small string section by then, and Mancini has said that this experience—learning to blend strings so that their voice (high violins, mid-range violas, low-strung cellos, and bottom basses) did not fight the four human voices but supported them—was his first chance to study string writing as deeply as any symphony orchestrator might and to eventually become one of Hollywood's best string advocates. Although the Beneke string section was hopelessly outweighed by the big brass section, Mancini found wise ways to blend them all. He was twenty-five now.

The sheath of Mancini's arrangements for Tex also contains certain Mancini original compositions: his "Bagatelle" became another popular *live* piece for Beneke. Usually the term *bagatelle* refers to a brief piano piece and literally means "a trifle." Mancini's trifle was a bouncy showpiece that derived its tension from the modal theme line over a simple modal bass figure. Heard first on tenor and baritone sax trading off, the theme was then taken by the band, lifted up a fourth (in this case from G♯ to C♯, which represents a four-note span on a piano). Mancini used the Beneke string section to shift into the major key that would be asserted, for a short time, by the brass. Then the distinctive leapfrog quality of the chromatic opening returned and a fast drum finish created a quick exit. A trifle it may be, but it appears to be the first original Mancini composition to be represented on disc, circa 1946 (although it was not published until six years later).

Perhaps the moment when both the Beneke band and Mancini came into their own was when they took on the old Glenn Miller hit "American Patrol" but completely recast it in a modern way. For a gig at the Hollywood Palladium Theater, Beneke had Mancini rethink the piece as a powerful showpiece they would call "Palladium Patrol." Miller's original (taken from Tchaikovsky's "March Slav") had been a straight 4/4 march with a touch of syncopation. Mancini's reimagining opened with a fast walking bass line, a high-hat cymbal keeping "cool" time. Then three trombones in unison played a swing version of the tune but with unexpected accents exaggerating the volume of one note in each phrase, saxes adding counterpoint. The second pass of this theme was joined by a Milleresque reed section playing a secondary theme, the Armed Services Hymn. Solos for tenor sax and full-bore trumpet were interspersed with effective reed-blend passages eventually leading smoothly back to the walking bass and, with the new energy of blaring trumpets and some deep jungle drumming, a final reference to the main theme, including a fragment of the army hymn in a different key. It was a fully original (and fun-to-play) chart that had some personal inflections and ideas encouraged by Beneke. That benevolent encouragement, as he had found with Max Adkins, was just what Mancini needed to get in touch with his more individualistic musical voice in postwar jazz-pop.

"Dancer's Delight" by Mancini was a slow, conventional soft-shoe rhythmic piece with just a few moments of modern jazz harmony involved. "Hop Scotch" played with an almost Scottish air for the full range of saxes before breaking out into a hard swing for the brass bridge. These pieces, too, were preserved on the various Tex Beneke record album sets of hard-wax 78 rpm discs on such labels as MGM (Metro-Goldwyn-Mayer) from the very early 1950s, always under the Tex Beneke moniker but with Mancini now being listed in parentheses as composer—proof to young Henry that perhaps he was on the right track for his career: arranging for bands on records and radio.

Those Palladium concerts and broadcasts had also given Mancini a taste of Southern California life and climate. He was hearing more about it from the Beneke band singer, Ginny O'Connor, a Californian by origin, who lately, it seems, had been singling him out from the rest of the band staff and trying to get his attention. Apparently that was no easy task: "No doubt because of a pattern set up by my father, I have never been very good at expressing my feelings for people in words," wrote Mancini years later.[1] So it was Ginny who, when not with her singing colleagues, the other three Mello-Larks, pursued Beneke's arranger and pianist. She and Henry were only months apart in age—they both loved movies and, of course, could trade musical enthusiasms. About the only difference between them was that Henry had experience with the Northeast winters and Ginny with the sun of the Pacific Coast. It was in those long conversations, as they grew closer and shared their private memories and postwar ambitions, that Henry began to rejuvenate his original vision of a career: to write music for the movies like the score he had heard on the soundtrack of *The Crusaders* in 1935. Ginny raised two ideas for Henry to consider, knowing that his basically passive personality might never formulate them without her: they should quit the Beneke band to settle near Los Angeles, and they should get married.

Henry took Ginny to meet his favorite cousins, Helen and Ralph Musengo, then to West Aliquippa to be with his parents, "who while they didn't exactly disapprove were surprised at our engagement," Mancini wrote.[2] Ginny resigned from Beneke's band first and moved back to California to live with her mother (a short, lively Mexican woman who had once played piano professionally). In time, Henry also gave his notice to Beneke and left the band as pianist, though for a couple of years he continued to ship back occasional arrangements to Tex. He had decided to go west, where his future wife was waiting and where he halfway hoped his own sun would rise. Ginny's mother, Jo, set up a separate room for Henry in her home until they were married. Because of Ginny's own half-Irish, half-Mexican heritage, and because her father had once driven trucks for MGM studios, she was known in many different enclaves of Hollywood, and she knew a lot of names around town. Singer Mel Torme was one of them. She had sung alto in his innovative, close-harmony quartet, the Mel-Tones, even before her time with the Beneke band. And through him she had become friends with other celebrities from Mickey Rooney and Sammy Davis Jr. (and Sr.) to Judy Garland and the actor/writer Blake Edwards, soon to be a bigger part of everyone's life as a hot TV and movie director.

Once Henry and Ginny married, Quinto and Annie moved out from Pennsylvania to live near their son, who, it seemed, would be able to make a living in the music business after all. Quinto resented that they were not all living together in the manner of big Italian households back home in Abruzzi, but it was just not the modern way. Annie understood; Quinto seemed amazed and affronted.

The year 1950 would bring two important milestones to Mancini's biography: a first-born son named Christopher, who would now cast Henry in the role that held such mixed emotions for him already, the role of father, and the first evidence we have of Mancini writing dramatic music for the media—in this case, orchestral background scores for a dramatic radio series called *Family Theater* over the Mutual Broadcasting Network out of Hollywood. Each episode of this series took the form of a half-hour narrated storybook featuring adapted classics—adventures or humorous family tales—with many top screen stars of the day donating their services. Scoring in these contexts was very elementary, requiring as few as seven or as many as twelve short orchestral cues (or entrances) per episode, some as brief as ten seconds (called "stings" because of the way they just appear for a sharp effect and then disappear), none ever as long as one minute. It is interesting, though, to hear Mancini's easy grasp of the clichés of scoring drama and his ability each week to fashion simple little identifying themes or motifs that more or less represent the story at hand.

For a January 11, 1950, adaptation of Dickens's *A Tale of Two Cities*, with Robert Ryan as narrator and Hans Conried as lawyer Sydney Carton, Mancini writes a generic-sounding formal opening based on the harmonic interval known as the "heroic fifth," which then descends as though to trace the failings of our would-be hero Carton, the sullen and drifting solicitor caught up in the French Revolution who will eventually sacrifice himself heroically for his beloved Lucy. After only a four-bar preface to that theme by the strings, narration comes in and the scoring darkens to a minor-key version of the theme itself (English horn, then clarinet soloing against a rather muddy, but at least competently scored, ensemble of winds and strings).

Following that narrative setup about hard times in the contexts of the revolution, the scoring transforms to a sea chantey for clarinet reminding us of the portside eighteenth-century setting of the story, which then rises in melodramatic details as the trial of Lucy's true love, Charles Darnay, starts going badly (full strings against brass with bassoon providing the bass line and string tremolos giving suspense). As mentioned earlier, these were all established devices of Hollywood romantic and adventure scoring in the quasi-operatic way optioned by Max Steiner in famous film scores like those for *King Kong* (1933) and *Gone with the Wind* (1939) and perpetuated especially into gothic romantic-thriller films and horror films produced throughout the 1940s. Mancini was giving the radio drama a sound that listeners would find familiar and that even this late in the history of radio programming might hold their imagination because it reminded them of the movies.

For a January 18, 1950, comedy script called *William the Terrified*, a mock fairy tale about a cowardly knight (Dennis Day), Mancini begins with a big brass fanfare and harp glissando announcing the milieu; then strings play a noble processional reminiscent of a past score that Mancini knew well: Alfred Newman's *Captain from Castille* (1947). As the façade of the knight errant is dismantled and we meet the meek and nervous Sir William behind the armor, Mancini allows his comic clichés to enter the score—the consecutive seconds (striking adjacent keys on the piano, comic because they sound like "wrong" notes) and *wah-wah* sound on muted brass with the muttering bassoon notes on the bottom; later, variations from the muted trombones and sliding strings carry the scoring. It does not stand out as music above the narration, but, heard for its own sake, it is a thoughtful accompaniment. Sir William sets out on a quest, seeking wisdom about how to be brave.

The king knows nothing about the subject but advises him to visit Mother Nature. The score strikes up a pleasant skipping theme as Sir William heads in her direction, strings providing the buoyancy. But to reach her he must pass by the purple castle in the forest, and there as he encounters a group of evil Swonks (three-eyed dragons), the trombones play a comic warning. Typical suspense music plays as the spooky forest grows darker. Pizzicato strings follow William as he sneaks around the purple castle, and a quick flourish of martial brass is barely heard in the background as he tries to bolster his courage with quotes from the knights' Code of Honor. Meeting Princess Anne inspires, over a smooth bed of muted strings, a brief duet between solo violin and the comic *wah-wah* muted trombone representing William's timid nature. There is a fetching waltz fragment as Father Time sends William off to the Watchmaker's Ball, where he can see Princess Anne again. And occasionally one can hear a sympathetic jazz chord or two in the string harmonies of these little scores that seems to suggest a composer who is beginning to think from his own personal perspective, beginning to use even a miniature radio drama to express himself.

The *Family Theater* broadcasts opened and closed with their own orchestral theme music (by Thomas Bruner), and Mancini's scores for the various episodes were not out of character with that corporate kind of music, yet there seemed to be a thoughtfully expressive musical dramatist behind them, no matter how modestly he projected himself.

By 1951 Mancini was working regularly, if not consistently, preparing music for club act performers (including Ann Miller, Anna Maria Alberghetti, Buddy Rich) and for more radio dramas. Once a week he would drive the nearly two hours from Hollywood to the small house his parents had bought in the town of Bell. His father, unfortunately, resented the job he had found in a shoe factory there, and after several heart attacks Annie's health was deteriorating. Ginny kept singing in studios around town and caring for baby Chris. The call came as a surprise, though, that Henry's mother was dying. "I have felt overwhelming sadness, the kind of pain you can't control, emotion that overwhelms you to the point that you break down and sob, once in my life," Henry wrote in 1989 about his mother's death.[3] She had been his ally against both the gruffness of his father and the "outsider" status of an immigrant boy in a prewar world. She had been the encouragement of his music, even more than the influence of Max Adkins. Losing her forced him to stand up alone with Ginny and with his own reserves of talent as his only strength. There was nothing to fall back on now; he could only fall forward into the future. From there came his strong sense of self-discipline.

In late 1951 Henry learned that Ginny was pregnant again. It was time to solidify his career and his daily life. First he coaxed his father to move up closer to Hollywood and bought him a mobile home and a new car. Then, through a few freelance jobs arranging music for club acts, he met choreographer Nick Castle, who had worked at MGM with headliners like Fred Astaire and Gene Kelly and was now putting together music and dance acts for the growing array of clubs and resort hotels in venues like Las Vegas and Reno. Nick (who later became godfather to the Mancini kids) liked Mancini's quick, clear ensemble writing and hired him often, but he had one piece of advice: if you want security for your family in this music business, you have to be more than just a clever and busy arranger. While orchestral arrangers were paid only once by the project boss, union composers were paid every time their music was used for profit. Each time a song was heard in public or on a broadcast, the music writer and/or the lyricist was paid a performance percentage; each time an orchestral or band composition was broadcast or issued as a record, the composer got a fee. Organizations like ASCAP (American Society of Composers, Authors, and Publishers) monitored the use of such music and then paid the member composers in royalties. Castle urged Mancini to write a song—anything would do—and submit it to ASCAP just so he could register as a published composer. So for one of Nick's client dancers, Arthur Duncan, later famous as a token tapper for *The Lawrence Welk Show*, Mancini quickly penned "The Soft Shoe Boogie." Though Mancini called it a "stupid little piece," he used it to join the union. On August 6, 1952, he became a lifelong member of ASCAP and eventually one of the largest royalty earners in the union's history with a forty-year catalog of published titles. The sheet music of his first published piece earned him just $14.73 that year, but he felt he was on his way. Far from being a boogie, the piece is really just a simple two-step tune similar to the wartime novelty "Three Little Fishies" and arranged by Mancini like an easygoing Count Basie chart.

That same year the continuing Tex Beneke orchestra issued an album with Mancini's original "Palladium Patrol" on it; his "Bagatelle" and "Dancer's Delight" would come out soon. But albums like those were the last gasps of the big band era. Multimedia music was the wave of the future, and a well-experienced composer/arranger with recordings and radio to his credit was the most likely to succeed.

— — —

In May 1952 Ginny gave birth to twin daughters, Monica and Felice. Son Chris was a lively two-year-old. With Ginny temporarily out of circulation as a studio singer, Henry's arranging and radio composing was their only income. He determined that if he wanted to become a successful and resourceful composer of dramatic and narrative music for the multimedia of the future, he ought to get more training in the classical basics and the modern musical grammar he had missed by having been drafted into the army out of his Juilliard scholarship. After all, a number of the best music teachers in the country had settled in Los Angeles, drawn for conflicting reasons (there was an active and innovative music community there, and there was that gorgeous climate) by the magnet of Hollywood.

Through the GI Bill, Mancini was able to sign up for study at the Westlake School of Music and, more importantly, to begin specialized studies with three famous tutors. "They really were private lessons, not classes," he has said.

> I went to these people's homes, not to a classroom. I studied music theory and harmony with Dr. Alfred Sendry, who was, you know, a classmate of [Béla] Bartók and for whom the interval of the fourth was a favorite. And that's a sound that's sprinkled through just about everything I do. . . . I studied mainly orchestration with Mario Castelnuovo-Tedesco [who wrote famous concertos for Jascha Heifetz and Andrés Segovia] and with Ernst Krenek [married to Gustav Mahler's daughter, wrote twenty operas, evolved from romanticism to atonality in his own musical language], mainly counterpoint and fugue. All private study. And they'd send me away with composing or transposing assignments, harmony tests and orchestrations, all that kind of thing.[4]

And so it was that Mancini, as the intuitive musician, acquired through one-on-one tutoring everything he would have received academically at Juilliard had the war not intervened. And he soaked it up now, being more mature and more focused than he would have been then. The one important course he missed was perhaps composition itself—delving into the classical repertoire and learning how great music of the past had been structured and personalized and thought out. He was not headed for any great intellectual music anyway—at least no long-form composition. He was hoping to be expressive in modern vernacular forms, and melody, harmony, instrumentation, and narrative correspondence (music behind a story) were the main elements of that expressiveness. The big bands had been a great ear-training ground for him, learning to hear how the subtle blends of instruments changed the mood, the tone, the meaning of a line of music, and which instruments sounded good together or slipped neatly in behind a particular solo instrument or voice. Music theory taught him the basics of Western music's piano octaves, the twelve tones of the Western scale, the common chords and modes within the scale that make up the basic musical vocabulary a composer needs. His orchestration study taught him not only more about blending instruments within an ensemble but also the specific range of each instrument—what scales or extreme notes are possible for each instrument; how much breath each wind instrument player needs, which in turn dictates how long phrases can be on the music paper; the bow strokes that create the smoothest phrasing in the strings; and so forth. Study in counterpoint and fugue, considered advanced grammar for composers, was more helpful than one might think in his future movie composing, finding new ways of combining two or more musical lines so that they spar and complement one another at the same time. Mancini absorbed all of those lessons with a novice's enthusiasm. He learned quickly and easily because, as he later said, he thought about little else except music, only marginally aware of daily practical affairs like financial planning or wider distractions like the Hollywood social scene or even the political climate of the times. Even as a kid of fourteen he had spent most of his mind on music; his friends had been few, and his social activities, except for a love of impromptu playground sports, had been all musical.

After an initial period of concentrated motherhood, Ginny rejoined the Mello-Larks, and once again it was her singing career that occasioned Henry's entry into the next step of his development: his introduction, at last, into the world of movie scoring. Down the street, so to speak, from Hollywood's major studios like MGM and Paramount was the home of the cheaper, more packaged type of film fare, Universal Studios, featuring stars who were not quite from the A-list. The term *B movie* was born here. Like the movie factory that it was, Universal employed a regular staff of in-house composers, just as it had staff camera crews and a revolving stock company of actors. At Universal in the early 1950s, the music staff, headed by Russian-born executive and conductor Joseph Gershenson, included Hans J. Salter, who had begun in Hollywood scoring silent films in the 1920s, and Frank Skinner, who had come up the ladder from a popular music background, written a book on movie scoring in 1950 called *Underscore*, and tackled most of Universal's big pictures from *Magnificent Obsession* to *Son of Frankenstein* and *The Man of a Thousand Faces*.

Along with other staff music men such as William Lava and Herman Stein, these composers would share scoring duties on any given film; one would write a main theme and prepare dramatic music for, say, reels 1–4 and 6–10, and one of the other staffers would score reels 5 and 11 using the given theme and trying to blend his bits with the rest of the other fellow's score. These group efforts, then, would be credited on screen not with the individual composers' names but with the phrase "Music Supervision by Joseph Gershenson." At Universal Studios most composers remained anonymous, and most scores were intentionally generic with a typically melodramatic nineteenth-century tone to them. But by the 1950s there was a desire to modernize. In fact, the studio's short-film unit was beginning to produce a few pop music entertainments (to be shown in theaters before the main feature) spotlighting big band music. As Mancini tells it, one of these Universal shorts was to feature the Jimmy Dorsey band and the Mello-Larks. Through Ginny, Mancini was brought in to write an arrangement for Dorsey of the old nursery tune "Skip to My Lou." His submission was clever and cool, and since he still remembered his failure with Benny Goodman when he had submitted a chart that was too complex for the band to bother, this time he made it easily playable.

Joe Gershenson's assistant heard a rehearsal of this chart and drew his boss's attention to it. They had been looking for a young composer with big band experience who also knew how to write for strings. Mancini was hired to finish the Dorsey short film and to get involved with a particular feature film they had coming up whose main character was a singer of the big band era. Their star was Frank Sinatra, currently in a career slump and looking to the movies for a way out—no longer a teen idol as in the 1940s, not yet an Oscar-winning actor as in *From Here to Eternity* (1955), nor the finger-snapping sophisticated singer he would eventually create. The film, *Meet Danny Wilson* (1952), told the story of a rising club singer whose career takes off as soon as he cuts a deal with a ruthless hoodlum boss (played by Raymond Burr). The club songs Sinatra would sing were the old standards, but Gershenson needed someone to compose transitional music between those songs and some background for the narrative scenes. Combining his Beneke experience with his desire to write for the movies, Mancini dug into his first feature film vehicle as a scorer—well, as a facilitator.

The Sinatra film was scored in 1951, but the next year marks the actual beginning of Mancini's career as a movie scorer. For a test period of two weeks, at a commission of $225 per week, Joe Gershenson called Mancini in to try his descriptive scoring abilities in a new comedy film featuring the broad slapstick vaudeville comics Bud Abbott and Lou Costello. *Lost in Alaska* presents Mancini's first real piece of cinema scoring in which the music is keyed directly and impulsively to the action on screen. First, Mancini scored the film's main title music, done very much in the big band style via the supper club acts he had done for Nick Castle, incorporating a couple of nods to the low-comedy Abbott and Costello shenanigans—xylophone-and-flute chatter, jokey gestures from the strings. But the main scene for which Mancini had to compose ("I agonized so over this sequence that I might have been scoring a battle in "War and Peace" . . . That bit of music took me two weeks to write."[5]) features Lou Costello searching for his runaway sled dog in the alleys of a small fur-trader town in the Yukon. At one point he peers into a tall crate at the back of the general store; it is full of someone's catch of Alaskan crabs. Like any classic vaudeville dunce, Costello leans far down inside the crate (as though his dog would be in there), where lots of crab pincers await him. One crab grabs Costello's hat, drawing him further in, then another latches onto his nose, eliciting the comedian's famous bawl. Well aware of Universal's past suspense music for thriller films, Mancini fills his cue with tremolo strings, alternating them with the usual comic consecutive seconds by a xylophone/piccolo combination. As soon as Costello's nose is firmly seized, slide trombones stretch the moment out. The *wah-wah* effect of cupped brass is used to make sure no one misses Costello's broad slapstick contortions while various-sized crabs nip at his fingers. But the most interesting aspect of this two-minute Mancini debut piece is that for all of its cartoonish exaggerated randomness, it at least has an overall shape. A motive phrase for woodwinds, twice breaking out of the fray and echoed in the end, acts as a kind of glue, convincing us that there was a thoughtful craftsman, albeit a novice, at work there.

Every comedy scene, even one as blatant and childish as this, should end with a "topper," the fulfillment of the laughs so far. Here, the climax comes with the unlikely sight of one huge crab now crawling down the alley toward us. Forget about all those little crustaceans in the crate; here is a monster crab on the loose and on the attack. Mancini hilariously references the scores of all those past Universal creature feature films—the blaring trombones and the menacing monster stomp coming from strings and brass. It is enough to encourage Costello to beat it from the alley, to get to the dog sled, and to mush.

Partly because of that knowing sense of humor, partly because the crab cue contains more detailed orchestration than the rest of the film's predictable patchwork score, and partly because Mancini's music demonstrated an awareness of how to fit in with the rest of the film's music, Gershenson was impressed. He decided that Mancini could be brought on board as a Universal Studios staff composer, at least for a trial run. Mancini may have been the junior member of the Universal music staff, but that in itself was the fulfillment of his early West Aliquippa dream. So at the age of thirty he had become a composer for the movies—a Hollywoodian.

CHAPTER 3

The Music Factory

The Universal Studios staff composers were a highly organized, well-oiled team, able to score any sort of film, any story or setting, albeit with fairly generic music and always in a rush. Indeed, film scoring assignments came crowding down the studio hallways toward their offices like cattle in a chute, like that huge crab in Costello's alley. Finish one film score and on to the next or, more often, finish one *while* working on the next. By the time Mancini arrived there, Joseph Gershenson had deputized Milt Rosen to help him run things—Rosen being a transplanted Juilliard graduate who had composed for theater and radio and even for Arthur Fiedler's Boston Pops in the 1930s. If Gershenson was the decision maker, often the orchestra conductor as well, Rosen was the guy who shepherded each film, and especially the younger staff composers, through the process of scoring. The first step was known as *spotting*, where the assigned composers would sit down, not with the men who had made the film (because in the Universal factory system they were already off working on the next picture), but with a music editor and with Rosen. Herman Stein was the staff composer with whom Mancini was most often paired in those days. Stein would be assigned the more classically or dramatically oriented cues, and Mancini would get the lighter ones—music for comic relief or love interest. An example is *Horizons West* (1952), a western about two brothers in post–Civil War cattle country. Mancini has a small string orchestra, split in two sections, playing sheepishly romantic meanderings underneath the dialogue of Robert Ryan and Julie Adams, while the bulk of Stein's scoring accompanies the outdoor action scenes.

By contrast, when Universal came to make its mildly popular Francis the Talking Mule comedies—for instance, *Francis in the Haunted House* (1956)—Mancini was scoring more than a third of its thirty-four music cues, partly because they trusted him more by that time and partly because this was the sort of lighter fare, full of amusing and colorful orchestral details, that was supposed to be his specialty. But regardless of how the scoring was split among the staff composers, the process of blending their various pieces into one score was always the same. Mancini has described it before:

> So the job was to divide up the film cues among the guys, the composers there, and they'd say to us, "Herman will do the opening main title, and the two themes, and all of reel one through four and this scene in reel six, and you do these five scenes," or "You do reels seven and eight." So you'd go back to the library and pick out some slow music for the love scene, or if you had a barroom piano scene you'd pick out a couple of those, and if the film had chases you went and you asked the librarian, "Give me the chase book." Universal's music library had folders full of sheet music already orchestrated marked "suspense," "lively," "fight," "dramatic," "pretty," "chase," "neutral . . . ," and one could consult those, choose some passages, and insert them into one's *own* scoring.
>
> You took it and you pieced together the parts of those library cues that you wanted. I had to lay it out on paper and do the timings first—that's the way we did it. You'd lay out the timings on a music sketch sheet in order to know how many bars you'll need and at what tempo, and then you proceeded to "borrow" bars six through ten from whatever library piece. But then you'd need a transitional moment between, say, some tense music and music that was expressive of some relief. So you would compose your own segue to bridge the gap and maybe stick in, under some line of dialogue, a reference to this particular film's main theme, then Scotch tape another transition of your own, leading back to a library ending. So they were real patchwork scores—making new cues out of pieces of past cues.
>
> Only a few Universal films in those days had specifically composed scores, but those were only assigned to the veterans like Skinner and Salter. We other staff guys scored the overflow and for very cheap. I was making, I guess, two fifty a week then and Herman maybe two seventy-five, and if another composer was in on it we'd do a film in two weeks. So for a six-reel western they'd have a score for under three thousand bucks, and, what is more, they didn't have to pay for the reuse of the music that we used out of the library or the later reuse of the music we were doing, because they owned it all.[1]

The instrumental parts would then be copied out for distribution among the members of the studio's own resident orchestra, and the score would be performed and recorded as though it were a seamless whole, credited in the end to Joe Gershenson as "supervisor" of scoring.

Hollywood historians have cast a disapproving eye on Gershenson's practice of taking screen credit for all of those collage scores done by his staff. But although Mancini reportedly once lobbied for composer autonomy at Universal, he and the others at that music factory considered Joe a fair boss. "He was a good musician," Mancini said much later, "and I think he never really got credit for his ability. He never composed a note, and yet he could conduct classical, jazz, and bebop scores with ease while running a tight administrative ship at the music department."[2] It is worth noting, too, that all of those individual music cues, the original transitional cues or the new melodies that the staff had composed on their own, *could* have been credited for copyright purposes under Gershenson's name, but he saw to it that at least for performance rights royalties they were carefully logged under each composer's name. Thus, even late in his life, Mancini was still earning royalties on all that music. "I don't know of any instance when Joe took cue sheet credit for anything," Mancini has said, "and I think that was the mark of an honest man. He could have had his name on everything if he'd wanted to."[3] In one sense, then, Mancini was being passed from one mentor, Max Adkins, to another, Joe Gershenson. The former had inspired his musical schooling, and the latter was overseeing his apprenticeship in the movies.

Mancini's daily routine at Universal, studying the clichés of Hollywood storytelling music, was the perfect on-the-job training for his career to come. Among his first assignments was to score the studio's glamorous two-reeler films with titles like *The World's Most Beautiful Girls*, *Fun for All*, and *Calypso Carnival*. The first feature-length film receiving more than a handful of music cues from Mancini was called *Willie and Joe Back at the Front* (1952). There he worked in tandem with Herman Stein. World War II cartoonist Bill Mauldin's famous comic strip characters, the army discontents Willie and Joe, had been previously packaged for the movies by Universal in a 1951 film called *Up Front*, meaning, of course, the not-so-long-past war front. *Back at the Front* served as its sequel, a plotless comedy about these two GIs, one of whom just wants to sleep away his army enlistment and perhaps do a little sightseeing, while the other longs for some female attention. Soon they are swept up in a plot to catch a smuggler working out of postwar Tokyo. Such films were a way of engaging the audience's continuing interest in military subjects while not actually talking about the war.

Because Mancini was just learning from Herman Stein; because Stein wrote in so many different styles, including some that sounded like Mancini's pop roots; and because all Universal scores, no matter who had composed their separate parts, had their final orchestrations filled out by the same man, David Tamkin, it would be hard to know for sure without seeing the studio's actual cue-assignment sheets which pieces were done by Mancini and which by Stein. And of course the two composers were working hard to achieve that very anonymity. In the case of *Back at the Front*, cue sheets do reveal that the broader, more formal opening and the ending music are by Stein, but an unusually large amount of the scoring that backs the various shenanigans of Willie and Joe is by Mancini. He relied on a lot of the old comedy score clichés right from the start: the old-fashioned use of bassoon chuckling or muted brass *wah-wahs* to cap a joke, even the cartoonish effect of two flutes and xylophone playing that comic *plink-plink* in half-step intervals as though winking at the audience. Two themes recur: one is Mancini's Tokyo theme, the other is a humorous Americanization of that theme, which rises on the scale one phrase at a time throughout the various hide-and-seek scenes in the story. The main Tokyo theme (first heard as the characters enter the city, then later in a rickshaw sequence, etc.), although based on the proper oriental-sounding scales, is more accurately in a Chinese style rather than Japanese as it was supposed to be—perky and noticeable but perhaps too often dependent in its arrangement on those comic winks and nudges from the woodwinds—and, of course, ethnically rude.

As a sign of growing confidence, Gershenson gradually gave Mancini a shot at writing the opening main title music for several films of that year— even dramatic pictures like *The Raiders, All I Desire*, and *City Beneath the Sea.* The latter title, starring Robert Ryan and Anthony Quinn as deep-sea treasure divers, featured less than half a score by Mancini, but it was an early chance for him to write some voodoo drum music, some pale romantic cues, even a bit of stereotypical Jamaican music not found in the Universal library. He also used the assignment to explore some thicker-than-usual clusters of tropical harmony attempting to evoke the depths (literally) to which men will go for gold.

It Came from Outer Space (1953), directed by Jack Arnold and starring Richard Carlson, contains some thirty-six cues of music spread among the three assigned composers, and there is much sharing of one another's musical material as the cues are shuffled throughout the film. Although Mancini's assigned music cues for this film amount to slightly more screen time than his two other colleagues were given, his contribution appears to mimic Stein's lead, which has been established in the main title, and he seeks only to carry it on. But bits of that score found their way into the next year's even bigger Universal hit, *Creature from the Black Lagoon* (1954), which told of an Amazonian expedition coming to terms with, and coming to blows with, the legend of a mysterious river-borne "gill-man" creature. The plain sight of a stuntman in a rubber creature costume was not considered especially embarrassing to movie audiences of that day, whose suspension of disbelief during all kinds of hokey matinee family films was nearly absolute. And viewer forgiveness extended to a lot of overwrought soundtrack music as well.

The most famous feature of the score to *Creature from the Black Lagoon* is Herman Stein's distinctive triplet motif for the creature: two half-step intervals in trumpets with a tongue flutter on the flatted third. Nearly every appearance of the creature was announced by that figure, making the soundtrack an integral part of the film's very style. Hans Salter's more dramatic cues and Mancini's more pastoral ones likewise add to the storytelling and the scene setting. The final music tally: Salter, twelve cues; Stein, only seven cues, but important ones; and Mancini, ten cues.

Stein's main title music is purposefully harsh, full of tragic brass lines, to announce the importance and danger of all they are planning to show us. His short music cue, as we first see one webbed claw emerge from the lagoon to paw at the muddy bank, is perfectly judged: the full force of the triplet creature motif we will come to know so well, then the deepening and empowering of it as the claw draws back—just outlandish enough to be matinee movie music, just dark and laconic enough to worry us a bit.

The next cue is Mancini: a rapturous description of the underwater world that cue sheets show to be titled "The Diver" for strings, winds in pairs, harp, celesta, and vibraphone. Its lyrical quality and its impressionistic Debussy style certainly make the shifting submarine currents come alive for us, and there is even a melodic feeling here that begins to sound like the personal Mancini. With this score, he was trying to prove to his boss and colleagues that he could write in dramatic styles and in the scene-setting (and perhaps scene-stealing) lyrical ways that can make even a crude action film attractive.

At the same time as he worked on scores for those Creature movies, Mancini also had to find ways to score the misadventures of Universal's resident homespun eccentric country farmer characters Ma and Pa Kettle (and their "13 to 15 children"), eventually a series of films sporting a low kind of quip humor, occasional knockabout gags, and a standing invitation to laugh at Pa Kettle's make-do schemes—all set to barnyard music. In one episode from the middle of the series, *Ma and Pa Kettle at Home* (1954), featuring more than the usual ratio of Mancini music, the Kettles have welcomed two New York magazine reporters—one snooty and anxiety-ridden about being in the country, the other a "regular guy" who acts as mediator and translator and falls for the Kettles's daughter. If the city slickers like the farm life, they will run a feature article and Kettle Jr. will win a scholarship of some kind. As the snobbish visitor, Mr. Mannering, begins his cursory inspection of the Kettle place, Mancini's music cue is a mock military march that comments on pompous authoritarianism as Mannering struts around the grounds, looking into corners, nosing into feed bags, dodging a runaway goat, and maintaining a sneer of superiority throughout. The march is, of course, constantly broken up by instrumental details matched to the gags on screen—the brief crescendo in the orchestra as the goat charges, the pizzicato strings in the background as the Kettles walk on eggshells hoping to impress. In the same way, Mancini teases Mannering, who stands in his ridiculous city pajamas, about to climb into bed next to a surprised chicken, with an oboe from the Universal orchestra serenading him in a snide version of "Brahms's Lullaby." These are miniature examples where Mancini was able to impose himself on the action, to step outside of mere accompaniment and offer comic asides. When a whole orchestra has to coax a creature out of a black lagoon, the composer's job is just to be larger than life and fairly convincing. Here in these quieter dumb comedies, Mancini could play around a bit.

One should be clear, though; this Kettle scoring as it stands by itself is nothing to praise in particular. In comparison with major comedy scores of that period from the larger studios (such as David Raksin's *Pat and Mike* or *The Secret Life of Walter Mitty* and Bronislau Kaper's *Auntie Mame*) this is trivial, just as Mancini's outer-space musings are menial next to, say, Bernard Herrmann's powerful scoring to the major flying-saucer flick *The Day the Earth Stood Still*. But seen as a scoring exercise in the lesson plan of Mancini's development in B-movie music circles, it carries a certain interest.

For Universal's World War II story *To Hell and Back* (1955), which starred Audie Murphy reenacting his own battle experiences, which had made him, at the age of nineteen, the most decorated American soldier of the war and would soon make him a successful movie star, Mancini revisited both his own war memories and his early West Aliquippa marching band days. This time he was allowed to score the film's opening main title sequence: a full military band rendition of the barracks song "Dog-Faced Soldier" with almost a swing feeling. Most of the dramatic scoring was still not Mancini's, but the shrewdly arranged accompaniment to an accordion as troops enter Italy, the sad oboe version of "Dog-Faced Soldier" as a comrade dies, and the guitar/celesta/

flute murmurings as raindrops fall on the GI's body are Mancini's—signs of his growing enthusiasm for the subtleties of movie scoring.

One by-product of scoring main title cues, though, may have been to start Mancini thinking in terms of the importance of a central, memorable tune to represent a film before the public. Thus, the 1955 Universal film *Foxfire* drew from Mancini his first distinct film song with lyrics and a straining vocal by the film's star Jeff Chandler. It is a typical minor-key torch song of that period, but more focused and natural, with that inevitable flow that would become a Mancini hallmark.

Mancini and lyricist Chandler teamed up for several more songs in 1955. The film *One Desire* featured a vocal by Gene Boyd in a Mancini arrangement that harkened back to the clarinet-led sax section of Glenn Miller. But their big song that year was surely "Six Bridges to Cross" from the film of the same name, starring Universal's Tony Curtis, about the rise of a Boston kid (played in youth by Sal Mineo in his first big role) into the crime scene. Mancini's opening melody starts high, trying to make the awkward title sound natural—"Six bridges to cross / which one is the right one"—then settles into the cloying but solid features of a mid-range love song. There are clear similarities, too, to a far more famous song of that day derived from Bronislau Kaper's score to *Green Dolphin Street* (1947). Still, Mancini's take on it seems original enough (Kaper ends his first phrase with an exotic interval leap of the augmented fourth where Mancini only jumps to the more traditional fourth). In any case, as a song, "Six Bridges to Cross" would become Mancini's first moderate hit, selling more than three hundred thousand copies on the Decca label.

≡ ≡ ≡

It is fitting that Mancini's first onscreen credit (even before *Foxfire* and *Bridges* showed his name as a songwriter) would come as an arranger in 1954 for the Universal bio-pic musical *The Glenn Miller Story* (the credit actually reads "Joseph Gershenson and Henry Mancini"). His wartime brush with Miller and his postwar stint in the Beneke-Miller band made him the ideal guy to handle this particular assignment. As with *Meet Danny Wilson* and other more orchestrally active Universal musicals (*So This Is Paris* features a good deal of Mancini orchestration), in *The Glenn Miller Story* he was being called on to supervise the music of other people, orchestrating and arranging the dance music and songs while composing bits of transitional music to keep the film moving dramatically—some were romantic in nature, some were lightly comic, like the bouncy strings and flutes in thirds as Miller (played by Jimmy Stewart) excitedly phones his wife, Helen, just after his first band success. Mancini thought an original melody was needed to underline the Millers's budding relationship as Glenn and Helen sit on her parents' porch swing. Glenn presents her with a necklace, and, on the soundtrack, a muted solo violin blends with warm string harmonies behind (they could get away with such sentiment in those days), introducing Mancini's latest important movie tune, later given words by Don Raye, called "Too Little Time." It is a melody reminiscent of the old Arthur Johnston and Sam Caslow song "My Old Flame" except that, again like the aforementioned Kaper example, it resolves more conventionally.

The Glenn Miller Story turned out to be one of Universal's biggest hits that year and, even more surprising, found itself on the Academy Awards list with a nomination for best score adaptation, Mancini's first Oscar possibility (the score lost to Adolph Deutsch and Saul Chaplin's orchestrations and arrangements for the major musical *Seven Brides for Seven Brothers*) and indeed his first contact with any kind of awards since winning the "First Flutist" recognition certificate in 1936's Pennsylvania All-Star Band. Even that mild fame brought a few freelance jobs arranging albums for other artists like clarinetist Gus Bivona, who included one original Mancini piece on his disc, the playful "Clarinet Parmesan." However, Mancini was still responsible for the normal run of other Universal films coming down the line, and his output during this period seems to be driven by his growing sense of optimism and individuality even though the plots and style of the films themselves would hardly warrant it.

The first of these cast Charlton Heston in a comic role as a by-the-book army major who is reassigned to take charge of the ROTC program at a Catholic boys' school. *The Private War of Major Benson* (1955) featured a tiny, toothy, squirmy kid whose accuracy in memorizing and delivering lines and whose contrast to the gruff Heston character earned laughs in the theater and earned him a multi-film contract at Universal. Six-year-old Tim Hovey was billed as the new Shirley Temple (meaning the next big child star), although he had nowhere near her range or charisma. Major Benson, after his initial surprise at being exiled to a boys' school, is appalled and bewildered at the lack of discipline in the ranks. The nuns are all wise and patient; the school nurse (Universal regular Julie Adams) falls for the new major, but the kids keep getting in the way, especially the needy Hovey character called Tiger. For him, Mancini wrote the charming miniature march heard in the film's opening titles and reprised nearly every time his character figures in the plot. Ideally suited to a muted toy trumpet with a light and springy accompaniment, the tune found a second life away from this film as a single 45 rpm record. Expanded with a bridge composed by Herman Stein, it was recorded under the title "Toy Tiger" and had a typical latter-day Mancini charm. Indeed, it proved so popular that Universal renamed young Hovey's later film in its honor, *Toy Tiger* (1956).

By Universal standards, Tim Hovey's Tiger and Henry Mancini's score were a success. Therefore it was Mancini who took over the music for 1956's next Hovey vehicle, *Everything But the Truth*. Its breezy main title music by Mancini begins with a flourish introducing the happy suburban life of children on their way to school. The tiny kid acting as a crossing guard is our hero, Tim Hovey, as orphan Willy Taylor, and for him Mancini creates a recurring three-flute phrase that is supposed to represent Hovey's nonchalant cuteness. Willy's teacher, played by Maureen O'Hara, has extracted a pledge from him that he will always tell the truth. That leads to nothing but trouble when, during his very public campaign for boy mayor, Willy casually mentions that his uncle once gave kickback money to a local politician. He is immediately suspended from the crossing guards and pushed by the mayor to retract his statement. Just tell a "white lie," he is urged if he cannot recant altogether. Only his teacher encourages him to stand fast. She enlists the help of a newspaper columnist (John Forsythe) to publicize the story and give Willy's dilemma a national airing.

Besides the happy opening tune, with its playground leap up a major sixth and then a romp down the scale, there are two subordinate themes to the score (mostly by Mancini but with some technical collaboration by Stein and Irving Gertz). One of these themes is a romantic piece as the teacher, Miss Wilson, and the columnist find a mutual attraction during their crusade to exonerate Willy, and the other is a sexier sax theme whenever Miss Wilson turns on her feminine wiles to gain some advantage over the enemy. But Mancini's real accomplishment here is the way in which his recognizable theme is woven into, and occasionally rises out of, the non-thematic functional music with increasing finesse and a fledgling sense of sophistication. Catch Mancini's brief minor-key phrase that momentarily darkens the main theme as Miss Wilson once tries to convince Willy to temporarily bend the truth (when she thinks the pressure has become too much for him), or hear another mock march as Forsythe's character dictates his plan of attack against the enemy. Instinctively, Mancini was doing more with this score than he had for that other David and Goliath story, *The Private War of Major Benson*, because he was getting more from the screen—not just an awkward army major among minors, but a little satire on power and corruption, on male ego, and on the incorruptible stuff of childhood.

Of course, even after all of his work on *Everything But the Truth*, there was still no screen credit for Mancini; the music is listed as having been supervised by Gershenson's assistant Milt Rosen. And yet, up in the main offices of Universal, it was decided that the time had come to talk with Mancini about plans to develop a new genre that was "hip" with the times: the teen musical. They had cost-analysis sheets for all the big teen dramatic films of the day, not only *Rebel Without a Cause* but also *Crime in the Streets* and *Blackboard Jungle*, all released within months of each other. All had groundbreaking music scores too—symphonic jazz-rock by Leonard Rosenman, urban jazz by Franz Waxman, and borrowed bebop records, respectively. The wartime consumers and big band listeners had had their day—these were the postwar babies coming of age, and they wanted to hear their kind of music. We can imagine the fear struck in the hearts of Universal's music department at a time like this. Mancini was the youngest guy there, and they were looking to him now as the conduit that might connect the orchestral traditions they had taught him, the band music from which he had come, and this new breed of garage pop. James Dean had just been martyred on the California highways to the "cause" of restlessness and recklessness. Southern rockers like Elvis Presley who had picked up black blues and gospel singing styles while loitering on the Mississippi street corners added a seductive quality to the mix.

As opportunistic as ever, Universal put together a package they thought would address all of those qualities and called it *Rock, Pretty Baby* (1956), the first rocker film musical. Naturally, in the same way they had homogenized the western film into a generic formula product, defanged the horror film, and domesticated the comedy film, they immediately de-radicalized their first teen musical past any question of rebelliousness or even impoliteness. Nor was the idea of a raucous music score ever really on the table. But Mancini could work with that. This was a chance to write original songs and to gain screen credit for them.

Mancini's main love song, original to this film, was called "What's It Gonna Be," with lyrics by Bill Carey, a gently reassuring and conservative tune preserving an atmosphere of safety around these movie kids. Only in its transitional phrase setting up the end, as Mancini passes from F through $A^{\flat 7}$ and $D^{\flat}$ to a suspended C^7 chord, is there a sense of something modern. More ambitious is the welcome touch of jazz that Mancini brings, if not to the main score, then through a device in the plot itself. In this case, Jim's girl, whose parents disapprove of Jim, secretly signals to him by placing her radio on his front porch. It is tuned to Mancini's first truly distinctive movie composition—a cool walking bass piece in D minor called "Free and Easy" for sax, vibes (vibraphones), and brushes on the drums that moves so smoothly between minor and major via augmented seventh chords that you can hear the echo of the new jazz school that was making the rounds called West Coast Cool. The piece is on screen for only forty-three seconds, and it does not seem the type of music that these self-centered teens would even understand, yet it does make itself known. *Rock, Pretty Baby* proved a big ticket seller for Universal that summer. For Mancini it meant another breakthrough—the first soundtrack record album ever issued of Mancini music.

A third film in the Creature series surfaced during that year as well, *The Creature Walks Among Us*. Although the cast and production values of each succeeding film in this series were gradually descending into self-parody, for Mancini they continued to be important assignments. But it was through just such preposterous monster movies, through those likable, sympathetic comedy scores for Tim Hovey and those few film songs Mancini was able to write, that he was finding his forte. This is not to say he was anyone's equal yet in the movie music field. Stein was still quicker and surer, Salter more serious. Irving Gertz was another at Universal who could still outdo Mancini. Gertz's score for, say, the first five reels (and reel 9) of *Monolith Monsters* (1957) amounts to a very cogent, intelligent, and expressive atonal canon well ahead of Mancini's own passive lazy music in reel 8 of the same film.

Mancini was still very much the apprentice, and yet new opportunities were approaching him fast. One more GIs-in-Japan comedy, *Joe Butterfly*, received Mancini scoring in this period, incorporating the usual jokey clichés in the orchestration and another ethnically wrongheaded (though admittedly cute) Chinese-sounding theme for the story's Tokyo locale. The film contains no space for a music score to gain a foothold beyond the half dozen references to that Tokyo theme and the introduction of a sort of love theme for the growing attraction between Audie Murphy as Private Joe Woodley and a local girl, Chieko. At last, in this latter gentle melody, composed on the pentatonic scale, there *is* an authentic Japanese sound, harmonized clearly and properly. As with most of this score, the Chieko theme (later extracted from the film and given lyrics by Rod McKuen as "Lonely Winter") is heard only faintly, briefly (three different times) behind dialogue. Mancini really only serves a mood-setting function here and helps with scene transitions. If it could be heard apart, the score might impress us with its likable, bright, and tuneful manner, in spite of all the clowning touches. Together, Mancini and McKuen recorded a demo disc of "Lonely Winter" in September 1957 with some hope of its release, but no one really cared. *Joe Butterfly* served its season and disappeared.

That same month, however, *would* finally see the Mancini name on a disc as the principal recording artist. Someone at L.A.-based Liberty Records had been listening to Mancini's quiet beach music in *Rock, Pretty Baby* and thought that a most "romantic" album of tropically soothing pop ballads for that teen-boy-and-girl market could be produced as a demonstration of Liberty's new Spectra-Sonic Sound recording process. They would call it *Driftwood and Dreams,* one whole album of a single beach-hammock mood in which Mancini the creative arranger made do with just four players and a small wordless chorus. The album had a clean sincerity about it; Mancini found thoughtful ways of exploring new bass lines on familiar songs like "The Breeze and I" and "Ebb Tide." And he contributed two original tunes, harmonically interesting if not quite authoritative yet—"Driftwood and Dreams" and "The Whispering Sea." Releasing one's own pop album was obviously a major career milestone. It suggested individuality as opposed to the studied anonymity of the Universal corporate style.

In 1957 came Universal's second try at a teen musical, *Summer Love,* and a related record album featuring fifteen Mancini tracks, including lots of bop rock, one cool jazz tune ("Theme for a Crazy Chick"), and one bland ballad. But what he wanted more than disc credits now was a dramatic film score, all his own, and his name finally up there in the credits as the sole composer.

— — —

The vehicle for Henry Mancini's first onscreen credit as composer of a complete dramatic film score was 1957's *Man Afraid,* Universal Studio's third attempt to make a child star of the *Toy Tiger* tyke, Tim Hovey. A burglar breaks into the home of Rev. Dan Collins (George Nader), scares his son Michael (Hovey), and injures his wife (Phyllis Thaxton). Collins struggles with the young intruder and kills him with the closest blunt object at hand: his son's glass snow globe. Later we discover that Simmons, the grief-stricken father (Edward Franz) of the burglar, has begun to stalk Rev. Collins's son, bent on retaliation—a son for a son.

Man Afraid uses its main title sequence to set up the home invasion scene. We see the late-night suburban neighborhood of the Collins house: an establishing shot of the property, then the approach of an intruder who frightens a cat off the picket fence. A smoothly gliding camera (by Universal's best cameraman, Russell Metty, whom Orson Welles would soon praise and utilize) takes us to the ground-level bedroom window of the room where young Michael sleeps. Mancini's music follows three lines that eventually converge. The first is a repeating ostinato of low piano notes doubled by basses in what seem to be alternating time signatures; the second, for unison strings, is the same apparently alternating statement delayed by half a measure so that the two lines clash and mesh in counterpoint like a round. Then as the film's title appears, unison trombones and trumpets present the third line, an urgent declarative sentence spanning the interval of the tritone, that ancient musical representation of evil or mystery or distress. As a police car rolls by in the street, oblivious to the scene, the soundtrack strings assume a double-time version of the opening motif, the trombones and a drum switch to a pattern of rhythmic punches in twos and threes, while the trumpets take over that opening declarative statement. Only when the strings smooth out to accompany the trumpets can we finally discern that all of that agitated, accented writing so far, with its apparently broken rhythms, has actually, ingeniously been contained within a standard 3/4 meter all along.

Just as the intruder reaches the house and manipulates the screen of the bedroom window, the soundtrack orchestra slows and trades aggression for a kind of watchful tension. This also coincides with the display of Mancini's name in the screen credits. A solo French horn leads to brass chords gradually bringing the tension down, though that opening piano/bass coupling still interjects occasional reminders of the danger at hand. As director Harry Keller cuts to an interior shot of the intruder climbing in through the window, Mancini brings out a brief exchange between two flutes, perhaps relating the two sons for their few moments together, one asleep, the other about to die.

The focus of the rest of the film is on the fathers, the demented despondency of the one and the conscience of the other. *Man Afraid*'s second music cue (low, searching strings) comes as the two fathers meet at the police station, one reaching out, the other turning away. Its third cue is a variation of the opening horn motif in the main title and is heard as Simmons sees a photograph of young Michael in a TV story about the burglary and comes up with his revenge idea. These are Mancini's intelligent and somewhat individualistic reactions to the Universal suspense formula, a cut above B-movie scoring per se, yet still part of the tradition. Where Mancini really begins to leave his mark, though, is the next music cue—a key musical set piece (an individual tune meant for one scene only) in the evolution of Mancini's own film language: the use of melody, here a humorous one, not just to accompany a scene but to influence it as well.

Young Michael is exploring the old derelict skiffs and paddleboats by the town wharf with some neighborhood kids. He alone has the courage to board one of the boats, declaring there may be pirates belowdecks. The other friends scatter, and as Michael walks the plank from shore to shipboard the music cue begins, a bassoon outlining a perky sea chantey against plucked strings. A threatening close-up shot of Simmons's footsteps on the plank behind Michael invites the return of the piano/bass motif from the film's opening, and a slow-building suspense commences. Now, as Mancini repeats the sea chantey, he adapts it into a minor key. Further echoes of the tune keep surfacing for oboe, then bass clarinet, but in this same darker garb. It is true that a couple of Simmons's threatening reappearances during the film are scored reflexively by Mancini with a bit too much melodrama, as though we were about to sight the Black Lagoon creature again, but most of *Man Afraid*'s score holds to a consistently serious and human level. It is the first genuine "Mancini score," and there, finally, is his name on screen to prove it.

Mancini's experience with scoring *Man Afraid* was a revelation to him, and he began to lobby for any solo-credited scoring jobs Universal would give him. The very next was a low-budget police drama called *Damn Citizen* (1957), shot cheaply on location in Louisiana with quick camera setups, crude lighting techniques that cast careless shadows, and using local townspeople in speaking roles. The film was touted as an exposé of corruption in the state police force and utilized a dry *Dragnet*-inspired narrator to tell the tale of a World War II vet who is unexpectedly elected superintendent of Louisiana's top cops. Predictably, the local crime bosses resent his interventionist philosophy. "He ain't no real cop," they say. "He's just a damn citizen." The film resorts to music only a few times, and Mancini seems to have volunteered for the assignment too quickly, having no idea how to approach it musically and so drawing heavily instead on the previous season's hit jazz soundtrack by Elmer Bernstein, *Man with the Golden Arm*. His entire score takes less than fifteen minutes and consists of a few brass stings derived from the film's opening (a low piano ostinato, four-to-the-bar, and the unison brass blowing against saxes, guitar, and trombones together—almost a paraphrase of the Bernstein style), two full reprises of the main theme, and several pieces of party/dance music: rock 'n' roll sax pieces mostly, imported from other films (at a party at the mob boss's house you can hear Mancini's "Too Little Time" from *The Glenn Miller Story* playing in the background). Later, Mancini even called the whole experience "my Bernstein moment."

He worked more confidently on two subsequent credited scores, even though for each he was asked to use a main theme contributed by someone else. In one case, a grim melodrama about alcoholism known by the oxy-moronic title of *Voice in the Mirror*, the opening song was written by Bobby Troup with a lyric and sultry vocal by the film's costar Julie London. Mancini's score often references the song (which is really just a blurry sort of "Bali Ha'i" phrase repeated three or four times) during scenes where London, as the worried wife, and Richard Egan, as the booze-tormented Jim Burton, try to relate to each other. Burton was once a top graphic artist; now he is just a desperate, coin-stealing, excuse-making, bottle-chasing alcoholic. He has variously sought help and advice from doctors, friends, and priests. His own physician, played by Walter Matthau, sympathizes but leaves it up to him to reform. Director Harry Keller from *Man Afraid* creates a fast-moving and fairly realistic narrative that admits the melodrama of the D.T.'s and the scary dreams (in this case, an effective nightmare sequence about being run down by a train in some abstract tunnel), but also allows a quietness and subtlety to form around some of the performances, especially Arthur O'Connell as Tobin, a fellow drinker to whose future sobriety Burton devotes himself before he can truly handle his own. They backslide together sometimes, but the effort to help another person seems to be building strength in Burton.

Mancini chooses a darkly clouded orchestra, sometimes employing the strings in two sections of twisted chromatic lines as Burton sets out in search of a bottle. Often Mancini kicks up the meter with a quick dissonant piccolo/piano effect that sounds like some flashing "danger" light going off in Burton's head: the addiction needing to be fed. Mancini cannot give those passages the fire and fearsomeness of Bernstein's scoring for the mania of heroin addiction as in *Man with the Golden Arm*. Instead he empathizes with the addict's experience of hopelessness, of feeling nagged and pursued. You hear that point of view in Mancini's string writing, which grovels like a whipped animal, or his high saxes, which wail like tortured souls as though Burton were being hounded by outside demons. "It's the middle of the night for us," says Tobin, referring to that feeling of lonely exile that all insomniacs dread and all alcoholics share. Mancini uses the clear, round sound of an alto sax to speak on behalf of Burton's wife—the voice of cool reason. When Burton's physician calls him a "classic alcoholic," we can hear the other-worldly sound of a bass flute in the background as mid-range strings play in slurred chromatic lines.

Burton's first day at a new graphic design job also happens to be his first dry day in a long while, and as he tries to concentrate at his desk he becomes obsessed with a bottle of whiskey standing near one of the file cabinets (it turns out to be a gag radio in the shape of a bottle). As he starts sweating over the proximity of his next drink, Mancini's score begins a loping, low piano rhythm. The sound of it starts to nag us as muted brass join in, then deep trombones, the whole structure building in volume and tightness. Finally, as Burton can take no more, the soundtrack climaxes in two high, piercing trumpet spurts, one of which is fed through a reverberation filter to sound like a cry of pain. It is clear that Burton is not ready to return to work yet—*and* that Mancini has discovered how music can control a dramatic scene.

Flood Tide (1958) was Mancini's other credited dramatic score of this period in which the main title theme was written by another composer, in this case veteran library contributor William Lava. Here, George Nader was the star, who as character Steve Martin rents a beach house and becomes involved with a widow next door and her crippled ten-year-old son, who has witnessed and then lied about a murder. At first Martin is just interested in the mother, but as he befriends the boy, questions arise about the murder, especially when an innocent man is arrested for it. Through Martin's probing and the boy's defensiveness, issues of trust become the subject of the film and the score. William Lava was a freelance composer who worked steadily in all media and occasionally wrote for Universal's library. Self-taught and simple in style, his themes often proceeded like anthems. His opening tune for *Flood Tide* has a sincere *life lesson* feeling to it, which Mancini exploits handily by casting it in his own warm string writing, thus making the music stand for the familial love that this defensive, confused child wishes he could share.

Major Mancini scenes in the score include a sailboat trip between Martin and the boy, where music suggests a sailor's delight as we first watch their skiff on the water: bright, zestful gestures in the orchestration as the two play at being offshore fishermen, then suddenly darker sounds at the low end of the orchestra when this unbalanced boy begins to act suspiciously, reaches for Martin's rifle and, for a moment, seems to threaten him with it so that we begin to wonder if he was involved somehow in the beach house murder. Waiting on shore for their return, his mother hears three shots from their direction (with low piano notes and dark strings in the music score). She meets their sailboat at the dock, and Martin tells her the boy was only target shooting at an old gas can floating on the tide. There is immediate relief in the music. But Mancini reasserts Lava's theme with a full range of feeling later as we watch the boy finally confess what he saw "that night." *Flood Tide* succeeds as an earnest little fable of ordinary people who wish they could admit their faults and feelings, but who are afraid to because to confess risks a flood tide of emotion, more than most can handle. Even working within the Lava material, there are traces of the emerging Mancini's personal voice as a passionate scorer.

— — —

It was at once discouraging and fortuitous that just as Mancini was beginning to enjoy credited recognition for solo dramatic scores, just as his name was beginning to circulate as a composer to watch, rumors were also starting to spread about troubled times for the studio itself as uninvited takeover bids pressed Universal executives to make changes in order to keep up with the majors. Probably only in such a climate of uncertainty would Universal brass have ever asked the brilliantly unpredictable Orson Welles to sign on as director of one of their floundering projects in 1958, *Touch of Evil*, hoping he might make it a surprise hit for them. He was originally slated to portray a corrupt sheriff in a Mexican border town, but with the blessing of the film's other star, Charlton Heston, they also signed Welles as director, and because of his own career lulls and stalls elsewhere, he agreed. The film he made has become a minor, if baffling, classic.

The two memorable elements from viewing *Touch of Evil* today are, first, the border town itself, with its shadowy (one critic called it "infected") atmosphere of decadence, its dark soiled alleys, its nightmarish hotel rooms and drug bosses and hungry wolf-pack delinquents, its bleak oil rigs at the edge of town, all given an extra feverish Latin touch by Mancini's most aggressive score at Universal; and, second, Welles's own corpulent self as the cigar-chomping, trench-coated, slit-eyed, amoral town sheriff, Hank Quinlan, who has made a career of coercing confessions, planting evidence, bullying and barking, and bellying up to the local politicians to be sure they look the other way. In addition to Heston as Mexican police agent Mike Vargas, there is Janet Leigh as Vargas's American wife and, working for union-scale wages in a role not in the original novel but added by Welles, the famous Marlene Dietrich as Tana, a madam from Quinlan's old brothel past, who has the last word on him at the end of the film and then does one of the great walk-offs in film history.

Welles was very happy to accept as his cinematographer Universal's regular salaried cameraman Russell Metty, because he had worked with him before (Metty had shot *The Stranger* for him) and because Metty was interested to try some of Welles's daring ideas. Indeed, *Touch of Evil*'s first shot has become famous: a long, complex, tracking/dollying/craning shot that runs three and a half minutes without a cut. (Check out Metty's opening uncut camera work in a film from 1947, *Ride the Pink Horse*, and compare it to this film's opening to see how much he must have contributed to Welles's vision here.) It opens on an extreme close-up of the numbered dial on a time bomb. Someone's hand sets the timer device, and as that person pivots away and runs offscreen right, the camera heads down an alley toward a parked car, catching the bomber's shadow as it darts across the alley wall. We see him slip the explosive into the car's trunk and dash off. Now the camera (still the same rolling take) pulls back and begins to rise on a crane just as a laughing, oblivious couple strolls up and gets into the car. As the car pulls away, our high perspective follows it slowly down the main street of this border town. It looks like a Saturday night; people are out wandering around, checking in at the bars, cruising and browsing and loitering. The doomed car overtakes our visual frame, and we catch up to Vargas and his wife walking along as part of the street crowd. Welles's original soundtrack concept was to run this whole opening-shot sequence using just fragments of ambient music emerging from clubs and bars along the street (he specified Afro-Cuban music rather than clichéd Mexicali pieces) that would fade in and out of one another as Vargas and his wife proceeded. And the shot itself would remain uncut and uncovered.

Instead, against Welles's wishes, the studio decided to use the shot in its entirety but run the film's opening credit graphics over it; thus it would become the background for the main title sequence. As such, they said it would need a three-and-a-half-minute piece of opening title music. It is not known what Welles thought of Mancini's beginning music here and the way it mixes with the visual action behind those opening titles. Undoubtedly he regretted their placing even these unobtrusive credits over his hard-won virtuoso first shot, and he probably preferred the subtlety of indirect inside-the-setting music rather than direct-to-the-audience music, which narrative scoring represents. But in truth, viewing both versions today, the Mancini-scored alternative, with its tapped bongos over the close-up of the time bomb's dial, its simmering sax lines as we view the shadowy street, and the powerful brass theme that predicts the dangerous game to come, accomplishes a lot more than Welles's ambient distant "source" music could have done to set up the story and the film's point of view.

Although Mancini reported attending only one studio staff meeting at which Welles actually appeared—and even then Welles had not spoken to him—he has said that his own plans for the rest of the music score were along the same lines that Welles later outlined. The ambient Latin band music that one would naturally hear coming from the bars, hotels, jukeboxes, and car radios on a typical border-town evening would gradually and subtly start to interact with, and become synchronized with, the story and action on screen—"source music" would imperceptibly take on the function of a narrative score.

Quinlan's murder of mob boss Uncle Joe Grandi is a good example. Quinlan has lured Grandi to a hotel room. Neon lights and wild dance music blast in through the window from the streets below. Slowly that music is being turned up on the soundtrack and grows in violence as though becoming involved in the killing to come. Two blaring opposing solo trumpets over a persistent honking sax are the elements of the dramatic score that appear to be up here with us at the scene of the crime, and then gradually the wild horns of the street music add in through the window and blend ecstatically with the functional scoring until the soundtrack is all one cauldron of hot Afro-Cuban chaos. Quinlan tears at, beats, and strangles Grandi while the music is at its most alarming pitch, "so that what had begun at a double rhythm goes into a triple time and then a quadruple time and, by the time he strangles the guy, the band's going crazy," as Mancini said. "Dramatic sequences in that score were really just another aspect of the source music that was already coming from the streets. That's exactly what Welles had wanted all along, although I must admit I was committed to that approach before I ever knew what Welles was thinking."[4] This was becoming too much for Universal executives screening the rough cut—too real and too surreal at the same time.

Another example of how Mancini's concept for the score fell in line with Welles's own is the old player-piano waltz that he wrote for Tana's brothel. Welles specified that it should be a somewhat tawdry-sounding tune yet have a certain nostalgia about it, hinting at Quinlan's distant past with her when they were both in better shape. "You're a mess honey; I didn't recognize you," she tells him now. "You should lay off the candy bars." And he sighs back at her, "Well, it's either the candy or the hooch," as Mancini's "good old days" tune plugs away in the background.

In the end, out on a decrepit bridge over a slurry creek by the oil rigs at the edge of town, Quinlan's Sergeant Menzies finally accuses him of graft and murder and playing him for a fool all these years. As Menzies threatens to expose the whole mess, Quinlan shoots him dead, and Mancini pegs the moment with the deepest trombone notes, given more ferocity by tubas doubling them. High trumpets pierce the ceiling—all of them playing in primitive chords that are related harmonically to those first three chords we heard opening the score. Menzies gets off one more gunshot before he collapses, aimed at his old boss. Tana is there as a witness and delivers her now-famous epitaph over Hank Quinlan's body with an existential shrug, saying, "He was some kind of a man. What does it matter what you say about people?" as we listen to that well-remembered player-piano waltz by Mancini, definitely a piece of commentary scoring with no obvious source on the screen except memory.

There is no definitive answer as to why Universal took the film's final cutting away from Welles. It is true that after Welles had submitted his initial edit for *Touch of Evil*, he had moved on to other prospects. At any rate, Universal was now a half million dollars in debt, and they had been hoping for a tight, hot salable thriller film from Welles, not this unclassifiable character study with its seedy amoral universe, dark look, and cast of crazies.

In any case, Universal had come to a crossroads, quite apart from Welles. They were actually starting to talk about closing, or at least reforming, their operation completely. One idea was to transfer their future efforts into the business of their parent company, Decca Records, and to run their movie business, Universal-International, in a new way—not as a factory, but deal by deal. Another scenario had them merging with a corporate arm of MCA (Music Corporation of America). For now they just made plans to break up their operation. First to go would be their music department. Imagine Mancini here, at the highest point in his career thus far, suddenly unemployed. The Universal orchestra, the music library, orchestrator David Tamkin, composers Stein and Skinner, Gertz and Salter and Rosen, and Mancini were given notice. The era of assembly-line films and patchwork scoring, at least as an officially sanctioned method of music for the movies, was over.

Mancini had been making $350 per week by that time. Now he was making nothing. With a trace of desperation, he went around town pedaling the tapes of his *Touch of Evil* score to see if he could interest anyone in releasing it as a Latin record album. Decca did not want it, but he managed to convince a small label, Challenge Records, to sign him, and without fanfare or many sales thereafter Mancini had his first soundtrack album of a dramatic score, released in June 1958—his fourth credited album if you include the two rock musicals and *Driftwood and Dreams*.

Universal Studios itself took on a new focus, that upstart industry of the age—television. At first they just used TV to rerun their old movies. Then, as had happened with 1930s and 1940s network radio, they began to produce certain recurring dramas and comedies specifically made for the home audience. And, following the same history as the movie factory approach, a TV factory system began to emerge. Among the component parts of those productions, then, would have to be some attention to background music scoring. They drew on the vast Universal music library at first, but soon, as their confidence grew, they began to think about commissioning some original scores.

CHAPTER 4

Big Screen, Little Screen

For baby boomer Americans of the late 1950s, television was taking the place of an evening at the movies. Young families liked the idea of dialing in two or three TV stations and choosing their own entertainment without having to drive into town. And thus it was decreed that television would become the new assembly line of prepackaged film and entertainment products, albeit in the new short form of the TV series. How ironic, then, that the studio that copied its product line so shamelessly from the mainstream studios—sci-fi tales after Twentieth Century Fox's success, musicals after MGM, cheap horror films after its own early classics—should now become influential on the programming that this new medium of television began to produce. The Universal formula, not only the quick shooting/producing/scoring of established genre films, but also their whole roster of familiar characters and plots, would become standard fare for TV through the 1960s. *Francis the Talking Mule* would become TV's *Mr. Ed*, a sarcastic talking horse in a modern suburban setting. *Ma and Pa Kettle* would translate into various shows from *The Beverly Hillbillies*, with a hayseed entering big city life, and *Green Acres*, with city folks adapting to the farm. Universal's various creature features became *The Outer Limits*, with silly costumed monsters and pseudo-scientific plots (with orchestral scores by Mancini's accordion player on *Driftwood and Dreams*, Dominic Frontiere). The beach musicals became teen series like *Dobie Gillis* or teen-centered family shows like *Father Knows Best* or *The Donna Reed Show*. All of those Universal westerns encouraged long-running TV series like *Gunsmoke, Wagon Train,* and *Wyatt Earp.* And it is likely that Universal's toothy tot Tim Hovey, especially as seen in *Everything But the Truth,* inspired Jerry Mathers as the similarly earnest kid Beaver Cleaver in TV's *Leave It to Beaver.* Notice, too, the similarities between Mancini's *Toy Tiger* theme for Hovey in *The Private War of Major Benson* and Dave Kahn's musical theme for "The Beaver" on weekly TV. (For another Universal movie theme from those days that is even *more* like "The Beaver," check Mancini's main title music to *Kelly and Me*). The Universal music factory may have been closing, but its influence lived on.

Even so, Mancini was out of a job. Ginny was still working as a freelance studio singer around Hollywood, but the pay, if generous, was not continuous. Meanwhile, at home were six-year-old twins and an eight-year-old son. On the table were contracts for Mancini to arrange and conduct record albums, including two discs of Sousa marches. His career seemed to be headed away from films. But as Mancini tells it, fate intervened. Although he was no longer a staff composer at Universal, he still retained his studio pass, with which he could enter the movie lot, use the cafeteria, mingle informally with producers, and, on one important occasion, visit the studio barber shop. There in mid-1958 he would meet, from Ginny's wider circle of friends, the aforementioned Blake Edwards, who had just come from a meeting at which plans were solidified for a new TV series slated for September at NBC. When Edwards asked Mancini if he would be interested in composing the music for the new show, to be called *Peter Gunn,* he had in mind Mancini's arranging and producing the club music that would be needed in the series, because one of the recurring settings of the show would be a small jazz cafe. Mancini had previously given him the kind of soft big band style needed for the soundtrack of 1957's *Mister Cory* at Universal and some dance arrangements on two other films, so the casual attitude of Edwards's offer here is understandable. At first, with the word *Gunn* in its title, Mancini thought the series sounded like a western, but it was quickly explained how Peter Gunn was going to be a slick, easygoing, cool-to-danger, intriguing-to-the-ladies, private investigator; that each episode in the series was going to be sharply and stylishly shot like a mini-movie; and that each script would be crisp and modern. Down with the world-weary Phillip Marlowe/Humphrey Bogart detective antihero of the 1940s or the playboy private eye of the 1950s like Edwards's own "Richard Diamond" on radio. Gunn was just cool, and the music in the club he frequented (to be known slyly as "Mother's") should be West Coast Cool jazz.

Edwards, too, has recalled that initial meeting on the Universal lot outside the barbershop and has said there were never any discussions about dramatic scoring for the series at that time. Mancini, on the other hand, was already thinking along the same lines as his work for Orson Welles on *Touch of Evil*, where the music that was emanating naturally from the film's setting could be exploited and dynamically manipulated into service as a dramatic score. Mancini intuited that he could write for the five or six players who might be pictured in a club scene and bring that music forward sometimes to take on the responsibilities of narrative scoring, with extensions, digressions, builds, and climaxes that matched the action on screen. He would use jazz in a storytelling capacity. Edwards started to like the idea, and Mancini proposed that every thirty-minute episode of *Peter Gunn* should begin with the same chromatic walking bass figure to cover the one-minute teaser in which some robbery, killing, or con was depicted to set up that night's show. A deal was struck; Mancini once again had a job.

After each week's teaser, animated graphic lettering introducing *Peter Gunn*'s star, Craig Stevens, was accompanied by the most aggressive and pounding theme music TV had ever heard—music that had both the sophistication of jazz and the harshness, the drive, the audacity of rock 'n' roll. The "*Peter Gunn* Theme" opens with a steady-stomping ostinato in E minor for bass guitar that could be in any rock band, but then low piano notes double it, giving a jazzy quality. The entire piece keeps repeating that one E-minor chord, bluntly but knowingly, never modulating. The theme is so intentionally primitive that it really is more of a rock fanfare, (four trombones, four trumpets, four horns, and sax solo, augmented with piano and bass), always with that perpetual pounding rhythm underneath, just ripe for some high-flying powerful trumpet or sax to solo above. And each phrase of that theme ends with a quick "fall"—that is, the players are instructed to slur the last note downward, an old blues player's gesture used throughout the "*Peter Gunn* Theme" that lent a further contemporary streetwise sense to the ensemble playing. At home as well as in the studio offices, people sat up and heads were turned.

The other innovation in the scoring of *Peter Gunn* besides its raucous jazz-rock opening music and the use of cool jazz as a scoring element was the notion of giving every single weekly episode its own tailor-made score, not relying at all on some cache of library music to be tracked in by some music editor. Mancini scored each particular story as though it were a short film and, even though he returned to a few established themes, scored each show separately: hard rock/jazz during a tough fight scene; then a rich ballad if, say, a swanky downtown woman came into the club; then a bright, humorous piccolo piece as, for instance, in the clever syncopated circus march he wrote for a novelty episode in which Gunn has to babysit a trained seal that has swallowed a gutful of smuggled diamonds. And using all of his experience at Universal, Mancini was able to apply the same tricks of the trade to scoring transitional moments between scenes or to underline Gunn's dry banter with clients, villains, or police—all still within the jazz idiom (or because true jazz includes long flights of improvisatory playing that these scores did not have, we should rightfully call the *Peter Gunn* music jazz-pop: basically melodic pop music but with jazz inflections and harmonies).

Over the course of the series' 114 episodes, Mancini found a way to adjust to the needs of each plot. Sometimes a walking bass line alone would serve to unite a whole crime sequence no matter what instrumental solo or ensemble was presented on top of that—sometimes an original Mancini melody would introduce a featured character and then return in various places when the character recurred. And, of course, as with the Universal film scores, sometimes only brief transitional music stings were needed as bridges between scenes or to make way for the inevitable break for a commercial.

Usually an ensemble of twelve players was all the show's weekly music budget of two thousand dollars could tolerate. Later, as music became more famous in the series, the ensemble was expanded to five saxes, four winds, four trombones, and two trumpets, with drums, piano, vibes, and guitar as sidemen. And because Mancini had become astute at both dramatic shorthand from the Universal days and band blends from the Beneke days, and because his players in the *Peter Gunn* ensemble were each band soloists in their own right, the music they played had a quick kick and confidence that propelled each episode, making viewers uncharacteristically aware of the role of music in the drama and, meanwhile, making Gunn seem even cooler than he was. Those players included a number of guys with whom Mancini had worked, and even bunked, in the army: bassist Rolly Bundock, who had encouraged Ginny to pursue the bashful Henry back in the day; drummer Jack Sperling; trumpeter Pete Candoli and his brother Conte; and the Nash brothers—Ted, with his mellifluous saxophone style, and Dick, the smoothest of trombones. On special occasions Mancini brought in the more subtly shaded and studied drum work of Shelly Manne. But everyone had his own band experience from the war years. For instance, Pete Candoli had been a veteran of both the Woody Herman and Stan Kenton bands. Other Hollywood studio men were added quickly—Larry Bunker on vibes and pianist John Williams, who was already a veteran playing on many film score sessions in "old Hollywood" for the likes of Alfred Newman and Adolph Deutsch (*Some Like It Hot*) and who, flashing forward twenty years, would eventually become the most famous film composer in the world.

Edwards stated for the record that he felt Mancini's scores were responsible for at least 50 percent of the show's success. Then, as now, that is a huge claim: that a mere background score should shoulder its way forward to such an impact. It was the fluency, the conversational naturalness, of Mancini's themes alongside the craft, color, and sheer "rightness" of his arrangements that struck listeners most about the *Peter Gunn* music, especially once that record album was released. On disc the music took on a new life of its own. "The Floater," a carefree major-key stroll, which actually includes a happy finger-snap in the rhythm section, and "Brief and Breezy," a minor-key club tune in the same meter, both seem to proceed as easily and organically as a prose sentence. On the record album, the walking bass line that opened each episode was built into a big band wailer called "Fallout!" and "Sorta Blue," the ultimate high-hat-cymbal haiku, was a nod to the beat generation whose A-minor theme spanned a primitive interval of the minor seventh and whose bridge a detached minor fourth—yet all harmonized to sound so natural. To find such music first in a television drama soundtrack and then in a state-of-the-art stereo home-listening album seemed like a great gift to listeners after what we have characterized as those musically dry 1950s.

The best example of this music, perhaps, is the melody that came to be known as "Dreamsville." It was actually written for the *Peter Gunn* record album that would be released after the success of the series, but it soon was being quoted in an assortment of different TV episodes to become part of the Gunn ethos: they used it as a kind of recurring theme for Pete and girlfriend Edie Hart as a couple. It had the sentiment of pop and the cool of jazz—sinuous, lithe, soulful, and intelligent at the same time, passing through sixteen chord changes in its dreamlike midsection alone, but mainly swaying back and forth between a luxurious Cmaj^9 chord and Gmin^7 with an added C. Predicting in its way the whole lovely lyrical revolution of the 1960s, it is Mancini's first great melody.

Music from Peter Gunn became the number one album in the country on *Billboard* magazine's charts and stayed there for 10 weeks, remaining charted for 117 weeks in all. It lost the Emmy Award for best TV scoring but wowed the recording industry Grammy Awards by earning Mancini two of his twenty lifetime Grammys—one for best arrangement and one for the most-coveted recognition, album of the year. More than a million copies would be sold, and the change in Mancini's world would be felt almost immediately. He later wrote about that period of unemployment between the demise of the Universal music department and the start of *Peter Gunn*. Even once the new show started, he was still struggling to make ends meet. He well remembered having only five dollars in the family bank account on the very day that his first royalty check for the *Peter Gunn* album (representing a number of accumulated months' album sales) arrived in the mail. He drove over to where Ginny was doing her charity work and showed her the check—for thirty-two thousand dollars.[1]

Out from under the benevolent control of the Universal music factory and at least a little more insulated from the discouraging undefined disapproval of his father, Mancini could start to make his own music, even if it was in service of someone else's TV shows. Listening to his musical evolution, beginning here in television and soon expanding (back) to the big screen, we can sense a new air of independence, relief, color, and even forgiveness in Mancini's music to come, a change that, again, serendipitously seems to match the growing optimism and expressivity of the young audiences for whom he was writing, the baby boomer generation and their short-lived but long-lasting Kennedy era.

— — —

Although the decade of the 1960s would simmer and quake with the restlessness of buzzwords like "the generation gap" and moral issues like the civil rights struggle and the peace movement, and although voters at the turn of the decade would purposefully (with all due respect) put away the Eisenhower administration of their parents and call up the second-youngest president in American history to represent their interests, musically the 1960s actually represented a reaffirmation of something old and reassuring (which has been hinted at already): a resurgence of lyricism in popular music, of thoughtfully composed melodies with interesting and original harmonic progressions and memorable matchups between the tune and the words. So it was natural that listeners would particularly value Mancini's brand of jazz-pop; it had optimism and empathy, sentiment and snap. By 1959 it was said that Mancini was receiving fully one-half of the *Peter Gunn* show's fan mail. CBS-TV approached Blake Edwards with a contract to produce a second series so long as the music of Mancini would be part of the package. Because Edwards conceived a more romantic crime-caper series, this time with a more lighthearted hero, and because Mancini himself was now working from a greater feeling of relief—with unemployment at bay and his personal confidence strong—the music for the new series would celebrate flowing melody, Latin rhythms, wit, and a sense of self-delight quite unlike anything coming from that cool, contained chap Gunn. The main quality one senses from this new music to the Blake Edwards TV series *Mr. Lucky* is Mancini's own joyous feeling of release.

Still infatuated with the Cary Grant persona of dapper charm and charisma, Blake Edwards borrowed his title from the 1943 Grant movie and cast a suave middle-aged actor, John Vivyan, to play the owner/operator of a gambling boat that had to stay anchored three miles offshore in order to operate a legal gaming venue. And to add another element of intrigue, Edwards invented a sidekick character named Andamo (Ross Martin), who, besides helping Lucky with his patrons and with the ladies, also seemed to have an ongoing loyalty to the exiled rebels of some unnamed Latin American country.

From the start, *Mr. Lucky* was a less focused series than *Peter Gunn*. With its rather bland hero and its indefinite locales (so many of the capers that happened ashore were shot at night in some vaguely Southern Californian streets and clubs, or they were confined to Lucky's boat, called the *Fortuna II*, and we could not see much more than the lower deck), there was little for the audience's imagination to grab. Only in the early episodes was there any real attempt to give Mr. Lucky a flippant Cary Grant edge to his dialogue (e.g., quips in the face of danger), but with Vivyan's inexpressive face and ill-defined character, he never registered strongly. Martin, on the other hand, with his mobile features and faked Latin accent could put a spin on the most dysfunctional lines. He was unpredictable; he was the sidekick who overshadowed his boss in much the same way that Mancini's warmly expressive music often swamped the not-quite-compelling stories on screen.

Like *Peter Gunn*, each *Mr. Lucky* episode opened with a teaser scored by a moody vamp. This time *Peter Gunn*'s walking bass was transformed into a recurring wharf-side Latin percussive motif: a Latin timbale drum being softly tapped on top and on the sides with a 6/8 *feel* on top of a 4/4 meter, coupled with tom-toms and then the final weight of timpani—all of it very quietly, waiting for some action to begin. Then the dark, almost sea-serpent sound of two bass clarinets, two bass flutes, and a bassoon played a little two-note call, twice, before an amplified guitar set up the A-minor key signature—and the week's show was under way. Thanks to even that short bit of music, the show was getting somewhere—or at least had a blank check from Mancini to make something happen.

Whereas background jazz-pop became the voice of *Peter Gunn*, *Mr. Lucky*'s constant sounds were the lightly Latin rhythms, the bright use of woodwinds in all combinations, and, at least in the main theme, lush string writing.

With his own apparent affinity for Latin music (through Ginny's heritage), Mancini brought something much more resonant, more personal, to those pieces than their function in the show as casino lounge music would seem to warrant. And when they were used specifically to delineate characters, build atmosphere, or match screen action, the whole series lifted. Warmth, elegance, and, once again, humor were the gifts of Mancini's *Mr. Lucky* music. The orchestra for the series also included a Hammond electric organ playing big, luxurious block chords in place of the usual brass punctuations. Strings were there to sell Edwards's idea of Lucky as a romantic hero (and for what the press release called his "suave, sophisticated, polished and international demeanor . . . He's a mystery man, intriguing to women and envied by men"). The *Mr. Lucky* sound was that of a ballroom orchestra as opposed to *Peter Gunn's* club combo sound, and yet it also had a sometimes-fiery, sometimes-sumptuous Latin atmosphere. In Mancini's hands the clichés were greatly avoided, the harmonies were never sappy—it was genuinely warm, sincere, and openhearted music.

As with the *Peter Gunn* music, some of Mancini's ballad themes for *Mr. Lucky* (see "Blue Satin" or "Softly" on the soundtrack disc) showed up in different background guises in different episodes. Richly scored on the album, they were presented as small casino ensemble pieces in an episode called "Dangerous Lady" one week, then as a guitar solo in "Money Game" the next week. In "That Stands for Pool," Mancini created another jazzy march (called "March of the Cue Balls" on the disc) to cover the billiard match between Mr. Lucky and a gangster's proxy. Andamo had his own theme with a gentle samba rhythm and a sympathetic bridge (in at least one episode being hummed by the character as he went about his business on the *Fortuna II*). Only during the biggest action scenes—the climax of a boat chase or some political showdown between Andamo and government agents—was the brass section admitted into the score apart from the organ. At times these sequences had tougher border-Latin scoring reminiscent of *Touch of Evil*, but the music was always tempered with the lyricism of Lucky's particular universe. It is in that lyricism that we find Mancini's sense of release, his sense of relief. Was that perhaps some kind of reconciliation with his own past coming out in the music? For him, tremendous success bred confidence and a feeling of expansion; he was able to exhale after a pressurized apprenticeship, both in his capacity as an overworked studio staffer and as an overlooked son. Is that what we hear in the music for *Mr. Lucky*?

The TV show did not care about the psychology of its composer—it just wanted elegant and breezy music. The "*Mr. Lucky* Theme" expresses all of that with strings and organ and a few brass. Like "Dreamsville," it is built on jazzy chords (D^{13} to $Dmin^7$ to $B\flat maj^9$) with all the chromatic asides that would later make it a favorite of jazz pianist Marian McPartland. There has probably never been an arrangement of that tune that did *not* work. In the show it was subjected to lounge style, to full organ fills as Lucky went jet-setting around the world, and as a cha-cha. Throughout the series, its first five notes were even used as the recurring "ringtone" of Lucky's expensive pocket watch.

Unfortunately, the changing premise of the *Mr. Lucky* show (first he was proprietor of a gambling boat; then a casino owner on shore when some Latin dictator sank the *Fortuna*; then the builder of *Fortuna II*; then, when network censors complained that gambling was illegal so how could a hero be engaged in it, he became a sort of restaurant owner) discouraged audience loyalty and the show lasted just that one season.

During *Mr. Lucky*'s run, Mancini was kept busy writing, scoring, and re-cording both Edwards shows at the same time, week by week, and it was both invigorating and depleting. "On Tuesday I would look at the next *Peter Gunn* episode in the schedule; that night I would go into MGM (where Edwards had rented recording facilities) and record the score for the episode before that. On Wednesday I would go in and watch the next *Mr. Lucky* episode and that night I would record the music for the current one."[2]

Perhaps because of that unforgiving itinerary, Mancini's work on those shows *had* to come from the gut, and his palpable sense of freedom and di-rectness comes through because of that. *Music from Mr. Lucky* was an album (again, the various themes from the show were rearranged into three-minute pop-orchestral charts) that other musicians were beginning to notice and even to study for its solid and natural melodies and for its arrangements brimming with color and ingenuity. As the *Peter Gunn* album had become a million seller, the *Mr. Lucky* album, recorded at the end of 1959, right in the middle of the show's brief run, went to number two on the charts and was nominated for more Grammy Awards than even the *Peter Gunn* album had boasted. Now Mancini was a recording artist in full. RCA wanted more jazz-pop albums out of him, whether or not they had anything to do with films.

Recorded during the summer of 1959 was a new disc meant to exploit Mancini's newfound fame, this one full of standard tunes right out of the big band tradition. *The Mancini Touch* (promo people were already packaging him) took advantage of all the regular soloists he had been employing in TV work—the Nash brothers, Ronnie Lang on sax and flutes, now Shelly Manne on drums, and John Williams on piano against a band of thirty-five players—four horns and four trombones (no trumpets this time); five rhythm players, including vibes; two solo wind players; and an active string section. The arrangements were bright and *Lucky*-lush, where every chord change acknowledged, with richness and clarity, the skill and accomplishment of the various pop composers being featured on the album. "Swing Softly" said the album cover. In addition to some big band standards ("Snowfall" was the theme of the Claude Thornhill band, and "Trav'lin Light" was Billie Holiday's old standby theme), there were some cool modern choices, too, such as André Previn's "Like Young" and four new Mancini originals: "Mostly for Lovers," a '30s-style ballad; "Let's Walk," a strutting vamp for marimba/piano/guitar, alto sax, alto flute, with a fingered-tremolo section from the strings; "A Cool Shade of Blue," straight cool jazz in the best Mancini vernacular and a younger cousin of "Free and Easy" (which was also one of the tracks here); and "Politely," a rather impolitely brash solo for trombone against a fast tramping rhythm. Mancini's arrangement of the Woody Herman band classic "Bijou" sparkled with contrast: piccolos and flutes challenging deep muted trombones with a tambourine kick-start and aggressive strings; "Snowfall" softened the strings to the texture of chemise; and "That's All" encouraged the normally ominous bass flutes to play sonorously. All in all, the album was an exercise in the most colorful of pop orchestral arranging—and again an expression of joy and some sort of relief.

On paper these orchestrations were precise models of balance and ingenuity, and yet they were easily played—lucid and legitimate in their harmonic and rhythmic ideas but somehow also original and tremendously satisfying for the players and listeners. Again, the coincidence of these albums with the advent of RCA's new high-fidelity stereo recording processes was another big factor in their success. RCA's studio engineers knew how to make the most of Mancini's carefully divided orchestras—how to close-mike the players, how to remix all the elements back together for the home stereo speaker system. Al Schmitt was in charge of engineering for these albums—an average of three studio days to record each twelve-song program—and to this day they still sound like recent recordings.

Critics found the Mancini orchestral albums fresh and impressive. His next was called *The Blues and the Beat*, recorded in February 1960, which featured twenty-five men—fourteen brass, five winds, and rhythm in a song set split between up-tempo numbers on one side (these were twelve-inch vinyl records, remember) of the disc. Baritone sax ambled through "How Could You Do a Thing Like That to Me"; high, giddy piccolos and flutes played around with "Big Noise from Winnetka" just before a fat brass sound entered the chart; while Pete Candoli's powerhouse trumpet carried Mancini's slowly building arrangement of "Sing, Sing, Sing" to the edge of frenzy. On the other side were darker, somewhat less distinctive ballad covers (the brass choir of four French horns blending with trumpets and trombones enriched tunes like "Smoke Rings" and "Mood Indigo").

By June of the same year, Mancini was exploring the exciting confines of the small instrumental ensemble for his next album, called *Combo!* trying to come up with harmonies that were both transparent and provocative and inspired by wartime combos like Artie Shaw's Gramercy Five or the Raymond Scott Quintette and by current artists like Gerry Mulligan or the Modern Jazz Quartet. Here Pete Candoli's terse, Dizzy Gillespie–like trumpet solos; Ted Nash's appealing sax; Dick Nash's always-fluid trombone playing; and John Williams on the piano (sometimes on harpsichord), all locked into a firm geometry as striking and detached as a Cubist painting. Bundock's bass and Shelly Manne's drums gave the rhythm section nothing so deep as *soul* but certainly a feeling of precision and naturalness. For the disc, Mancini and producer Dick Peirce again mixed standards ("Dream of You") with new tunes (Cy Coleman's "Playboy's Theme") and two more Mancini originals. Some of Mancini's widely spaced harmonies around the solo trumpet/alto sax duo, or around the piano, had a truly modernist feel to them as did the very close harmonies among the winds. *Combo!* was all about the admiration of the arranger's craft—how to make eleven players sound like a fully balanced orchestra *and* do justice to the songs as well.

In an interview, Mancini talked about the process of putting music together:

> I have always been a creature of texture, the way instruments blend with each other, the voicing, the way the chords are voiced. I'm very aware of that . . . to feel when you should make the weight of the strings heavier, to feel when you need the oboe doubling the flute or the bass clarinet and the bassoon together, or just the bassoon and the bass—those little varying adjustments that you talk to yourself about when you're looking at the drama of an arrangement or the balance of a piece. Knowing the orchestra is like my mechanic's set of tools—and I think I know it pretty well.[3]

Combo! was Mancini's most erudite album yet. The same wit and wisdom that made the *Peter Gunn* albums so sharp and the *Mr. Lucky* album so friendly was now enjoying the freedom of not having to tell a screen story. These were self-descriptive charts, absorbed only in music-making, enjoying their own skill. The opening track, "Moanin'," perfectly set out the album's premise of soloists (Larry Bunker's marimba) working in front of the ultramodern harmonies of the ensemble, one player on each note of the chord. The two Mancini originals made great jazzy use of the ancient harpsichord sound: the prim staccato melody of "A Powdered Wig," with its swinging midsection, and the brooding "Far East Blues."

Together, those three albums, *The Mancini Touch*, *The Blues and the Beat*, and *Combo!*—especially in the wake of the *Peter Gunn* and *Mr. Lucky* projects—seemed to be establishing Mancini's reputation beyond films. Other composers were listening; other arrangers were starting to study his charts. Again, people were thinking to themselves, *Here was something fresh.*

— — —

By all accounts Mancini settled into the demands of early fame and his new publicly scrutinized life fairly contentedly. It was, however, an existence on a different level. As all movie stars know, having to rouse one's energy to absorb a hit or accept a disappointment makes for a lot of uncertainty—just this side of chaos. And for the freelance composer, never knowing whether more opportunities are coming or what the subject of each new score may be, it is a life of some suspense. Perhaps it was that need for an anchor, as he looked back over his career since those study days with Max Adkins and Krenek and Castelnuovo-Tedesco, that the thought came to him: maybe he should write a book—trace and reaffirm for himself what he had learned along the way—which could also then serve as a sort of road map for aspiring musicians. Orchestration is a subject all music students need to know if they want to graduate from conservatory. To past generations, books on that subject by Hector Berlioz and Nikolai Rimsky-Korsakov were paramount. In the twentieth century, Roger Sessions and Walter Piston wrote famous texts. At first it seems implausible that Mancini, as a relative newcomer, with only a handful of successes and supposedly modest about his accomplishments, would suddenly decide he was astute enough to teach a course like this in print, what eventually would become his 1962 self-published book, *Sounds and Scores: A Practical Guide to Professional Orchestration.*

The fact is, though, that he had been receiving a lot of student requests for printed orchestration excerpts from his thus far six jazz-pop albums (*The Music from Peter Gunn, More Music from Peter Gunn, The Music from Mr. Lucky, The Blues and the Beat, The Mancini Touch*, and *Combo!*) that could be studied alongside the recordings themselves. The idea here was to create a text that would discuss the different sections of the standard orchestra and pop band, display printed musical sketches from his album charts, and include with the book three seven-inch discs containing snatches of the recordings that corresponded to the print excerpts (on subsequent editions, the vinyl discs became cassettes and then a CD). Once he had obtained a waiver from RCA and the musicians union to use excerpts from his own recordings as demos with the book, he set to work on the teaching text, proceeding in the most disciplined way, as was natural to a task-oriented person like himself—both like a professor planning a syllabus and like an exam-cram student. His typist for each day's work was the future writer, singer, and music critic Morgan Ames. She later recalled her secretarial experience with Mancini: "Arriving each day with a neat stack of score paper and penciled notes to himself, he dictated the book nearly as a whole, within about two weeks—evidence of a rich and organized mind. . . . He was unsure of the title but I liked it. And he was also fluid, just as he wrote music. Sometimes he would go off on improvisations as he laid the work out. He liked input."[4]

Now students could hear the piano/bass/ride cymbal/guitar opening to *Peter Gunn*, see on the printed page exactly where and how the brass enter, and get Henry Mancini's advice: "When approaching an instrument do a little ground work before you start filling in: lightly pencil in your leads and spot your solos on the score paper from beginning to end if possible. Using the 'Peter Gunn' theme as an example, here are two ways of doing this."[5] And then we see a twenty-two-staff orchestration of the *Peter Gunn* opening, showing how to number the bars, how to mark them for rehearsal and cutting purposes, how to notate ad-lib solos in jazz-pop music, and how to notate the exact value of notes—for example, how to indicate that the player ends on a downbeat or a fourth beat. This is all under the chapter he calls "The Essentials." He then breaks down the book into sections: "The Saxophones," "The Woodwinds" (nine instruments and ensemble writing), "The Brass" (four instruments and ensembles, different kinds of brass mutes, and brass blends with saxes), "Show and Act Music" (with practical advice on what he calls the "typical requests of a stage arranger such as 'Write the arrangement for fifteen players but it must be playable for six in case the budget is cut or guys don't show.'"[6] Final chapters include information on the twelve-member rhythm section, a look at Latin rhythms and instruments, a section on "combo" writing, and one on the string section.

He writes a good deal about "dramatic contrast"—using, for instance, major-key bridges to relieve minor-key melodies, light percussive sounds to contrast a dark brass section, transparent wind combos to break up thick string passages. And for insight into the sounds that seem to personify Mancini, his book spends important space parsing his own style of strings, like the 12/4/4 division of the string section (violins, violas, cellos) for the *Mr. Lucky* orchestra. He shows the close violin voicing that sounds rich in a *Mr. Lucky* tune like "Chime Time" and then how the harmony opens up along the line. And with advice on muting the strings (called *sordini*), which produces what he calls "a haunting and somewhat hollow sound," he writes about the special effect of the lower-toned violas and cellos playing *divisi* passages, "a well-sounding change of color" from the norm.

Rather than some kind of brag from a nouveau-riche celebrity, *Sounds and Scores* was really a gesture of mutuality. Thanks to Mancini's sharing tone, rather than pontificating, *Sounds and Scores* delivers a ready education, not like an academic lecture but like a summer seminar out on the campus lawn with musicians at hand to play instant examples. "The wonderful thing about the saxes," Mancini enthuses in the book, "is that they blend so well with each other—in practically any combination. This brings up the question of how we 'voice' or distribute a given chord. The closest of all voicings is the cluster [a section of the chromatic chords in "Blues for Mothers" is demonstrated]."[7] "The clarinet probably rates second only to the violin in the number of things it can do well."[8] "The trombones can be very funny fellows on occasion. The introduction of 'Timothy' had them pumping away at the humorous marching figure making fine contrast to the four piccolos that enter shortly after with the theme."[9] "The union of horns and trombones is a sound that has been used quite freely in the *Peter Gunn* and *Mr. Lucky* music. It is confined almost exclusively to sustained and pretty passages. Beauty and phrasing are the big considerations here."[10] He goes on to demonstrate the major phrasing of the "brass choir" in "Dreamsville," where players are instructed to breathe right in the middle of a line at bar seven, which ought to feel wrong but instead instinctively gives just the right relaxed pace.

Sounds and Scores proved to be a helpful course to audit for both beginners and professionals and, with the recorded examples, a unique guide. The book still holds value today, although jazz-pop arranging has moved on to include electronics and in a sense has moved backward to prefer rhythm and repetition over harmony and nuance. Mancini's book was well received in its day by an insider readership of aspiring or admiring musicians. It sold out its first self-subsidized printing, went to its second edition five years later, and remains in print with a mainstream publisher after generations.

Of course, not everything Mancini tried was successful even in these "high times." Sometime in 1960, during the glow of popularity for the *Peter Gunn/Mr. Lucky* albums, someone at RCA Victor's handling company decided that Mancini ought to go out on the road for a ten- or twelve-city tour to conduct whatever contract musicians and freelance symphony players could be found at each venue in a program of his own TV music. As Mancini later told it, he very soon regretted the idea. He certainly had all of those rich, colorful, jazzy-yet-accessible arrangements to offer a sit-down audience, but what he sorely lacked was any kind of a public stage presence or personality. His modest, flat announcements at the stage microphone between each piece made the whole event seem like an awkward recital. Nor was his box office draw established at all. People knew the albums and had heard the phrase "The Mancini Touch," but he was not thought of as a performer whom people would park their cars to go see in concert. An even bigger blunder in the plan was the difficulty of finding concert-worthy musicians who were fluent in playing even mildly swinging charts. As we have seen, Mancini's arrangements tread a fine line between formal structure and easygoing conversational delivery. With just one hour of rehearsal in each city and a whole new orchestra each time, the music sounded fairly bad to Mancini's ear. Giving sixteen or thirty-two bars to an inexperienced soloist for a jazz improv proved disastrous more than once.

Reluctantly, two of the last concerts were simply canceled, and Mancini came back to Los Angeles a bit puzzled and feeling chastised; even great success did not insulate one from reality. He was not a concert act yet, if ever. He was a media scorer and a studio arranger. That this failure did not offend him, that he took it with a shrug and went back to the business at hand, is a sign of his natural modesty. He had the good sense to pace his career and concentrate on the music. With that kind of balance, Mancini survived and evolved through four decades to come. Ginny remembered those days, years later:

> Well, it just had never occurred to him to go out and be a performer/conductor at that time, because, you know, he was a relatively shy person. And anyway I don't think his ambition went beyond just writing music for films. It wasn't until after *Peter Gunn* that he was even encouraged to go out and give concerts. It seemed a very foreign idea to him, and when it wasn't immediately successful, all he could do was take it in stride. There was more work waiting for him when he got back anyway.[11]

Waiting for him in January 1961 were twelve new pieces he had recently written as part of his ongoing contract with RCA Victor to be recorded in what he later pronounced to be his favorite album from among the ninety-plus discs he would release over a lifetime. It was a program of Latin-themed original miniatures with his familiar studio band, enriched by the same large string section used on *The Mancini Touch* album and augmented by a distinctive dais of Latin instruments. Because it opened with an up-tempo cha-cha arrangement of the "*Mr. Lucky* Theme," the album was given the overall title of *Mr. Lucky Goes Latin*, though none of the eleven tracks that followed had anything to do with that TV series. These were studio originals, as sharp as *Peter Gunn* and as warm as *Mr. Lucky*. Mancini would draw on this same material for other albums in years to come.

Album producer Dick Peirce made sure to take advantage of both Mancini's colorful, detailed arrangements and RCA's state-of-the-art recording studio. Of the familiar Mancini band, Dick Nash returned on baritone horn, Vince De Rosa led the French horns, Laurindo Almeida appeared on mandolin, with Bob Bain on electric guitar. And beginning a long association with Mancini, the great jazz minimalist piano player Jimmy Rowles sat in for the *tinpanola* solos (a kind of Brazilian piano with a tinny, off-tuned feel) while concertmaster Erno Neufeld led the string section. Those faintly exotic sounds and all kinds of quiet Latin percussion gave this new album a special charisma, but the strength of the album, what made it so distinctive to Mancini so many years later as to cite it as his favorite, lay in the warmth and generosity of its melodies and the solid resourceful arrangements—it was another collection of songs without words.

The luminous album track "Lujon," an atmospheric nocturne with an Fmin to D♭min hammock-swing melody and a sighing major-key release, is one track that might well represent the entire personal pop language Mancini was developing. After its quiet introduction, which becomes a counter line played on the *lujon* (a simple Latin instrument in the form of a tall rectangular box fixed with metal plates bolted on one side and arranged in a five-note scale to be struck by soft mallets, producing a sound similar to a metallic bass marimba), the seductive melody wafts in from the strings with such a tropical ambiance that in years to follow lyricist Norman Gimbel would retitle it "Slow Hot Wind." Mancini's orchestration for the string parts further exploits seductive qualities; he scores in eight-part harmony like his choral writing but with a French air that he described as "strictly a Ravel take-off . . . the blocks of four in the harmony: it's just eight parts, starting four parts in the violins and then the four parts doubled an octave lower in the violas and the cellos. It's a very sensuous sound that Ravel made famous. But he was my influence there."[12] (Alert listeners could have heard him hinting at that sort of French harmony even in the mid-parts of the main title music to *Congo Crossing*, from his Universal days, aiming at a kind of sultry jungle ambiance.) The track called "The Dancing Cat" is more rhythmic and edgy with its *tinpanola* main chorus and its minor-key melody relieved by a major-key bridge. "Speedy Gonzales" is conceived as a nimble-fingered guitar solo for Bob Bain. "Cow Bells and Coffee Beans," with its chromatic raised eyebrow and its dancerlike pauses at the end of each line, was actually first written to accompany a piece of ultimately unproduced Gene Kelly choreography in a television special, while "Blue Mantilla" was written with the cold, stark tone of Vince De Rosa's French horn in mind, set against a black background that glistens with celesta and the intimate side of Latin percussion, soon joined by a sultry alto sax.

This was Mancini the arranger, the mood miniaturist, the melodist at his best. And the album continued the same sense of relief, sympathy, freedom, even reconciliation, previously noted in the *Mr. Lucky* project; it sounded like the appreciation of a man who had found his independent voice at the same lucky moment when there was an audience to receive it. This empathy, which is in all of Mancini's more personal music, seems to parallel not the kinds of assignments he was given in each period of his life, but rather the life experiences he was going through all along. His mother's death had come at the very beginning of his Universal days and perhaps thrust him into that impersonal factory/school with a kind of determination and focus he would not otherwise have had, being such a passive fellow. By that time his father was still a big pressure and a source of constant challenge, even contention. When his concert tour failed, Quinto was there to warn him, "You should take conducting lessons." Some of that chill and lots of that yearning found its way into pieces like "Lujon" and certainly, soon, the song "Moon River." And yet all of this music was still within the confines of simple, salable pop—smooth of surface but true to a certain depth. The simple flowing and wise tune "The Sound of Silver" from this same *Mr. Lucky Goes Latin* album—with its sympathetic melody perfectly sketched out in two long lines without a bridge, first as a trombone solo against a bed of mid-range strings, then as a truly "silvery" passage for those Ravellian strings—is a great example of "the personal" in pop music. No wonder this was Mancini's favorite album.

But what he really wanted to do was to score more movies, to move up the ladder of prestigious motion pictures and see how far his style, sophistication, and talent could evolve. He even accepted an offer to return to his old stomping grounds, Universal Studios, for a one-time-only scoring assignment for a new low-budget Tony Curtis picture. The studio was only producing flicks one deal at a time these days—no more stock company contracts for actors or musicians—but they did have this one not-quite-major motion picture called

The Great Impostor, and Mancini agreed to write a theme and variations for it. This was the true story of Ferdinand Demara, who, wanting to get ahead in life and finding various unguarded doors open, simply barged through to assume a series of false identities, eventually masquerading as a surgeon, an assistant prison warden, an army officer—and ending up both a hero and a fugitive from justice. Half the people who had contact with Demara wanted him to be honored for his service to humanity, and the other half wanted him arrested as a scoundrel. Later, in 2002, Steven Spielberg recast the same basic story with Leonardo DiCaprio as *Catch Me If You Can*, concentrating on the psychological enigma of the main character and using a super-cool score by John Williams. But director Robert Mulligan's 1961 version seemed satisfied with the entertainment value of the con-man scenario, and, accordingly, Mancini's musical setting assumed the tone of a romantic comedy.

The main theme was introduced on alto flute with marimba keeping up a quietly busy meter in the background, sounding like a mind at work and, when spiked with higher winds and celesta, having an air of mischief. Already we were put on notice that no deep exposé was planned, but Mancini treated that theme to a clever range of disguises, much like the main character, during the film while never essentially varying it in truth. It was made into a brief sea chantey (two flutes, bassoon, vibes) as Demara illegally became a navy surgeon aboard ship; it took on a baroque liturgical feeling when he tried to enter a monastery and adhere to the monks' code of self-denial (muted violins play the twining baroque figure). But even when the theme was not fully evidenced, its marimba rhythm introduction was used as the ongoing pulse of the Demara character. A placid accordion waltz and some other functional music as in the old Universal days filled out Mancini's obligations to *The Great Impostor*.

Writer Irwin Bazelon lamented that Mancini should have exploited the assignment about a character who repeatedly dissimulates himself with an authentic theme-and-variations score but that "his idea of variations is to orchestrate the tune in different ways for different scenes. . . . A more enterprising approach would not only have made the audience more aware of the impostor's virtuosity but would have underscored his obsession."[13] Of course, Mancini the dramatist was not up to such tricks yet. In the end, the producers were happy, but the studio had no more work for him. Then, almost immediately, Blake Edwards was on the phone telling him about a new feature film that would star no less than Bing Crosby and was in need of some big band blasts. It seemed that this Edwards/Mancini combination was developing into something very much like a partnership.

CHAPTER 5

Blake Edwards
and the High Times

The rising star of Mancini was also bringing Blake Edwards up in the world. Edwards's success in television more or less assured he could return to the movies with a lot more clout than he had known just a few years before at Universal. Of course, he had begun as an actor (see him in *Strangler of the Swamp* [1946]) and after that as a successful radio writer; then film writing, then TV. He first directed film in 1955, *Bring Your Smile Along*, while the aforementioned *Mister Cory* was his first professional contact with Henry Mancini. Personally, they were a study in contrasts; on the one side, Mancini was curious and disciplined at work, deferential and ingenuous in person, and on the other, Edwards was conceptual and uncompromising in his profession, friendly and explosive and inscrutable in private. That natural clash is almost completely masked in the work they eventually did together, but we will see later some problems it raised in regard to Mancini's output. Mostly, though, the presence of Blake Edwards in Mancini's career had a wildly positive and prosperous effect.

Now, at Twentieth Century Fox Bing Crosby's production company was planning a new comedy set on a college campus starring the old crooner himself as self-made millionaire Harvey Howard, CEO of a burger chain, who, now that his kids are grown, decides to go back to school and earn his degree. In *High Time* (1960) Crosby as Harvey chooses to live on campus, pledge to a fraternity, and revel in the undergraduate culture. So the ongoing joke of the film is how this fifty-one-year-old tycoon (Crosby was fifty-four at the time) fits in with the college kids. Mancini responded with easygoing big band swing and, as a recurring theme, "The *High Time* March," the most joyous high-stepper he ever wrote.

Capitalizing on the prestige of just having directed King Crosby, Edwards was now quickly able to talk his way into landing a major A-level theatrical feature for his next project, this one to star Audrey Hepburn. It would be based on an old Truman Capote story about a country girl who comes to the big, bad city of New York to reinvent herself as a swinger, *Breakfast at Tiffany's* (1961). Hepburn was well past her best actress Oscar for *Roman Holiday* (1953) but had proven durable and charismatic in several films since, including *Funny Face* and *The Nun's Story*. Edwards's personal frankness and likability had won Hepburn's confidence, so the deal was going ahead, to be produced by Marty Jurow and Richard Shepherd from a screenplay by George Axelrod. There was never any question about who would do the music score, but with such a multilayered story line there would have to be some detailed discussions between director and composer this time, not just the tacit approval that had covered *High Time*'s jazz-pop. Their talk began with how best to evoke the film's Manhattan setting in music. Where so many past soundtracks had tried to quickly embody New York in music, composers were prone to invoke Gershwin clichés, usually those urbane 1920s chords out of his "Rhapsody in Blue," or those busy metropolitan syncopations in his "An American in Paris." Alfred Newman paraphrased Gershwin in *Street Scene* (1931), Steiner did it in *Four Daughters* (1938), and almost everyone in movies and television has succumbed at least once since.

Mancini saw the rousing, striving city of the 1960s—all glass and steel and plastic; all vertical space, as though the whole city were one big building with the streets as corridors, the alleys as breezeways, the populace as one big, youthful, jostling workforce—and made *his* theme for New York a piece of cool jazz-pop. Vibes, warm strings, a cocktail sax, and a wordless chorus teach us Mancini's city theme, which has both the sophisticated awareness of the party culture and a bit of yearning as unresolved phrases remain suspended at the end of each line (on a B♭min^7 chord, for instance). At first the chorus articulates the theme in a scat style, singing "do-doot-do-doo" like the cheapest kind of television commercial singers. It was a jazzy and sophisticated approach for that middle-class cultural moment, but it sounds uncomfortably uncool today. (This is beautifully avoided and smoothed out on the record album of the score, and it does settle down during the film, too.) Elsewhere in the score, big band jazz underlies party scenes and Manhattan traffic shots, and outdated comic musical effects learned at Universal's music library underscore the antics of an outrageous landlord or a mock shoplifting spree. But it became increasingly clear that the best way to suggest the complicated emotional history of the main character would be to represent her through identification with a recurring song.

In the original script, Hepburn's character, calling herself Holly Golightly, is overheard casually singing some wistful ballad from her rural past as she sits in the windowsill overlooking the fire escape of her Manhattan apartment building. Mancini considered what it might sound like. For instance, if Audrey Hepburn, hardly a vocalist, was going to sing this piece by herself and not be dubbed by some studio substitute, it would have to be a melody within her vocal range. She had done her own singing when she costarred with Fred Astaire in the musical *Funny Face*. In screening that film Mancini discovered that she had been able to sing the thirteen-note span of the Gershwin song "How Long Has This Been Going On?" So he set that spread as his limit. He has said that it took him thirty days and thirty minutes to compose "Moon River" as a melody—a month to get a sense of what kind of piece it should be and then half an hour to put it down on paper. The first bars capture the concept—an interval of the *perfect fifth* is scribed, then down a step while (if you cast the song in the key of C) the chord base moves from C major up to A minor, then down to F on the next phrase and back to C.

The lyric by Johnny Mercer, whom Mancini had requested, perfectly matches both the folk-wisdom sense of the tune and the yearning quality of the chords through metaphysical references to life as a passing river with its surface flow and its unseen depths. As the lyric suggests, Holly Golightly has set herself adrift in the big city on a shaky raft, looking for companionship and a sense of self. Mancini's melody so peaceably, so sincerely ruminates on that wandering mood. Yet while its simple harmonies sometimes reflect the innocent country girl ("dream maker, you heartbreaker"), at other times they pass through some pretty sophisticated modulations, more jazzlike than any simple folk melody would encompass (Fmaj to Dmin to B♭ through to Gmin^6, etc.) before leading us, longingly, up through a transitional series of sixth and seventh chords under the words "wherever you're goin' I'm goin' your way." Then, continuing the metaphor of the river-as-companion, Mercer's lyric calls them "two drifters off to see the world" and seems to lead Mancini's melody line up to its climactic phrase in Dminor, then to the high G against a B♭ chord before heading back down gradually through a series of gracefully descending chords to the home key of F. "My Huckleberry friend," says Mercer's lyric against Mancini's eighth notes for the ultimate "river-companion" reference straight out of Mark Twain. At the time, some singers claimed to be baffled by the Twain-ish phrase, as though it were too abstract for them, yet its assumptive familiarity and deep recognition is its strength and should not require further explanation except by the most compulsively methodical listeners. (If there is a fault in the lyric to "Moon River," it is rather the second phrase, which runs "moon river, wider than a mile," sounding like an awkward kid's poem. It is immeasurably redeemed, though, by the genuine longing of the very next line, "I'm crossing you in style someday.")

It was Mancini's own sense of "someday" and "waitin' round the bend" while stuck in his small town of West Aliquippa that brought out this simple, clear melody once he had traced the still-unfinished character of Holly back to the universals in himself and, through this song, passed them onto us. Mancini's own December 1960 choral recording of the song would become a million seller, and his arrangement seems ideal. It begins with the graceful waltz strum of guitar and mandolin, then George Fields's amplified harmonica enters warmly with the melody until strings, split into two streams, take it over. A formal studio chorus (with Ginny as one of the altos) then presents the lyric, sometimes in smooth unison, then breaking off into rich eight-part harmony, which became a familiar Mancini sound. The choral crescendo on the rising phrase "We're after the same rainbow's end" gradually leads back down to calm when the harmonica returns for a perfect coda. As Mancini described it: "My choral writing has always been fairly simple; basically it came out of my experience writing for the Mello-Larks and other tight-harmony groups. But on 'Moon River' it was more full—with basically four girl parts, with one girl being on the lead, and four boy parts. Sometimes I can go to eight-part tight harmony with one person on each part."[1]

But Mancini's score for *Breakfast at Tiffany's* is more than just one song repeated and one bright modern city theme. As mentioned above, Truman Capote's original story was about a mercurial Manhattan playgirl who, with a certain charm and joie de vivre and a carefully hidden sense of desperation, makes the rounds of elegant parties, jet-set gigolos, and lonely businessmen, collecting patrons (she calls them "rats") in exchange for some unspecified service she provides them—all of this being observed by an anonymous narrator who lives in her apartment building. She shares her flat with a nameless cat and a nameless past, but casts both of them aside and disappears without so much as a backward glance, leaving the narrator with an unexpected sense of great loss. It is a novella about the impermanence of "belonging"—all of us being nameless alley cats belonging to no one while, of course, longing to belong.

Although probably miscast in the first place (she never really does convey Holly's capacity for decadence; also her drunk scenes are just silly), Audrey Hepburn does a terrific job of showing the desultory nature of the girl, alias Loula Mae from Texas, in her witty wordiness, her impersonation of shallow glamour, and her panic when all defenses fail and she has to come up with something real about herself. Enough cannot be said for the way in which Mancini's heartfelt hometown tune "Moon River" provides a constant source of conscience to support and explore her character. It is a tremendously sympathetic reminder that she is already a whole and lovable person if she will only put away all the claptrap, all the party posing, all the street cruising and the pretense of not caring that hides her. The song's most moving appearance in the film, then, comes in the scene during which Holly's much older common-law husband "Doc" (played by Buddy Ebsen) has come from back home to the big city to reclaim her. He talks about how her brother and all the kin miss her and how the hills of home are where she belongs. In the bus station Holly is trying to explain herself. "I love you, Doc, but I'm just not Loula Mae anymore," she pleads. Strained chromatic chords from Mancini's string section divided into two streams, which have already accompanied Holly's troubled moments before, begin a long circuitous search and arrive finally at a minor-key statement of "Moon River." As Doc resigns himself to losing her and moves off in bewilderment to board the bus, that harmonica enters again, coaxing the melody back into a major key. And there, as Holly seems torn, the score offers its most impassioned statement of the song in highly emotional harmonies (with a hint of country guitar buried behind them) and then sobering horns and piano chords as the bus pulls away, leaving her with her boyfriend Paul (George Peppard) and her own decisions. She has made up her mind to stay but now has no idea what to do with her newly declared self. This scene, flagged and supported by the music, is the heart of the film.

By this point in the story, "Moon River" has become our own poignant, nostalgic anthem, and one would be wrong to avoid using it as a reprise to cap the whole show—it is a hinted-at, longed-for fulfillment. To the extent that the audience ultimately cares more for Audrey Hepburn than for Holly Golightly, the film has to set her right in the end, Capote's original purposes notwithstanding. Mancini's score has to follow with the big, emotional, Tchaikovsky-like play-out to bring us to that point. "Yeah, of course," Mancini explained later, "pulling out all the stops, bringing in the chorus at the end and all of that business is an old romanticized ideal, but for those contexts, and after that particular story, it seemed right. If a soaring tune works there, you're expecting the recapitulation and there's no stopping it."[2]

Just before that melodic and emotional catharsis, though, Holly struggles with the notion of dumping everything—running off with a Brazilian millionaire. Paul argues with her in a taxi on her way to the airport. In that scene we get all the expected 1960s dialogue that equates "love" with "lockdown." Hepburn performs the rather self-conscious speeches with great integrity by letting the words tumble out as though Holly does not want to think them through too closely lest she discover their flaws. It is, of course, pouring rain during the taxi ride, and at her most desperate she tells the driver to stop and throws Cat, her symbol of Self, out into a waterlogged alley. Paul gives up on her at this point, and as he slams her cab door Mancini's last music cue begins—a blurred chord for horns and trombones under which low strings navigate an exploratory passage punctuated by the same piano/vibes/guitar chords that once seemed airy and bright. Here they begin to repeat a tricky alternating 7/4 and 5/4 (12/8) meter against a minor-key fragment of "Moon River's" first phrase.

Overcome with remorse, spurred by that unsettled music, Holly abandons her cab and runs back along the sidewalk to search for Cat. Paul joins her and that ostinato drops out of the scoring, leaving just the strings in two sections, marking time as we begin to believe that Cat is lost forever. The scoring struggles with that possibility for a time, then tips its hand by a shift to our familiar main melody in a major key just as Cat's forlorn meow is heard from behind an alley trash can. All three characters come together then and all seems well. There *is* "no stopping" a big romantic musical ending to a scene like that. Audiences then—and new college student viewers now, generations after the fact—seem to find the score's admission of such emotion appropriate and even affecting. Music, as it had for *Peter Gunn*, answers for nearly half of this movie's power.

For Mancini, *Breakfast at Tiffany's* meant three new vehicles of public fame: a hit song, a best-selling jazz-pop soundtrack album, and the respect of his colleagues for the knowledgeable orchestral writing behind such scenes as the taxi sequence. And yet, while *Breakfast at Tiffany's* was not just a pop score using a single repeating melody as its heart and soul, neither was it quite a traditional orchestral score with horizontal logic and interwoven motifs such as two generations of Mancini's older colleagues had espoused. A look at the other film scores nominated for the Academy Award that same year shows the difference. The epic scores of Miklos Rozsa and Dimitri

Tiomkin for *El Cid* and *The Guns of Navarone*; the swooning romantic score of Elmer Bernstein for *Summer and Smoke*, full of complex violin solos; and the old-fashioned matinee strings of a musical like *Fanny*, co-scored by Morris Stoloff and Harry Sukman, all succeeded for their films in traditional terms but would have been stylistically all wrong for a girl like Holly. And so it was that for the baby boomer audience of *Breakfast at Tiffany's*, Mancini's musical language—cool, optimistic, yet with an honest sentiment—was what seemed the most true to the moment. Mancini won his first Oscar award for best score and, that same night, his second for best song.

For RCA Victor the record album of *Breakfast at Tiffany's* quickly went to number one on the *Billboard* album charts. In keeping with the new film-score-as-entertainment trend, Mancini had recast the music into twelve three-minute tracks. The party music became five Latin-spiced big band tunes; a shoplifting cue translated into a humorous novelty piece that moved between that sneaking motif and a walking bass; the softer Latin themes were channeled into lounge music; the city theme became a breezy pop *cantabale*; and the song "Moon River" became a choral anthem and a million-selling single on its own and at the Grammy Awards became record of the year. For all the advantages of rearranging these scores into pop albums, much was lost, too. That 12/8 taxi scene would have been more interesting to hear on a disc than "Moon River" as a cha-cha. But as Mancini later said:

> Because the albums were made up of the most melodic material from each film, a lot of the dramatic music, which is what I really loved to do and really thought I had a feeling for, was left out. . . . It may have hurt my reputation as a writer of serious film music. To this day I would love to have an album of some of those scores as they were heard in the films. The albums gave me a reputation, even among producers, as a writer of light comedy and light suspense, and at that time it was not easy for them to think of me for the more dramatic assignments. I did that to myself.[3]

And yet, because of those listenable soundtrack albums, Mancini was on his way to becoming the most recognizable—perhaps the *first* recognizable—film composer ever.

--- --- ---

Mancini has said that although Blake Edwards's directing an A film like *Breakfast at Tiffany's* was what brought both of them into the major leagues of Hollywood, Edwards's true penchant was for lesser movies of physical comedy and for sinister stories with psychological suspense elements. In that way he may have been more suited to his next two stark black-and-white films, the first of which was the crime thriller, more reflective of his TV work, *Experiment in Terror* (1962). Glenn Ford starred as FBI agent John Ripley with Lee Remick as young bank teller Kelly Sherwood, whose younger sister, Toby, is kidnapped. Edwards's cohort Ross Martin played the asthmatic sadist/extortionist Red Lynch. Working from a novel by Gordon and Mildred Gordon called *Operation Terror*, Edwards aimed for a dual style, hoping to unite black-and-white realism (TV cinematographer Philip Lathrop's documentary-like exteriors of San Francisco) and some very unrealistic, eerie, and stylized settings: dark, shadowy parking garages; the heroine's bedroom with silhouettes outside the window; and an artist's studio hung with mannequins. Edwards discussed the film's scoring needs but sent Mancini off alone to muse over a concept.

Seeing that black-and-white world, thinking of nerves stretched and tension high, Mancini imagined the cold, taut steel strings of the obscure zither-like instrument, the autoharp. Usually held across one's lap and strummed with a pick, associated with summer camp and classroom sing-alongs, the autoharp has a nostalgic, folksy sound when strummed, but Mancini noted that it also had a brittle, somewhat sinister feel to it when it was plucked with a metal pick. Mancini explained:

> This was the period of the hootenanny, you remember, the folk music craze. And I got one of these things and started playing with it, and I saw that it could only hit certain chords. It was not chromatic—I don't even know if it had a dominant seventh—but at any rate I strummed it, and I said, geez, forget the hootenanny, this is a *very* chilling instrument. So I strummed a chord, and what I liked was that the decay [how a note hangs in the air, fading] was forever. And then I started plucking single strings and comparing that to the strum, and that started me off.[4]

Two autoharps, one plucked and one strummed very slowly so that the notes of the chord peel off in an ominous way, all backed by a repeating line on electric bass, would form the theme for *Experiment in Terror* and its central motif between Dmin and Gmin/D.

The film's main titles show Kelly driving home at night across the streets of San Francisco. The routine nature of the action—stopping at traffic lights, passing other cars—is, of course, being troubled by the creepy music we are hearing and the nightmarish quality of the autoharp sound. Double basses add a harmony for the second chorus of the "terror" theme, then open brass chords support the bridge (E♭⁹ to Emin⁷) under an aerial shot of

Kelly proceeding through town to the suburbs where she lives. Bass flutes join for the final statement of the theme as her car pulls into the driveway and, when her automatic door opens, into the garage. But as she climbs out of her car she senses there is something in the dark around her. Edwards allows a moment of silence, and then comes her question (which no heroine should ask)—"Is anyone there?" We hear a sudden swipe of the metal pick across the autoharp and a hand grabs her from behind and holds her mouth, Mancini now fully complicit with Edwards in creating the fright show. We can hear only Mancini's ground note and the heavy breathing of the man as Edwards's shot holds on an extreme close-up of Kelly's eyes and the gloved hand that now covers much of her face. The man tells Kelly he knows all about her and her sister and that he will do them both harm unless she gets one hundred thousand dollars from the bank and transfers it to him tomorrow.

Throughout the film, with all of its cat-and-mouse police work, the frightened sister, and the dodges and disguises of the villain, one recurring musical device begins many scenes: it is that low ground note on electric organ over which we then hear the slow arpeggiated notes of the autoharp.

Kelly contacts Agent Ripley, in spite of being warned not to, so that he becomes a participant in the process of trying to second-guess and trap Red Lynch. During Kelly's first night at home alone, with agents already on a stakeout of her neighborhood, the scoring lays down a bed of muted string chords dotted with a few low notes on the vibes, further detailed by a unique chromatic phraseology that Mancini would exploit elsewhere in the 1960s: a trumpet and sax playing together in a twisted duet that is almost a unison line but keeps baiting itself.

One other frightened woman claiming to be stalked by Red Lynch is Nancy (Patricia Houston). Fearing for her life, she phones Ripley and begs him to hurry over. Nancy is a mannequin dresser for no other reason than that it provides Edwards with a weird, eerie setting for her murder. Waiting for Ripley to come, she locks her door and, rather illogically, begins to work on one of the mannequins; then, even less logically, she begins to take off her dress (not the behavior of a frightened woman). Wearing only her slip, she sits thoughtfully in front of her dressing table mirror, which reflects the whole room, mannequin heads, limbs, and busts behind her.

Taking that scene as an isolated set piece, Mancini provides a spooky, reflective piano piece entirely quarantined from the rest of the score, made up of a dissonant, slow-rocking arpeggio in the left hand and an equally spectral, delicately nontonal melody in the right hand underscoring the strangeness of the mannequin room and adding altogether a kind of distant sadness and a sense of doom so that we begin to feel that Nancy's very casualness, her undressing, and her last mirror gaze are preparatory self-sacrificial acts. The only obvious translation of such a scene into the rest of the film is the notion that this is how Red Lynch sees all women: as interchangeable body parts. Edwards's clever payoff for the scene, despite its contrived nature, is the climax, where suddenly one of the many mannequin heads in the room appears to turn, and we realize that it is Lynch and that Nancy is a goner. When the piano motif is repeated, it comes with low strings and bass flute to give an emotional underpinning to that sense of doom. A single French horn plays a lonely counterpoint over everything in chromatic opposition to it all. Then the solemnity of the whole cue is broken by one piano/vibes chord; the deep organ-pedal point is heard again (which seems to always signal death), and the brass enter with one crescendo that caps Nancy's coffin.

Mancini much more efficiently depicts danger and dread here than he did for the same sort of stalking scenes in the broader, bigger scoring of *Man Afraid* just five years earlier. His education has come from those years of scoring television noir and from the freedom and encouragement granted him now by working with Blake Edwards. With its conventional story, *Experiment in Terror* performed conventionally at the box office when it opened in April 1962. Mancini's soundtrack album, lacking exploitable pop tunes, was likewise a mediocre seller. But Edwards had expected that; he was more interested in directing that kind of small-scale film than in a career of fashion-plate romantic tales. His second black-and-white film of this period would prove to be even more unfashionable in nature.

This time the script came from a recent TV drama about a couple's descent into alcoholism, here expanded for theatrical release and starring again Lee Remick and new friend-for-life Jack Lemmon, who had been wanting to follow up his success in light comedy (such as *Mr. Roberts* [1955]) with some serious acting. *Days of Wine and Roses* (1963) would be Edwards's most daring film yet. And it was Mancini's second foray into scoring a film about drinking. His music for *Voice in the Mirror* had stressed the cravings, the dread and suffering of alcohol addiction. Conversely, Mancini believed that this new film would need a score, a very sparse and modest score, that would stress the *relationship* between the two maimed main characters and all the regrets that follow their descent into mutual dipsomania. Lemmon's character, Joe Clay, drinks to escape pressures and doubts on the job; Remick's Kirsten joins him to get closer, then gets caught in her own drinking. Joe and Kirsten soon marry and have a daughter together.

The script and Edwards's unsqueamish direction take us step by step through Joe's decline—the cover-ups and excuses, the lapsed promises, the hysterical thirsts when he tries to quit drinking but then can think of nothing else, the panic when the bottles he has hidden cannot be found, and the stripped degradation of the drunk tank into which he finally lands exhausted and, thence, into Alcoholics Anonymous. Kirsten, who has followed him into the abyss, begins to resent his eventual sobriety, and the story shifts to his efforts to redeem her. Along the way of that emotional teeter-totter, one character up when the other is down, the only constant is their enduring marriage, which is being savaged by alcohol-the-interloper but not ever being killed by it. With Edwards's approval Mancini figured that to represent their relationship by a single nostalgic melody—one whose chord modulations seemed to be luxuriating in the "days of wine and roses"—would lend this film and these characters the emotional continuity that was needed.

Mancini has said that he found the melody idea easily in half an hour by the very structure of the words in the title. The first two notes, C up to A, mimic the phonology of the words "The days," and from there it was all a matter of his own personal sympathies. The film's opening song, performed by chorus over the main titles and then fragmented and repeated instrumentally throughout the film, was his most sophisticated melody line since *Dreamsville*, and for all of its stark story contexts it had the same casual nostalgic, almost passive, harmonic flow to it. The first phrase is in the pure key of F major, but those seventh and ninth harmonies that lead the rest of the song, so naturally, into a minor key are the essence of jazz naturalness, supporting Mercer's now-famous lyric about "a closing door / a door marked Nevermore, that wasn't there before." ("I guess those minor ninths I was brought up with still get to me at times—you know, when the big band era was being influenced by Ravel and Debussy, when all the ballads took lush modulations like that."[3]) The second chorus follows suit, playing with the major/minor edge under lyrics like "a passing breeze filled with memories," and ends with a sense of reconciliation (seventh chords again) toward the initial key of F major.

Although Mancini's choral version and all the pop singers who later recorded the song to great success accompanied it with a moderate beat to maintain its shape over the long whole notes in the arch of the melody, "The Days of Wine and Roses" is really a free-rubato ballad that may be best performed at its own conversational pace outside of tempo. As Mercer's whole lyric was actually two long (and strikingly abstract) sentences, so Mancini's melody line contained just two broad arches without the usual bridge or verse. It can pack a real emotional wallop if presented with modesty and restraint, precisely because of the reminiscent quality of its casual rises and falls—like very personal and only half-regretful sighs.

"Seeing scores in sounds," as Mancini once described, often led him to conceive particular melodies with certain studio players in mind. "Often I see scores in sounds before I start composing. Sometimes when I hear people play, especially if they're very distinctive players, I actually try to incorporate their sound into a particular score."[6] For the first yawning notes of this song, he was hearing the solid round tone of studio veteran French horn soloist Vincent De Rosa, and that became the voice of solitude in the film. Its lonely "face yourself" connotations became important to the whole message inherent in the story. Thus Mancini was scoring not the issue of alcoholism but a character study. Besides that melody—heard on French horn at the start, later as a choral pop song, later on a cozy fireside electric guitar, and later played by different groupings of strings slowly working up and down the line of the tune in a reflective manner—the other memorable voicing in the score is the jazzy, slurring sax-against-trumpet combos, sometimes playing languorous phrases associated with the late-night bars and damp backwater wharfs of the setting, sometimes heightened and disturbed into a few blurred climactic chords associated with the horrors of delirium tremens. The composer is telling us better than any dialogue the difference between social drinking and needful drinking, and how booze can sneak up on you.

Mancini brings his strings into the scoring whenever the message of the film reaches beyond the immediate action—for instance, as Joe catches sight of his own reflection in a storefront window and at first wonders who "that bum" is and then realizes how far he has slid. Brass and strings in dark dissonant chords overwhelm the simple insouciant jazz we have been hearing on the street before that moment.

After losing his job, Joe stays with Kirsten's father for a while, sober one month, and the string writing gets lighter around him. But music is absent altogether during his relapse scene, played out in his father-in-law's greenhouse. Joe has lost track of the one security bottle of booze he had hidden in a potted plant, and he tears the place apart in search of it, ending up on the floor panting and raving with no sympathy this time from the score. The scene, supposedly the dramatic high point of the film, seems showy and indulgent today and might actually have played better with some orchestral perspective behind it. The laconic nature of what scoring there is proves most effective at the very end of the film, though. Kirsten begs Joe to take her back. He is living sober with their daughter, but Kirsten is still on the precipice. Joe says she must be committed to sobriety before he can live anywhere near her again; he is still and forever vulnerable, of course, to drink. It is a promise she cannot make yet; she walks off into the night streets to the now familiar call of Vince De Rosa's solo French horn playing the first phrase of the "wine and roses" song. The child wakes, a celesta plays a phrase of the song; she asks Joe when her mommy might be coming home. He tries to reassure her, then goes to the window to watch Kirsten walk away. The last shot is of Joe looking out his window. The French horn recalls the film's opening musical phrase—but this time minus its last note. The film and the score end suspended like that.

It was a perfect and adroit way to, at once, support and comment on the scene and fully incorporate the spirit of that main song into the drama, all without gushing forth with the "love song." Shallow critics, without considering or even investigating Mancini's use of the melody throughout the film, were quick to reprove him as a "cheap pop guy" for trying to shove a love song into a searing dramatic movie "just to get another hit record." As we have seen, music is one of the most effective elements about the film today, even if its acting histrionics have not aged as well. (It is worth comparing Jack Lemmon's hysterical greenhouse scene with Arthur O'Connell's hesitant, sad, helpless barstool scene in *Voice in the Mirror* as he sits there longing for both the drink in front of him and the drinkless days behind him. Which says more about the alcoholic's reality?)

If anything, Mancini's theme-based score for *Days of Wine and Roses*, far from being "cheapened" by a pop music approach was, certainly in that final scene, more narrative and orchestral (and understated) in its concept than most film scores of that same year. Both Lemmon and Remick were nominated for performance Oscars for 1962; Mancini and Mercer's song took them up to the Academy stage to accept the best song award for the second year in a row.

"Just a word about the songwriting thing," Mancini once said:

It's strange, but all of the so-called hits I've had, like "Days of Wine and Roses," have been outgrowths of dramatic situations. I mean, there were very few that were written as songs like "Moon River" was, but even that had to be a dramatic, narrative melody that could also double as a song. But with "Wine and Roses," that was a theme first that I could work with for scoring and that did its job narratively throughout the film. Then on top of that, it got great lyrics and was sung at the beginning of the film. Lots of times people don't even notice a score unless there's a song in it; if it's just doing its job no one pays attention. But I can't worry about that. The main thing is . . . for this film a song was important because it was not an issue-oriented story; it was at the bottom about a relationship.[7]

= = =

As Mancini had predicted, Blake Edwards decided to alternate his preference for dark films with his other passion for farcical comedy full of physical gags as elaborate as those of the silent film era. By 1964 he had written a comedy script with Maurice Richlin and secured the participation of David Niven as a debonair playboy thief, Sir Charles Lytton, scheming to charm a princess (Claudia Cardinale) out of a huge diamond in her possession while she vacations at a ski resort in Cortina, Italy. The jewel has one flaw embedded in it, which, when held to the light, has a pink hew and resembles a leaping panther. *The Pink Panther* (1964) was born. British actor/writer Peter Ustinov was to play a French detective, Jacques Clouseau, who trades wits with the Niven character, hoping to prove that Lytton is really the thief known as The Phantom. Shortly before production began, however, Ustinov bowed out only to be replaced by the much wilder comic style of the British farceur and mimic Peter Sellers. Sellers was already famous in Britain as part of TV's *The Goon Show*—forerunner to irreverent music-hall absurdist comedies like *Monty Python*—and in a series of comic films like *The Ladykillers, The Mouse That Roared, The Wrong Arm of the Law,* and, soon, *Dr. Strangelove,* each of which stressed his gifts for playing awkward, hilariously out-of-place characters. Initially he meshed well with Edwards's ideas for creating the Clouseau character.

Throughout the film and the eventual series of Panther titles, much comic mileage is gained through the notion that Clouseau fancies himself to be a master of logical deduction and a real clue hound, but in fact he spends more time and energy trying to rationalize the completely illogical things he says. "Everything I do is carefully planned," he explains in the embarrassing silence after falling off a couch. "I suspect everyone, I suspect no one," he answers as though it made sense. Looking for clues, he picks up a jar of cold cream in the suspect's room and holds it up to check its scent. When he pulls the jar away, a large glob of white cream still clings to his nose. It stays there through several more exchanges until someone quite casually brings it to his attention. He simply wipes it off. "It's just that thing over there," he says, motioning toward the jar on the dresser.

In the original Panther film there is, of course, somewhat less attention on him than in subsequent films, where he will be elevated to the main character. In the original, though, he is just a comically bungling cop, an inept force majeure among the suave mystery story being told. Attempting to greet the princess with some panache, Clouseau reaches out to kiss her hand, but, delaying a beat behind his assistant, who has reached her first, in the pile-up he kisses his assistant's hand instead. Even on the way out from that interview, Clouseau defers to let his assistant pass through the doorway first, pauses as his assistant pauses, but then moves forward just as his assistant does; they bunch up in the doorjamb anyway, which cannot accommodate two abreast. Edwards shoots all of this subtly, with the camera away across the room, allowing the audience to discover the gag while other characters are still in the foreground of the shot. That kind of slapstick had not been seen on screen for decades, and Edwards's way of offering those gags in passing during an otherwise straight mystery story seemed delightful. The one other element, then, that seemed fresh and perfectly conceived for the project was the sly, witty, and silver-chic music score by Mancini.

Mancini could have treated *The Pink Panther* as a thriller film like, say, Lynn Murray's score to Hitchcock's *To Catch a Thief*, or as a glamour show like John Williams's music for *How to Steal a Million*, or as an authentic *comedie français* like Laurence Rosenthal's *Hotel Paradiso*. Instead, Mancini saw the score in the same way Edwards was planning for it: as a series of separate scenes to be charmed by isolated jazz-pop melodies, all hosted, as it were, by one recurring representative piece.

Mancini has said that the theme for *The Pink Panther* was suggested to him by two things. First, in watching the intended main character played by David Niven sneaking in and out of hotel rooms, simultaneously seducing women and safecracking in a stylish dinner jacket, Mancini was reminded of an old song about a "sentimental crook" called Jimmy Valentine. That song's musical line, though in a major key, had the same stealthy gestures, pauses, and climbs that the piano players in old silent movie days would use to accompany villains and espionage scenes. Out of that, and somehow translated through his own ear (go back to Peter Gunn's "Sorta Blue" or *Tiffany's* shoplifting music for precedent), you have the sly jazzy E-minor Panther piece that seems so familiar today. Second, even as he was writing, he heard the specifically throaty tenor sax sound and phrasing of his colleague Plas Johnson, who had so recently made a strong impression (with his Ben Webster–like approach) on Mancini's big band albums and as part of the *Peter Gunn* band. Mancini cited this as another example of how he "saw scores in sounds," heard even a particular player in his head when he was writing for the screen.

That sound and that theme became great examples of an important Mancini principle of scoring: intentionally "funny" music behind a comedy scene is redundant and destructive. The "*Pink Panther* Theme," though witty in itself, is not a joke, not a novelty number. It is, besides its grin, a seriously swinging piece of jazz-pop with an invigorating sense of both fun and sophistication. So it does not overkill the comedy. We first hear the theme during the film's animated main title sequence, which, famously, morphs that panther-shaped flaw in the stolen gem into a wry, mischievous cartoon panther, which spends the credit sequence taking great liberties with the graphic lettering that spells out the movie's cast and crew.

Early in the film's postproduction process, once the idea of an animated main title sequence was discussed, the animators asked to hear a finished piece of main title music against which they could time their cartoon sketches. At that stage Mancini had not yet fixed his own ideas, but he said he would give them at least a rhythm. They created the panther, Bugs Bunny–like in the long ancestry of animated anarchists, to that bass line alone. The theme itself came after. It begins with a suspended chord of open fifths by the piano and a small hand chime with a triangle tapping out the tempo for three bars until a low piano/vibe/two basses/guitar combo plays the sneaking motif, first ascending, then descending unresolved. This creates, most efficiently, the suspense of a detective story while also making fun of it. At bar 12, or where Peter Sellers's name appears in the credits (already undermining Niven's supremacy as the star), we hear Plas Johnson's tenor sax with its unmistakably jazzy accents as it moves so naturally up in parallel fifths and then does a dying fall, slurring the last note like a bluesman.

Two kinds of scoring follow: (1) a series of background instrumental ballads in the genial, chic language that was almost a separate genre for Mancini and that one can either overlook as being generic cocktail Muzak or recognize as exquisitely scored songs without words, and (2) the continuing deconstruction of the "*Pink Panther* Theme" as the story unwinds. Sir Charles's first attempted seduction of Princess Dahla (only she knows the whereabouts of the panther jewel) is scored with music from the first category: a light samba tune ("Champagne and Quail") for alto sax and flute backed by easygoing strings and an occasional wordless chorus used as brass might have been used in the big band days. Then comes a slower, more elegant and dreamy piece ("Piano and Strings"), which features the light touch of Jimmy Rowles on the keyboard. Later we hear an accordion playing another sad Mancini waltz ("The Lonely Princess") as Dahla blithers

on, drunk, about her life while Sir Charles, stone sober, tries to grill her ever
so elegantly for information.

— — —

It so happened that just as *The Pink Panther* was showing its initial surge of
success, its bankrollers, the Mirisch brothers, Marvin and Harold, approached
Edwards again for help with another property they had acquired: a play by
Harry Kurnitz and Marcel Achard called *A Shot in the Dark*. The assigned
director, Anatole Litvak, had just quit. Edwards agreed to take over only if
he could recast the screenplay with his own vision. And with only five days
to work on it before shooting needed to begin, his one inspired solution was
to change the original play's detective lead character into Inspector Jacques
Clouseau and turn the mildly comic mystery into a Peter Sellers farce.

Gone from the film *A Shot in the Dark* (1964) are the Phantom character
and Clouseau's wife; gone are the Pink Panther diamond and the princess;
gone, too (for the only time in the Panther series), is Mancini's "*Pink Panther* Theme." In its place is a new opening theme with a more deliberate,
terse rock rhythm by Mancini that seems almost a parody of his own "*Peter
Gunn* Theme" with its eight-to-the-bar tempo on a heavy, plugging bass
guitar. This theme is introduced by an odd unpredictable instrument, the
latest selection in Mancini's search for unique voicings: an antique Indian
pump organ he had seen in the window of a shop in London. This strange
contraption produces a pitch in an extremely low and dynamically unstable
register, rather like the ground notes of a comically asthmatic accordion.
His mystery theme this time, absent the feline grace of the panther, relies
on the famous tonal interval of the tritone, a span of three whole tones on
the piano keyboard (it is also known as an augmented fourth) that has such
a basic tonal instability that in the Middle Ages it was known as "the devil
in music" and church composers were forbidden to make use of it. To today's
listeners it just has the sound of intrigue.

The main theme to *A Shot in the Dark* shares the key of E minor with the
original "*Pink Panther* Theme," but it is intentionally heavier, more plodding,
promising a tougher, cruder kind of comedy. The full score is less colorful,
less available, than the original Panther scoring, consisting of two main
themes and a few overt comic musical effects produced instrumentally. Yet
from thinner materials it actually represents a stronger example of film
scoring than the largely decorative panther music. Edwards and Mancini
together decided that this score would be more involved in the comedy;
indeed it assumes the director's point of view on more than one occasion, not

by offending the comedy law about never duplicating a joke on screen but by, sometimes, even creating the joke. The film's opening sequence, coming before the main title cartoon, is one example of the music score helping the director to flaunt convention this time with a complicit parody of the movie love song.

As we watch, from a distance, a murder-from-jealousy occur on screen, we hear vocalist Fran Jeffries's florid performance of Mancini's gauche melody (complete with flowery violin solo) and Robert Wells's syrupy lyric to the song "Shadows of Paris." We cannot quite tell what is going on behind closed doors, but we hear an argument and then a shot in the dark. The scene cuts to the main title cartoon, animated by the same team who had drawn the Panther character, David DePatie and Friz Freleng. After that song, Mancini's main theme on that bizarre pump organ is a welcome relief and a knowing gag in itself. At one point a grande dame hearts-and-flowers exaggeration of "Shadows of Paris" tries to interrupt the pump organ just as Mancini's own credit comes on screen; at another point a shimmering, descending string tremolo follows Blake Edwards's own credit as it comes parachuting down from the top of the frame. But the main theme wins out, and its opening bass guitar vamp is mimicked by pizzicato strings to the end of the opening credits.

We cut to live action now: the sight of Peter Sellers riding in a police car with a look of vacant detachment, heading to the scene of the Ballon Chateau murder. A muted trumpet plays the "Marseillaise" again (Clouseau's mock fanfare from the first Panther film) to set the scene; the car pulls up before the chateau but so close to the courtyard fountain that when Clouseau exits the vehicle his first step trips him into the water. Mancini lets this gag alone. Similarly, music never interferes with the long, droll scenes between Clouseau and his passive (seen-it-all-before) assistant, Hercule, who stands obediently aside with us as Clouseau stupidly reviews the suspect list at a chalkboard or tries in vain to synchronize his wristwatch to reality. The Universal style of scoring comedy might have relied on lots of winks and slurs to break up those long set pieces of character humor, but having graduated from those freshman habits, Mancini (and, of course, Edwards) knew to let those scenes play out on their own sans music. There *are* some tremolo strings together with *tinpanola* and alto flute playing around with fragments of the main theme when Clouseau first enters the room where the murder happened and ineptly questions the butler and the household staff. Then when the maid, Maria Gambrelli (Elke Sommer), comes into the shot and Clouseau is shaken by her sexiness, three slow celesta arpeggios over a bed of suspense strings spotlight the moment. Later, celesta accompanies just a whiff of her perfume as she passes by. This is cooperative, not intrusive, scoring annotation.

During the sequence when Inspector Clouseau attempts to trail Maria (hoping to prove her innocence, so infatuated is he with her), he dons different disguises in order to affect a number of stakeouts wherever she goes. He is a sidewalk painter, a balloon vendor, and so forth—each time halted by a passing cop and arrested for hawking without a permit (referencing a similar series of comic arrests in Charlie Chaplin's *Modern Times*). The continuing joke of those arrests is capped each time on the soundtrack by a single note on the guitar that bends sour. That is a cartoon scoring device, but here it is an allowed indulgence and becomes its own gag rather than just duplicating the one on screen.

— — —

The fantastic success of the two Clouseau films seduced Blake Edwards into the notion of perhaps single-handedly inspiring a renaissance of slapstick comedy on screen. He secured a huge budget from Warner Brothers Studios to produce *The Great Race* (1965), an elaborate knockabout road movie set at the turn of the century, and he plunged ahead in spite of skeptics around him. One thing he knew was that he would never get away with such a big, crude, intentionally old-fashioned, outrageous pageant without the constant support, sustenance, and active participation of a colorful music score—one that would not be afraid this time to draw attention to itself.

In its basic template of a plot, *The Great Race* presents Tony Curtis (his fourth film with Edwards) as the impossibly chaste, white-suited daredevil known as The Great Leslie (when he flashes his power smile, an animated sparkle shines off his teeth) and Jack Lemmon as the gravelly voiced snarling villain Professor Fate, with his handlebar moustache and megalomaniacal cackling laugh, who delights in diabolical schemes and contraptions to make himself master of the world. Each man has his requisite manservant—for Leslie, a bald strongman named Hezekiah (Keenan Wynn), and for Fate, the skittering, rodentlike loyal Max (Peter Falk). Fate, naturally, creates his own bad luck and then refuses to learn from the consequences. Leslie, on the other hand, assumes his charmed place in the scheme of things and lives a winning life. As we all know, there *are* such maddening people in the world and must always be, for the balance of nature. No wonder Fate throws so many tantrums at the unfairness of it all. The tremendous struggle between conceited Good and frustrated Evil is one comic theme of *The Great Race*. The other is that turn-of-the-century (and now turn-of-the-generation) competition between the traditional definitions of masculinity (which Edwards has always been challenging and which he mocks here through Leslie's glib perfection and Fate's angry impotence) and the emerging role of the militantly independent woman. Here she is represented by one newspaper reporter, Maggie Dubois (Natalie Wood), who insists on accompanying Leslie once the Great Race has been proposed by her publisher, the *New York Sentinel.* Edwards really respects none of these characters and reserves only a smirking form of sympathy for Professor Fate, because he is so cruelly and predictably the victim of all his own schemes.

Although this time Edwards does not try to mix moods of storytelling as he has been known to do—there are no suddenly serious or even sincere moments interjected into the basic farce of *The Great Race*—he does play fast and loose with several movie genres and throws them into the pot. Thus elaborate slapstick gags alternate with screwball verbal comedy as all the hot-button issues of the day (the rise of the suffragette movement, the invasion of the automobile, the imperial American male syndrome, the new monopoly of corporate greed) come together into a preposterous plan for an intercontinental car race sponsored by the publicity hounds of the print industry, winner take all. For a time as the drivers pass through the American West, the film becomes a comedy western—saloons, gun-toting varmints, and fake Indians—and later it drifts into a swashbuckling style. Eventually it switches back to the race rivalry and begins to channel yet another film classic, *Around the World in 80 Days* (1956). No matter what the setting, though, Edwards keeps invoking the masculine/feminine role-reversal subtext throughout. Maggie regularly upbraids Leslie for his arrogant assumption of superiority, but his complete unflappability frustrates her more. He never engages in anything so lowdown as a real argument—nothing that might muss his hair. Somehow their continuing spats along the race course make Fate even more jealous of Leslie's advantages. All Fate has is Max. Even Hezekiah seems a bit jealous of the woman in the midst of their "man's world." And Edwards further undermines the expectations of masculinity by making the crown prince (a second role for Jack Lemmon) in the kingdom of Carpania, where the racers stop overnight for refueling, an embarrassingly effeminate sod simpering for his mother.

Critics and audiences of the time appreciated the return of physical comedy to the big screen (the Clouseau films only whetted people's appetite for it, and Stanley Kramer's then-recent slapstick epic, *It's a Mad, Mad World* [1963], was considered overdone), but at the same time they grew restless with the random nature of the plot, the basically annoying characters, and the undercurrents of nastiness that seemed to belie the breezy nonchalance of the long (two and a half hours) series of gags. It was often laborious (and obviously expensive) to set up the laughs as the race went along, and it often felt more furious than fun.

But ignoring any rumble of discontent and taking the film at its best possible face value, Mancini moved in and, as it were, set up shop, unwrapping all kinds of music from his past experience to colorize the film. Almost everything he had learned in film scoring could be useful in such a story (except music with any depth): two songs to be performed on camera during the film, at least four set pieces with individual melodies that would not recur elsewhere, a patriotic march, a number of purely narrative pieces of dramatic scoring, and a dour piece for slide trombone that *does* recur whenever Fate and Max appear with a new strategy to sabotage the Great Race. With nearly half the film's 150 minutes using some kind of scoring (399 actual score pages), Mancini had turned Edwards's pratfall comedy into a musical—a pastiche operetta.

Three recurring themes supply a sense of continuity as the race progresses. First heard (after the overture) is the quaint player-piano waltz "The Sweetheart Tree," which is used variously as a parlor song, a western banjo trail tune, and a love ballad for Maggie Dubois to strum on guitar around a campfire. The second, "The Great Race March," is basically a jingoistic band proclamation (the first three notes of America's national anthem) followed by an answering phrase from some well-known patriotic song, then the first phrase repeated up a step and a second patriotic snippet. Played with lots of fife-and-drum exuberance and a brace of trombones, it propels the most competitive legs of the race. Crowds, confetti, and cheers inspired it, though one can enjoy its clever patchwork of all of those macho military-icon tunes from "Hail to the Chief" to "Dixieland."

The third recurring theme is, of course, the unique, comically skulking and slimy tune for Professor Fate, later recorded under the title "Push the Button, Max" for solo baritone horn with a baritone sax bass line, strummed banjo and tin piano for details. It accompanies and also lampoons Fate's dozen dastardly inventions and conspiracies as he tries to beat Leslie at his own games. The smarmy lines of the minor-key melody and the satiric determination of the counter figure in the bass make it clear what petty tyrants, doomed to foolishness, are Professor Fate and his hapless assistant. It has the same sneaking quality as the "*Pink Panther* Theme," but it exchanges the Panther's sophistication for a loping and myopic quality that fits Fate better. (Actually it is first heard as a kind of acrobatic circus waltz during the film's opening balloon stunt, but ever after it becomes the 4/4 skulk we will come to know.)

With those three themes available for continual reference, Mancini interposes the aforementioned set pieces: a barroom song with rollicking lyrics by Johnny Mercer, a grand royal waltz (his loveliest of the kind) for the racers' stopover in the kingdom of Carpania, and a vigorous clarinet polka for an impromptu pie fight in the royal bakery. A rundown of the film's scattered story reveals how much Mancini's scoring has lent the film mood, momentum, and extra humor. The signal for the great race to start is yet another set piece by Mancini: the banjo-pumping, brass-band gallop called "They're Off!" with more echoes of the old Keystone Kops.

Narrative scoring has its place in *The Great Race*, too. While in Carpania, Professor Fate is kidnapped because of his uncanny resemblance to the incumbent king (as in A. H. Hawkins's classic novel *The Prisoner of Zenda*). An evil baron (Ross Martin) wants to gain power by installing Fate as his puppet and stashing the bumbling effeminate prince in some permanent dungeon. The Great Leslie discovers the plot and confronts the baron in an upper alcove of the palace. An impromptu sword fight begins with foils. The kind of music common to fencing scenes—certainly in the original *Prisoner of Zenda* film but more famously in Erich Korngold's scoring of such films as *The Adventures of Robin Hood* (1938), in whose style Edwards staged this duel—is, of course, highly active vivace scoring for orchestra, full of heroic leaps and the energy of thrusts and parries. It is music to mirror the athleticism of the two-man contest. Mancini's scoring for the start of *this* duel, however, begins with low strings, low brass, and bass flutes in dim but rising blots of sound. Once Leslie and the baron switch from flexible foils to steel sabers, the sound of the clashing metal is more threatening. The brass are harmonized in thick suspended clusters, almost clotted, between muted brass and winds, holding the tension, then sliding up the scale to the next plateau chord as the swordsmen back off to regain balance and then come at one another again. That holding-rising-holding pattern in the scoring parallels the backing-thrusting-backing rhythm of a sword fight and makes for much more tension in the scene than a gallant, galloping swashbuckling music cue could have achieved. Partly because of this musical dramatization, where the inner feeling of the moment is what is being scored rather than the outer action, the sword fight becomes the one scene in the whole movie where the characters seem a bit real.

The two concluding jokes of the whole film are (1) that Leslie and Maggie are arguing so much that Fate's car can skim past them to win the race at the finish line, and (2) that Fate is so outraged that he did not win fairly that he proposes another race back the way they came. "Here we go again" is the message that Edwards wanted the audience to be laughing about as they left the theater. For Mancini, at this stage in his career when he was still responding to film stories with multi-themed pop scores, this movie gave him a good chance to score many different episodes and not worry about having to tie them together. It was a great playground, and it was made possible only with the collaboration, inspiration, and freedoms associated with the Blake Edwards team. Mancini's chance to write a delightfully unctuous gag piece like Professor Fate's theme, a clever jazzy gem like the "*Pink Panther* Theme," a frosty dirge like "Experiment in Terror," or the reverie of "Moon River"—not to mention his personal emancipation achieved through the success of the *Peter Gunn/Mr. Lucky* days—came only through Edwards's efforts and energies. That near-partnership of opposite characters did not come without eventual dissension, but from the late 1950s throughout the mid-1960s it produced some high times indeed.

CHAPTER 6

Career Crescendos

One major outcome of Mancini's success with Blake Edwards, his best-selling albums, and the growing shelf of his awards was that now other directors, even famous classic veteran directors, the past kings of the cinema, were starting to take notice of his music, trying to get him on the phone to talk about the musical possibilities of *their* next pictures. Again, he was writing traditionally satisfying music that they could understand, yet it had a modern slant toward the younger audiences they wanted to court. The great Howard Hawks was one of those directors. Just now he was hoping to find a workable composer for his own new, overlong, under-structured John Wayne adventure film set in Africa about a group of wild game hunters who collect specimens for zoos and circuses around the world, to be called *Hatari!*—the Swahili word for "danger."

Hawks, who had started in silent films as early as 1926 and went on to make a handful of the greatest classics of American cinema, such as *To Have and Have Not* (1944), *The Big Sleep* (1946), *Sergeant York* (1941), *Dawn Patrol* (1939), and *Red River* (1948), was a pal of John Wayne, and this whole project had been loosely built around the Wayne image, trumping even the need for a cogent script. The idea of Duke Wayne as a modern big game hunter chasing down rhinos from an armor-plated jeep seemed enough: just him and a series of animal chases separated by casual conversation scenes among the chase crew (Red Buttons, Hardy Krüger, Elsa Martinelli) back at base camp. After location shooting in Tanganyika, the filmmakers returned with a lot of footage and no sequential story, save for one subplot about wanting to find the meanest rhino, which had gored one of the team members early on. Hawks talked with his most frequent composer compatriot, Dimitri Tiomkin, about what music might do for such a picture, and he floated the idea that the soundtrack might keep away from the usual symphonic action scoring for which Tiomkin was famous, that it might concentrate on more authentic African rhythms and sounds. Hawks had brought back two large boxes of African percussive and tonal instruments for that very purpose. Initially Tiomkin nodded, but he never really took the suggestion seriously. He was a two-fisted, large-scale orchestral composer, famous for compelling themes like those for *High Noon* and *The High and the Mighty* and for blunt adventure scores like *55 Days at Peking* and *Duel in the Sun*. That was his kind of music, and no matter how the director re-explained his needs, Tiomkin remained intractable. Hawks began to think he had a soundtrack crisis on his hands.

His second choice for the music to *Hatari!* was most peculiar. But as tinkering went on during the film's editing process, trying to make it fall together into some kind of a story, Hawks was hoping that some new approach to the music might spark the whole project in the right direction. He had a few conversations with another old friend from the 1930s, songwriter Hoagy Carmichael, to see if there was some other way to go with the music. Trying to connect the kind of nostalgic, romantic, southern-flavored blues tunes for which Carmichael was known with this film's African savannah setting seems a misguided idea at best. It is hard to know what Hawks was expecting there.

In Richard Sudhalter's biography of Carmichael and in Todd McCarthy's life of Howard Hawks it is mentioned that Hawks wanted a score that would be by turns dramatic and tuneful. Because Carmichael's career had been mostly a 1930s-to-1950s event, he had been particularly pleased with this unexpected attention now in the early 1960s. Carmichael's son has told how Hoagy would get up in the middle of the night to jot down musical ideas for *Hatari!* "You'd hear it and you'd know you were in Tanganyika." As gloriously American as Carmichael's songs were, it is baffling to think about what scoring he was devising that might evoke John Wayne on the African veldt. According to Sudhalter, the Carmichael archives contain music and manuscript material for *Hatari!* "indicating work on a main theme, a song, and bits of connective tissue."[1] Hawks soon asked to see some of this material, took it away, and apparently added some hack lyrics to one melody, intending to bolster the rest of the score later by bringing in some offsite composer/orchestrator. Carmichael protested that he had not even finished his ideas for the music yet and was not willing to surrender it to other hands. The two parted ways, and Hawks had his big sprawling film back on the cutting table—scoreless.[2]

Mancini was the studio's suggestion to Hawks, since both *Breakfast at Tiffany's* and *Hatari!* were Paramount products. He jumped at the chance to meet the famous director of *Red River* and, perhaps, to score an exotic dramatic picture. "I saw it as a way to open up and broaden my image, an image that was so far associated with romantic strings and flutes and jazz," he said.[3] At Hawks's office Mancini saw a rough cut of the film and was presented with the same boxes of African percussion instruments that Tiomkin had ignored. He was also given an outline of Hawks's scoring boundaries: the score should avoid conventional European string passages or symphonic affectations, it should ignore the traditional ideas of movie action music, and yet it should have its own inherent sense of drama. What Tiomkin had found annoying and Carmichael had found discouraging, Mancini welcomed.

In the boxes he found giant peapod shakers, a thumb piano, shell gourds, and some tapes of native Masai tribal chants that seemed to repeat a certain two-note span Mancini would incorporate as a major motif in his eventual scoring. To those percussive devices he decided to add hollow drums, flat skin-sheathed tom-toms, and a cheap upright piano slightly detuned so that each note has a strained quality to it.

The score he fashioned opens with two chords taken from that Masai chant—presented as a crescendo in the deep brass accompanied by a gong display. This quickly recedes, leaving a background of quiet, expectant percussive sounds—plucked and clicking and tapping noises evocative of dry brush and insect life on the African plains. We are shown introductory shots of the hunters, Wayne and each cast member, standing by their pursuit vehicles out on the hunt, scanning the distant wildebeest herds for any sign of the big game animals on their capture list—today they are hunting rhino. The finger piano, *lujon*, and seashell gourd are making their first comments very slowly, layering up on one another. Soon the sustained tones of bass flutes bring their own peculiarly ominous voice to the scene with long falls at the end of their lines. Someone spots a rhino in the herd, and everyone climbs into the jeeps to begin the chase. The scoring, too, rouses in anticipation; the detuned upright piano doubled by guitar and mandolin bring not only tonality but also crispness to the now-steady galloping, gradually quickening foundation of African drums.

Even though Hawks had said he wanted no traditional woodwinds in his score, Mancini was betting on the idea that he had been thinking of the typical lightening effect of flutes and clarinets. No one had used bass flutes to such a dramatic range in films as Mancini. To the six bass flutes were added six trombones, six horns, and vibes as the chase truly takes off. Hawks's wide open shots from a speeding camera truck keeping pace with the chase vehicle, which is in turn keeping pace with the galloping rhino as the flat endless plain skims by, are the best thing about this film, and the discretion with which Mancini's music introduces these scenes (the hushed percussion and exotic tones) and the power with which it shortly parallels the chase seem to promise a great dramatic score—all before the opening credits have even begun. One complex blurry chord from brass and saxes (three alto, three tenor) blares out at the climax of the action just as one of the hunters is gored by the rhino's horn and the chase is abandoned. There is some discussion about getting the fellow to a hospital, and the whole party heads back to base camp. At last the main title music begins here and the credits roll.

Mancini's main theme for *Hatari!* has a somber, primitive, ancient-wisdom quality to it, based in a minor-seventh variation on the Masai chant (not to mention its tonal debt to the primitive phraseology found in Stravinsky's *Le Sacre du Printemps*). He has scored it for unison horns with occasional trombone fills and the same kind of exotica as the rhino chase displayed—the *lujon*, the bass flutes, the peapod shakers, native drums, and mandolin.

But Mancini's music gained its biggest notice for one satiric idea in the score linked to a truly optional scene that otherwise made no contribution to the film whatsoever. During the shooting, when a trio of baby elephants seemed to take a liking to actress Elsa Martinelli, Hawks thought to shoot a sequence of her leading them down to the river for a bath. Mildly amusing, the sequence itself goes nowhere. But Mancini, taking advantage of Hawks's blanket approval to try anything, combined two whimsical inspirations. On the one hand, the sight of three pachyderms forming a conga line behind Martinelli and following her down the slope to the water's edge put Mancini in mind of circus music; on the other hand, the syncopated shuffling gait of the animals suggested a boogie-woogie rhythm to him, eight beats to the bar. He had in his head an old novelty big band record by Will Bradley called "Down the Road a Piece." Putting the two notions together with his own free and easy sense of humor, he created what came to be called the "Baby Elephant Walk." An electric circus calliope set the meter, then an E♭ clarinet played the droll, perky melody. Timed perfectly to the whole self-contained scene, this music shapes what was really a random incident into a film highlight. Though it comes late in the already overlong movie, the sequence made people talk more about the music score than they would about the film, and when the soundtrack record (or rather rerecording) was released, the "Baby Elephant

Walk" became a famous single record on its own. Mancini had struck a chord with the public again—right over the head of the veteran director.

Obviously grateful, Hawks called on Mancini again for his next picture, a romantic comedy called *Man's Favorite Sport* (1964), liberally based on his own 1938 screwball classic, *Bringing Up Baby*. It would star Rock Hudson as an average guy pretending to be an expert fisherman for the duration of a big tournament, egged on by and gradually attracted to his coach, Paula Prentiss. Mancini penned an emblematic song for it and played the score off of that, with a mix of comedy gestures and sweet moments, a throwback to soundtracks like *Everything But the Truth*, except that this tune is far more sophisticated, beginning on an upbeat Bdim chord and launching from Cmin^9 to B♭maj^9 just in its first phrase as lyricist Johnny Mercer has a ball rhyming *pearls, curls*, and *hurls* with "the favorite sport of man is girls!" Mancini contributed a similar score in these same few months to another sitcom film by veteran director Henry Koster and starring James Stewart, *Mr. Hobbs Takes a Vacation*, again relying on a single attractive theme, scored for a relaxed electric guitar with a quasi–big band backing.

Two more veteran director kings from cinema's aristocracy sought scores from Mancini for their very different romantic tales during this period—one a discreet fable of middle-age courtship, the other a torrid melodrama of a lover's murder and cover-up among spoiled rich folk on the Riviera. For the latter, *Moment to Moment* (1966), directed by Mervyn LeRoy, Mancini's main melody intuitively and intentionally picks up the purple prose of the film's script; he gives the film a strong, firmly crafted straight-ahead tune in A minor that mirrors the movie's self-consciousness. One of Johnny Mercer's rare bad lyrics ("Every moment that I live / I live for every moment with you") likewise mirrors the film's sordid tale. The tune works best when used as dramatic scoring, a blatant but knowing magnet for melodrama sometimes backed by dark, blurred cluster-chords for strings and brass and punctuated with vibes as the heroine struggles between conscience and desperation.

The other romance, the shy, discreet one directed by Delbert Mann, *Dear Heart* (1964), seems miles away from all that melodrama. It was originally a Ted Mosel play called *The Out-of-Towners*. Its movie version offered Glenn Ford as Harry, a mild-mannered minor executive with a greeting card company come to New York for a convention, meanwhile trying to deal with a shallow, demanding fiancée back home. Across the hotel corridor comes Geraldine Page as Evie, booked in for a convention of her own—the Postmasters of America. The question is, can two middle-agers fall in love in a strange city? Mancini's soon-to-be-famous opening theme song seems strange at first, beginning with what appears to be a country pastorale piano figure, then during the main titles rolling into a sort of bicycle-built-for-two, turn-of-the-century ballad whose association with the modern Manhattan setting is unclear. Tremolo strings and a wordless chorus offer this theme to us during the film's five-minute opening sequence orienting us to the locale and characters. The whole show is mostly a filmed stage script, so music cues are scarce throughout. There *are* some important moments, as when Evie checks in to her hotel room and calls downstairs for a hairdresser. Flutes repeat what was the main theme's piano introduction, and celesta and strings make the melody light and pure; later the same sounds are used to suggest a closening of the relationship between her and Harry. In their own ways these two people are brittle and self-defensive for all their politeness, and the music, with its air of nostalgia, seems to soften them and entice them nearer. As Harry and Evie talk, on the verge of mutual affection, about life's regrets and hopes, a solo violin even poses, without embarrassment, its own version of the main theme. They stand at some upper-floor window looking out over the city and their hands touch. On the soundtrack the emotional pull of a few leaning chords (appoggiaturas) makes the theme a bit more poignant than its many subsequent pop recordings apart from the film ever did.

The question of applying that old-fashioned tune to a contemporary story is finally answered within the movie when, from down the hotel corridor, we can hear the half-tipsy late-night conventioneers strike up a slurry version of Mancini's melody with simple folksy lyrics (by Jay Livingston and Ray Evans). Evie refers to it nostalgically as "that old song." Mancini's task, therefore, so beautifully accomplished, was to write an original song that sounded like a comfortable old heirloom. Evie says its lyrics are about "a man writing a letter to his wife from far away." In that context it sounds like an old parlor-piano piece of Americana. And since Evie is basically an old-fashioned, abandoned turn-of-the-century romantic, the song, and therefore the whole score, suddenly feels right. The producers were going to call the film by its original theater title, but at the last minute, having fallen in love with Mancini's tune and the homesick lyric ("Dear heart, wish you were here . . . / a single room, a table for one, / it's a lonesome town all right"), they decided to rename the whole film for its representative song, "Dear Heart."

The experience of working with all those old-guard directors, Hawks and Koster, LeRoy and Mann, had been something quite different from collaborating with Blake Edwards. They had appreciated how easy Mancini had made their collaboration, and, of course, they were fairly agreeable elder statesmen by that time anyway, working on their last films and not prone to argue. What is more, Mancini's music for them seemed so likable, so respectful, so right. It is also true to say that during these high times Mancini was writing fairly easily for everyone—for films and for albums. The music he had stored up over all those West Aliquippa years, the war years, and the Universal experience was finally coming out—directly and sincerely.

Mancini's daughter Monica recalls this as a time of easy creativity for her father:

> His studio was upstairs at the house, and so when we kids would walk up and just visit or say hello, he'd be there writing. In his right hand would be the pencil and the score paper in front of him, and his left hand would be working out chords at the keyboard, and he'd play just little sections of music and kind of hear them again and start writing them down. And he was very fast—I never remember walking in and seeing him struggling or plodding along or being that much in his head. I just remember his pencil going pretty quickly on that paper, and it seemed to me my perception of the way he composed was that it was just sort of a free-flowing thing. It was kind of the way he was in life: things just flowed. He had a very good temperament for just about anything and anyone. Very disciplined and yet intuitive too. I never saw him out of balance.[4]

- - -

Sometime in 1962 the veteran director Stanley Donen had heard and been charmed by the "Baby Elephant Walk," so he decided to phone Mancini from London to tell him about his current picture, a comedy/mystery starring Audrey Hepburn and Cary Grant called *Charade*. Of course, Donen had been directing famous musical films throughout the 1950s (*Singing in the Rain, On the Town*), but he had done non-musicals as well (*Once More with Feeling, The Grass Is Greener*). With writer Peter Stone, he now intended to put his own slant on a Hitchcock-like thriller mixed with amusing dialogue, high fashion, and a strong sense of melody in the background score. Mancini seemed the perfect choice for a collaborator—not to make *Charade* a mini-musical but to provide a colorful musical transition from scene to scene, ambient music for the many clubs and glamorous Parisian backdrops against which the characters would move, and some sort of identifying theme to tie it all together. Once the project was under way, Donen was impressed with Mancini as a working partner, using phrases like "just a lovely man to work with" and "elegant, meticulous, very organized" to describe him.[5]

The plot of *Charade* presents Hepburn as Regina Lampert, who is trying to recover from her husband's apparent murder. She finds two strange men eager to help her: Carson Dyle (Walter Matthau) seems to be a representative of the American embassy in Paris investigating the case, and Peter Joshua (Cary Grant) appears to be a passerby, who meets Regina at a ski resort called Megeve and then reappears as if by chance throughout the film, often to rescue her from unknown assailants. But why does he keep asking about her husband's missing fortune? Regina finds both men confusing, not knowing whom to trust, and therein is the intrigue, played out as a romantic confectionary entertainment. Mancini's Continental-flavored pop score accurately admits the three main elements of Donen's concept: the faddish Paris setting, the likability of the romance/comedy/mystery genre as filtered through the casual polish of the Cary Grant style, and the elegant femininity of Audrey Hepburn.

One can wish there had been a strong, integrated orchestral score to *Charade*, for instance, in some of the fight scenes or action climaxes where Mancini provides only sustained vibe chords or rhythmic vamps instead of real music-making to equal the strength of the pop themes that abound here. Yet one critic declared that Mancini was showing "unusual restraint" in such laconic scoring with his "telling use of solo vibraphone (a few notes on which, in a simple gesture later much imitated, can conjure up eerie, expectant or tense atmospheres)" and his "ability to move rapidly between jazz idioms and dissonant modernist gestures."[6] In truth, the music for one of those fight scenes—the one between Cary Grant's character and a hook-hand villain, was left unscored by Mancini, yet Donen laid in a suspense-music cue from some other scene to keep the tension going—not Mancini's idea. But regardless, for purposes of this study, there are two main strengths to *Charade*'s score that lift it from the ordinary and make it both one of Mancini's most celebrated "high times" efforts and a big part of people's memories of the film. One is the multiplicity of melodies—a tasty array of bistro dance pieces, a mock-classical string quartet adagio for a gangster funeral, carousel music, Les Halles cancans, and a romantic duet for solo violin and French accordion (musette). The other is the recurring *Charade* theme, a lonely A-minor waltz with a lovely major-key bridge flirting with the key of C, then passing through diminished, to minor, to major seventh chords, finding its way back to A minor for the chorus—and all the while giving the impression of some sad and stylized carousel tune. As with "Moon River" and "The Days of Wine and Roses," the melody for "Charade" is subjugated, at various places in the film, to the role of source music, heard as though it were the tune of a merry-go-round in the park or ambient music from a tour boat passing on the Seine. But as a straight melody it also has a wistful, woeful feeling, which lyricist Johnny Mercer perfectly caught in yet another song-poem. He said this was his favorite Mancini melody, and, again, he made a metaphor out of the implications of the film's dissimulating characters with lines like "When we played our charade, / we were like children posing" and then carrying that into the universal of *everyone's* mendacity and longing for a simpler time with lines like "sad little serenade, / song of my heart's composing; / I hear it still, I always will."

Our first experience with that tune, though, comes at the abrupt opening of the picture. A train comes out of the distance in the French countryside and screams past us. Our vantage beside the tracks reveals a body thrown from one of the train cars and rolling down the embankment. A second cut shows us the dead man's face. It is Regina Lampert's late husband, though we know nothing of that yet. The shot is then covered by Maurice Binder's swirling, geometric animated graphics, which take over the screen as the main titles begin. On the soundtrack, emerging from the roar of the train is a loud knocking on a Tahitian wood block from Mancini's percussion section, marking out the fashionable Continental dance-craze rhythm of that season, the *tamoure*. A bass line and bongos add in, and then a sharp electric guitar (doubled by *tinpanola* and very low musette) states the melody as a driving dramatic action piece. It is a compelling overture, one of Mancini's strongest. And the tune itself stays in your head forever.

Mancini has said that the idea for the tune first suggested itself (the hardest thing about film scoring is not the composing, the timing, or the orchestration but deciding what *kind* of music, what point of view) as he watched an early shot of Regina in an empty apartment where she had expected to reunite with her husband. Instead, she finds all the furniture has been hocked. A police inspector appears to say that her husband has been murdered and shows her a suspicious collection of passports her husband had been using under different names. Obviously he was involved in some international thievery about which she knows nothing. As she tries to absorb this scenario, alone in the apartment, Mancini plays the *Charade* theme as a simple piano waltz, and it is that image of isolation for which he conjured the tune in the first place.

Charade, as another easily noticeable score, enhanced Mancini's reputation even further; the film was a hit and the song itself (heard as a lyric only during the riverboat scene with male chorus singing in the distance behind dialogue, then again briefly at the end of the film) won another Oscar nomination for the Mancini-Mercer team, though it lost to a more traditional love song, Jimmy Van Heusen's "Call Me Irresponsible." Nevertheless, Donen was pleased. An Oscar-nominated song and a best-selling soundtrack album generated much goodwill toward his hit movie. He immediately signed on with Mancini for his next picture, a story similar to *Charade*—again an innocent drawn into international intrigue—part mystery, part romantic fantasy scripted by the same guy, Peter Stone, but under the pseudonym Pierre Martin. Another middle-aged couple takes the Grant/Hepburn roles, this time Gregory Peck and Sophia Loren, this time the male hero being the pawn and the female lead being the deceiver: is she friend or double-crosser? Peck plays British professor David Pollack of a university Department of Ancient Arabic Languages, who is accidentally caught up in an assassination plot against an Arab sheik. Authorities on both sides want Pollack to decipher a hieroglyph embedded on a chip of microfilm that will reveal the assassination plan. In keeping with the exotic gyrations and coded poses of Arabian dance, mirrored also in the twists and turns of this film's contrived story, they called it *Arabesque* (1966).

With a much less elegant setting (gray London instead of pastel Paris) and a single obvious villain, *Arabesque* offered less opportunity for an active music score. Here, Mancini's pounding saber dance opening music and then a succession of seductive (yet also strangely solemn) background melodies referencing the Arab musical scale are nearly all there is to establish the film's intended exotic milieu. Donen's framing of his leading lady, Yasmin Azir, is worshipful—her image reflected in mirrors or shards of cut glass, seen behind crystal décor and before sumptuous draperies and, of course, in a series of gorgeous gowns. And likewise she is always being visually devoured by the abashed Professor Pollack; we are made to identify with his first soft-focus admiring view of her as she enters the library where he is working on the cipher. Peck performs a love-struck double take at the sight of her, and the soundtrack abruptly dials up two chords of muted strings that lead to the main Yasmin melody playing languidly on the soundtrack behind their first conversation.

This sudden music entrance shows how uncertain Donen was in how to best use the music tracks he was given, and yet we can also see how it is working, not reacting specifically to their talk but just supporting the atmosphere that Loren embodies. And all the while, Mancini manages to personalize this music even though he keeps within the particular language of the Arabic scale—speaking personally and directly out of a foreign dialect. The song (later called "We've Loved Before [Yasmin's Theme]" with a "wonders of the world" lyric by Jay Livingston and Ray Evans) tilts back and forth between major (D⁷) and minor (Amin⁷) until a mood at once Arabic and romantic is affected. Three other such melodies are spaced throughout the film, though they are never given lyrics nor much chance to be noticed; each of them is distinctive, and each is scored for muted string orchestra, the mandola (half-brother of the mandolin), and a solo oboe. These cues, with their lovely Scheherazade quality and that sober sense of sadness, are among Mancini's most attractive set pieces, but since they were written in response to Donen's already finished film, it is not fair, or at least not beneficial, to wish that *Arabesque* should have done more with them—could have built whole scenes, romantic or spy-charged, around their strength. Instead, those three pieces and "Yasmin's Theme" are simply laid in behind a long dinner scene with Pollack at a table in a London mansion as the villain Beshraavi serves his guests a plate of roast lark.

The main feature of the *Arabesque* soundtrack, though, is its opening theme; three English horns in unison play under the main title, sounding for all the world like some snake charmer's reed pipe. Mancini begins with a pounding of hollow drums and a set of tunable tom-toms so that each of the six notes in the scale of his percussive counter line can be tonal, not just rhythmic. ("They're tuned in parallel fifths, hand-tuned by my percussionist so that they were not only rhythmic but also struck specific tones."⁷) Add to that a bass line on low *tinpanola* and basses with a bright two-beat feeling, then the overarching *alle breve* melody in A minor that moves toward G minor, and you have as gripping an opening as Mancini ever wrote for a film. This, then, becomes the perfect orchestral potion for the central action episode in the picture, the zoo chase.

Pollack and Yasmin escape from Beshraavi's house arrest but are pursued by his thug and also by a counteragent. They run into the Regent's Park Zoo, giving Donen another chance to shoot his action through reflective mirror surfaces, such as glass turtle tanks and reptile cages. The zoo chase (Mancini labels it "Animal Crackers" on his score sheets) begins as the thug punches his way through the locked mansion door. On the punch there is a sharp chord from vibes/*tinpanola*/jangle percussion and a visual cut to Pollack and Yasmin dashing down a spiral staircase, shot through a crystal chandelier. A vigorous sforzando passage for sixteen violins, then violas and cellos, spurs their escape. It pauses (with a held tremolo of strings) to accommodate some dialogue where Yasmin convinces Pollack that they had best stick together, then the pounding beat, the tom-toms, and the counter bass line all kick in again and the chase begins in earnest. Only when they enter the zoo proper do the three English horns come in with the main theme. Pollack and Yasmin dash through a number of animal exhibits, upsetting the predator cats in their cages, exciting the monkeys, alarming the elephants. Donen makes soundtrack use of all the animal shrieks and voices over Mancini's tense music, and he cuts in close-ups of mad primate faces and threatening serpent tongues. Mancini keeps the strings running underneath as brass chords punch out a jagged rhythm over them, and the English horns, four French horns and saxes ("as many as we have," Mancini writes on the music sketch) build to a crescendo in half notes on top. Donen, hearing the tremendous excitation produced by these two and a half minutes and twenty-nine sketch pages of Mancini music, actually went back to the editing room after the scoring session and recut the film of the zoo chase climax so that it might end with five serpent close-ups cut precisely on Mancini's last five brass punches—an expensive and somewhat unprecedented (and most generous on Donen's part) tribute to the importance of good scoring in the filmmaker's collective art.

When the chase gives way to a hide-and-seek game in the reptile/water tank rooms, only the bed of strings remains after bar 131, and the soundtrack switches to a studio-tape overlay of some cloudy atonal murmurings as Donen abstracts his images even more. Indistinct chords are pierced by solo instruments like bass flutes, autoharp, and small percussive devices, each playing random notes fed through a crude tape-delay echo effect. Not only compared with the sophistications of today but even in 1966 it sounded more watery than scary—a vague mishmash of sounds. It is still strongly atmospheric scoring, though. As with *Charade*, Mancini does not try to build a broad architecture for this soundtrack. *Arabesque* remains a gallery of themes. The pleasure lies in hearing him take an ethnic musical language and personalize it to his own tone of voice. Donen certainly got his money's worth.

Thus, by being dependable, adjustable, sentient, and clever, Mancini successfully served a whole range of respected filmmakers during the early 1960s, men well outside of the generation and milieu of Blake Edwards. If Mancini had been active only with Edwards, he would have been called a specialist. Now, having proven himself valuable to so many different camps so that even cinema kings were considering him part of their entourage, he could perhaps be called one of the major (if not quite yet mature) film composers.

CHAPTER 7

First Cadence

hus far in his film scoring career Mancini had been pursuing the multi-melodic approach with great success, but what he wanted was to evolve beyond that, to write a more consolidated kind of score, music with its own internal order that proceeds like a parallel narrative to the film's own. After all, contemporary composers like Elmer Bernstein (*To Kill a Mockingbird*) and Jerry Goldsmith (*A Patch of Blue, Freud*) were doing just that. All Mancini lacked was a strong storytelling film. It did not matter if it was in a pop melodic language or a descriptive orchestral form; he just felt ready to dig deeper.

Certainly in Mancini's recording career, he had been writing at the top of his game as an arranger. He produced some best-selling discs of other people's film themes, like *Our Man in Hollywood*, where he made sure that traces of his own recent scores, which had not been issued as soundtrack albums, survived at least in representative tracks, including his own choral rendition of "The Days of Wine and Roses" (preserving the Vince De Rosa French horn introduction), "Bachelor in Paradise" and "Dreamsville" from *Peter Gunn*, and even the old porch-swing tune from *The Glenn Miller Story* done as a trombone solo, "Too Little Time." Even more impressive were four bass flutes and Plas Johnson's tenor sax that gave a dark, lurking quality to "Walk on the Wild Side" by Bernstein, and Bronislau Kaper's island love theme from 1962's *Mutiny on the Bounty*, scored for delicate Tahitian percussion and Mancini's special way with strings in Ravellian harmony. Sprightly piccolos and bells in his arrangement of Nino Rota's "Drink More Milk" from

Boccaccio '70 added color to what was a bright showcase of pop orchestration as well as an effective proclamation of how much good film-related music now existed—so many composers having been loosened up by the example of Mancini. And there was a second charismatic album of *The Latin Sound of Henry Mancini* in answer to the rise of the Brazilian school of pop headed by Antonio Carlos Jobim.

A trio of pop choral albums kept up Mancini's subscription as a middle-of-the-road recording artist for RCA Victor. One was his only showcase for the "*Dear Heart* Theme," also including a rollicking reading of the old barroom round "Frankie and Johnny"; second was a two-disc set of the Oscar-winning songs from 1934 to the present; third, an album of holiday music called *A Merry Mancini Christmas*, split between one side of secular seasonal songs and one of religious carols. There, the sixteen-voice blend against brass choir was his chorus's best controlled performance yet.

More telling perhaps of Mancini's conscious personal and musical evolution during this period are the two albums of big band music he produced. *Uniquely Mancini* featured a band of twenty-four with high intensity in the brass section and a major commitment to electric guitars of various ranges (pumping bass lines and racy solos), with Plas Johnson's powerfully funky tenor solos on cover tunes like "Night Train" and "Green Onions." Also included on the album were two strong Mancini originals: "Lonesome," a plain ballad complaint for De Rosa's solo French horn, and "Cheers!" a bright, boisterous show-starter full of punchy brass block chords and frenetic drumming. The other band album, called *Mancini '67* even though it was recorded in early 1966, ranged more widely and offered on one bill music from the late 1930s, like Charlie Barnett's "Cherokee," and the 1940s, with Claude Thornhill's "Autumn Nocturne," up through the 1960s' Quincy Jones and Lalo Schifrin—and even a couple of rock citations. Likewise, the band was a blend of the old and the new. On hand were Mancini veterans Dick Nash, offering a smooth trombone solo on Johnny Mandel's "The Shadow of Your Smile"; Jimmy Rowles's delicate, dotted piano style (always a man of few notes that go a long way, playing slightly behind the beat in the style of Teddy Wilson); Pete Candoli's power-trumpet solos; Jack Sperling's active drumming; and Ted Nash, Ronny Lang, and Plas Johnson on saxes. Vince De Rosa provided a chilling French horn solo against bass flutes for Mancini's dark, mysterious, and potent arrangement of the rocker "House of the Rising Sun." But new to the band were top sidemen like Jimmy Priddy on trombone and the breathy, groggy, sometimes stoned sound (inspired by Miles Davis) of Jack Sheldon's trumpet. Here Mancini gave Sheldon a full eight-bar unaccompanied solo introduction to Thelonious Monk's saddest tune ever written, "'Round Midnight," before the rest of the rhythm section enters to lay down the meter.

The *Mancini '67* album would reach number 65 on the *Billboard* 200 pop charts, but there was little attention paid to its Grammy Award potential, whereas eight years earlier they had swarmed all over the *Peter Gunn* album. He did gain one Grammy nomination for the previous year's Oscar songs choral album. It was as though the awards culture was saying, "Mancini is popular enough. Let's move on to someone else." And anyway, Mancini still did not want to be thought of as a pops composer. He was impatient for and, it seemed, ready for more serious film scoring chances. He did decide to prop up at least one aspect of his ongoing fame as a pop culture figure: the concert tour. Since his early failure on the road, he had gained more confidence, developed a modest kind of audience rapport from the stage microphone (at awards ceremonies, etc.), and soon, thinking of the audiences out there, learned to program not the jazzy, improvisational specialty music that Gunn represented but more generic suites of film themes and tribute medleys that were easy for any municipal symphony to sight-read, yet solidly crafted. And he would bring a few soloists with him to blow the jazz bits with ease. As a result, these gigs had the comfort of home listening and made the local orchestras sound good. He knew by now that concerts were not the place to challenge listeners or try to grow. He knew that those concert audiences did not want to hear the latest dramatic film cue of which he was so proud—they wanted to hear the hits and familiar melodies. So he played into their hands knowingly and, let it be said, quite well.

And yet the two pernicious troubles of those concerts were that they brought him no nearer to finding the serious narrative film scoring jobs he was seeking, and that being on the road meant he often had to be away from home just as the first signs of teenage rebellion were showing from his son, Chris. Working with Stanley Donen in London for two months had meant more time absent, and Mancini felt responsible for any family problems it created. And even at home, the very fact of Mancini's celebrity was pushing the whole Mancini clan out into the Hollywood social world more than ever. It seemed an important step to take, because, after all, being seen at parties could lead to more work. Still a reactor rather than a natural self-starter, Mancini relied on Ginny's solid practicality, endless charm, and social savvy to navigate the cocktail circuit for both of them. Organizer, mediator, elegant, yet down-to-earth hostess that she was, Ginny was able to steer Henry in and out of the right events, where he could simply show up, do his own ingenuous bits of chameleon party chat—sly verbal wit for some, boyish interplay with others—and bow out. He had successfully made the transition from working musician to the ranks of the famous without losing his center. By the middle of 1962, *Time* magazine was calling him "Hollywood's hottest music man." And yet Chris was nearing the age of thirteen and definitely showing signs of looking for the exit, especially at the particular school where he had been placed. The twins, Felice and Monica, were at the happy, mischievous age of ten, enjoying the power they had to confuse adults, who so often could not tell them apart. ("They have slightly different speech rhythms but they can imitate each other and I've been taken in enough times," Mancini has written.[1]) Musically, they were taking piano lessons and vocal coaching. But Chris was feeling like an outsider. His hero was Bob Dylan—the inner rebel without claws, self-ordained curate of the disgruntled soul, counterculture observer. Mancini music per se, although it was facilitating family trips east to the ski resorts and west to Hawaiian vacations, was not much on the kids' minds, being merely agreeable to the girls, fully irrelevant to Chris. It was up to Ginny to arbitrate between the big public career of Dad and the immediate family needs day to day.

"Chris was wanting to be a musician but he resisted any kind of formal music training that I wanted to give him. He had a great ear and a great sense of time but he had a block. And I think I created it," Mancini wrote later with admirable honesty, almost amounting to self-chastening. He worried about being absent; he worried about trying to be more demonstrative with his son than his own father had been with him. "He was trying to stay out of trouble but he just couldn't and when he got into scrapes I was never there to advise him and he resented it."[2] A subtle gesture of Mancini reaching out to his son can be seen in the headstrong rock-influenced track from the *Uniquely Mancini* album called "Bonzai Pipeline." His desire to rock outright with a powerful electric bass guitar ostinato against deep trombones and rebellious tenor sax seems like a kind of unspoken message from father to son, especially since he had given it the title of a famously dangerous surfing beach in Hawaii that Chris admired for its impossible curls and lethal undertow. Meanwhile, there is Chris pictured on the original cover of the Mancini Christmas album, standing by the piano in what purports to be the Mancini family home, looking uncomfortable with this whole "limelight" thing.

"The problem," Mancini confessed finally, "was compounded by one of my own problems: being the son of a father who could not communicate love. I was not always able to communicate it myself. Sometimes I think I expressed it all in the music."[3] Indeed, for someone who could write so clearly, directly and, when fully engaged, so personally, that last part seems a fair statement. And it seems a possible explanation, then, for the sense of mourning and empathy he wrote into the main theme for an otherwise crass and clumsy comedy/drama about a type of father-son relationship in the peacetime army, *Soldier in the Rain*, from a couple of years earlier. Blake Edwards had written the script, but television director Ralph Nelson helmed the film version, in which Jackie Gleason played an army sergeant, Maxwell Slaughter, trying to live a high life in the midst of his petty aimless Cold War military stint. Assisting him, worshipping him, and, occasionally, needing rescue by him, is his lunkhead junior, played by Steve McQueen (struggling to give a comic spin to his performance) as country boy Eustis Clay.

To attribute genuine feeling to this material, one would have to bring one's own projections onto it, and that must be what Mancini was doing to have created such a wistful, lonely, and intimate theme for the film—a stark piano solo (as spare, pure, and melancholy as one of Satie's *Gymnopédies*), whose chord base rocks back and forth between Gmin and Cmin⁶/E♭ in sober waltz time until a solo trumpet (voice of the lonely soldier) introduces the main melody, the saddest that Mancini ever wrote. Given the subtle sixth and seventh chords that this theme uses as its foundation ("I had to get a kind of timeless harmonic structure, almost modal—almost all on the white keys of the piano"[4]), the melody on top of it is more tentative, impressionistic, than Mancini's usual direct conversational tone—it is almost a melody of arpeggiations based on the harmony rather than a self-reliant tune. Fragile ballads like this—the suspended chords, the gestures toward major-key relief before returning resigned to the stark G-minor waltz with which it began—are composed from inner materials. This music remains one of Mancini's essentials.

By 1966 the Mancinis had moved to a more central part of the county, from Northridge to Holmby Hills and a two-story Georgian brick house with a pool and circular drive just off Sunset Boulevard. The traffic was heavier, the kids had less freedom to hang around the neighborhood, but it was closer to the studios where Mancini was working and the clubs and charity offices where Ginny was so active. It was during these days that Chris was placed in Catholic school in the hope that his edgy behavior might be pointed toward some positive direction or at least disciplined until some other force of maturity or good counsel might settle him down. But as his father later related, "Then, we made another mistake."[5] He and Ginny decided to pull Chris out of parochial education and send him to military school. At the time they considered it a prudent and proactive thing to do. When something moves beyond your control, you call in the experts, or, in this case, you send the problem away to an expert. This was Henry's passive, reactionary way of trying to be the most help to his son—sending Chris away to a whole new landscape rather than simply facing him where they stood and duking it out. Maybe because of all such unsettlement, Mancini's very sense of compositional language seems to undergo a cadence at about this time.

If the word *cadence* can be defined as the notes or chords that resolve a melody, or at least lead to a new development, then this next transitional period in Mancini's career can be seen as his first cadence. It was the first sign of real evolution since he had come into his own as a jazz-pop film composer, demonstrating not only a contemporary enrichment of the harmonies and instrumental blends he had learned in the big band era (even allowing ethnic influences to enter naturally) but also a broadening of the dramatic architecture of his orchestral writing into scores that were not just collections of admirable tunes and isolated film scenes but more cohesive compositions as well. Something was stirring.

It is only speculative to connect this maturity in Mancini's writing to any one event in his personal life. Nevertheless, it was also at this time that his father, Quinto, died suddenly of a heart attack at the age of nearly seventy. "The feeling," he wrote later, "was not like the grief of my mother's death. I was just numb."[6] His father had been a source of both inspiration and criticism all Henry's life. Now that father-son struggle had passed. But just as Henry's relief and self-empowerment at his first career success had seemed evident in his cheerful, colorful *Mr. Lucky* recording, so now perhaps there was a link between his father's passing and the progress that was about to show in his work, taking on, after years of color and fun, a deeper purpose. Who knows what these events meant to Mancini? News of his father's death reached him on the road. There was a concert to be given that night, and Mancini elected to go ahead with it anyway. It was, to him, a willing sacrifice and an expression of ambivalent feelings, both avoiding and honoring Quinto in one action by carrying on with his career.

So now there was a brand-new sense of being orphaned, surely, but also of being freed. Maybe this opened Mancini up to a more mature awareness of being a storyteller himself, of writing with more serious intentions and trying to connect the individual cues that make up a film score into a single work. He was hearing that director Stanley Donen was in contact with Audrey Hepburn again, showing her a script about an ultrachic British couple whose marriage is on the rocks and whom we follow throughout Europe, first during their early Bohemian days, then through their marital bliss, and third into their mid-marriage crisis. Albert Finney would play the male lead. Everyone shared Donen's real enthusiasm for the script by Frederic Raphael, with its rapid-fire articulate, cynical, brittle but ultimately humanist tone. He called it *Two for the Road*, and it followed this young married couple as observed in an energetic jumble of vignettes spread over a period of twelve years. A kind of verbal fencing match between the couple was kept up throughout the film, with dialogue more akin to the Cambridge University Debate Society, with which Raphael was familiar, than to the typical love story, but entertaining nonetheless. Sometimes the persistence of such cutting dialogue could be annoying, but it provided what Hepburn and Donen were looking for: a story not about ciphers and missing loot like *Arabesque* or *Charade*, but rather about the secret messages and lost treasures of a relationship, how things of value get lost over the years and how we have to spar sometimes—and travel far afield—to get them back. This film would be *about* something. On the set Hepburn and Donen agreed there was only one person to do the music score for such a film. She cabled to ask Mancini to come aboard the project: "Dearest Hank, please won't you do the music? . . . Can't imagine anyone else but you scoring."[7]

So here was an adult project about grown-ups living real life, told by A-list talents, and in need of a music score that could not rely on splash and color but had to be honest, mature, and single-minded. Mancini pulled from his own store of recent emotion and conflict and, at least on the music page, mastered the issue with a wise reply. Besides a few cues of background music, dinner music, poolside tunes, and a bit of cool jazz underneath a certain skirt-chasing moment, everyone agreed that what this score needed was one strong, all-encompassing theme that would both express what was most human in these characters and tie together the story, which kept leaping back and forth in time and geography over the years of their courtship and marriage. Mancini sensed that this was one of those substantive projects he had been wanting, so he tried to write very close to the bone. But what he was feeling, intuitively, out of his recent saddening and maddening personal experiences, was still a bit raw. In movie music it came out as a rather sad, rather hurt-sounding melody, trying to be redolent of the film characters' regrets but rather indulging his own. After hearing it once, Donen said no.

All set to push ahead with what he intended to be a serious pop essay on relationships and the shallowness of the jet-set life, Mancini was taken aback. He had not experienced rejection through all the recent high times. This was a new thing. The rejected melody had a slower meditative brooding quality. ("It was a bit more reflective, a little more pathos; it was 'down' more, let me put it that way," Mancini has remembered. "And what was wanted was something that moved a little more, had more notes in it, so Stanley's the one who set me on that direction.") What Donen had wanted was something that had an underlying pull and tension to it.[8]

That simple act of rejection woke Mancini and brought him face-to-face with his more adult newly orphaned self. So, with that fine sense of self-discipline and fear of disappointment, he planned a second attack at a theme that would not only have more lateral physical movement but would also be more complex, more searching vertically—that is, it would be built on a more complex harmonic scheme. In sum, Mancini understood what Donen had wanted was not a love song, but a road song.

He reached back for the old perpetual-motion device, such as the circular bass lines from *Peter Gunn* to *Arabesque*, and wrote an eight-to-the-bar figure that corresponded to the turning car wheels in Maurice Binder's opening animated collage during the main title sequence of *Two for the Road*. That, then, became a counterpoint to the main melody, which begins unexpectedly with a dominant rather than the usual tonic chord and, likewise, begins on the upbeat before establishing its first regular-count measure on $F\sharp min^{9-5}$. There are two chord changes for almost every bar thereafter—yearning, plying chords. ("It starts on a question-mark chord, but then it resolves immediately, and it keeps going back and forth like that.") The feeling is one of a constant journey, including the major/minor shifts within the lines. ("Not only the theme had more motion to it in my second version, but the tune's harmony is constantly changing, and the bass line is going downward contrary to the melody.")[9] And although it is mainly a G-major melody, it maintains an almost constant state of appoggiatura—those "leaning" chords that beg to be resolved but, until they find resolution, express such longing.

This deeply personal and substantively intelligent song without words certainly has the road-song quality that Donen wanted, but it also has the strength and resilience to tie this whole jet-setting, scrapbooking, part comic, part romantic, part peeving, part charming story together and make us care. (Only later, and apart from the finished film, did Leslie Bricusse supply a sweet lyric to Mancini's melody ["two for the road we'll travel down the years / collecting precious memories"]. As Bricusse said, "One of the great advantages of writing songs *after* a film has been shot is that the complete mood is already there for you, everything is laid out, which made the lyric of "Two for the Road" particularly easy to write—really just a romantic jigsaw puzzle."[10])

In any case, when wedded to the verbal intensity and visual vogue of the film, the constancy, wisdom, and authority of Mancini's recurring theme not only ties all the energies of the other elements together, but it also actually makes it seem as though the score existed already and the film had been constructed *around* the music—as though the whole film were one long music video, shot to Mancini's music. This is not to diminish any single element of the film but to observe how completely Mancini's score (based on different presentations, extensions, fragments of that one theme) becomes the voice of the picture. Its feeling of coming home, of utter sincerity and truth-speaking made it both Henry's and Ginny's own favorite of all themes he would ever write for films. It is also the most lush and openly generous of his theme-based scores.

Two identifiable voices typify this score for us: the French accordion and the solo violin. Because Donen has set such a level of elegance and *recherché* style for the whole project, Mancini thought it plausible to ask for a specific violin player to handle the most emotional parts of the score. He wanted the great jazz violinist Stephane Grappelli, from Django Reinhardt's legendary group, Quintete du Hot Club de France. Donen said yes. Grappelli's sound of bow to string was so French and sensuous that each time a solo statement of the road theme emerged from this film's score it caused its own momentary enchantment. Respectfully, Mancini writes "Mr. Grappelli" in his sketch sheets whenever the violin enters the scoring page. The music proceeds through thirty-seven separate cues, which is about the average quantity for a film of that length and that era (*Charade* used thirty-two while *Days of Wine and Roses* had only twenty-four; *The Great Race*, with its operetta aspirations, ballooned to sixty-one music cues). Still, the dispersal of music throughout *Two for the Road* and the instant binding of the theme to the characters make it seem far more active and present than it actually is. In any case, none of this work was even nominated for 1967's Academy Awards, probably because the score clung to its film so devotedly, rather than stood away from it to be noticed.

— — —

The other major Mancini score that marks this year of 1967 as Mancini's cadential pass into deeper film scoring was the very next Audrey Hepburn project (for which she again specified Mancini for the soundtrack score, lobbying directly this time to her husband, the film's producer, Mel Ferrer), called *Wait Until Dark*, a thriller about a blind woman terrorized in her apartment by drug thugs. Taken together, these two Hepburn films show Mancini at his best—in one the supremacy of a fine interpretive melody, in the other the concoction of an eerie orchestral context.

For the world of the blind, Mancini imagined the hypersensitive faculty of hearing that must develop to compensate for a person's loss of eyesight. Listening carefully, not just for identifiable sounds but also for the nuances of those sounds, can reveal their character—whether the voice that is speaking to you or the car that is heading in your direction, which may be either a routine passerby or a potential danger. If the finger touch on the keys of a piano reminded Mancini of the tactile touch of the Braille reader, then the idea of quietly playing on a slightly out-of-tune piano seemed to him to suggest the peril and trepidation that this particular blind girl, Audrey Hepburn's "Suzie Hendricks," was about to go through. He had used the exotic effects of an out-of-phase tin piano in *Hatari!* A new idea struck him for *Wait Until Dark*. Always searching for those unique instrumental sounds that might characterize each film—the solitary French horn in *Days of Wine and Roses*, the autoharps in *Experiment in Terror*, the circus calliope in *Hatari!* the tenor sax in *The Pink Panther*, the tunable tom-toms in *Arabesque*, Grappelli's very French violin in *Two for the Road*—he now began to think about writing for two pianos in *Wait Until Dark*, one normal and one not, to get at a villain's schizoid psychology. He requisitioned twin Baldwin pianos owned by the Warner Brothers Studio. One was tuned to the standard tuning-fork pitch of 440 cps (cycles per second); the other he detuned so that every note was a quarter-tone flat. The beginning of *Wait Until Dark* displays this effect: a simple A-minor triad played on one piano, then repeated by the other "flat" piano, alternating the in-tune chord with the off-tune chord. The payoff is instant and viscerally disturbing. The studio pianists recording the music (Pearl Kaufman and Jimmy Rowles) said they were experiencing vertigo as the session went on, so disorienting was the effect.

For the viewer/listener of the film, that sound goes a long way toward recreating the unsettling world of Suzie, under attack from forces she certainly cannot see nor barely comprehend. Composer and writer Irwin Bazelon declared, "The tonal distortion convincingly delineates the villain's disturbed psychoneurotic personality; it does this by an economy of means infinitely superior to the illustrative sounds and ominous musical announcements usually associated with this type of dramatic scene."[11] It certainly creates what Mancini liked to call the "question mark" at the beginning of this film, raising the audience's curiosity about "what is going on here and what is going to happen."[12] The detuned piano effect is even more striking when Mancini plays a phrase of single notes echoed by its own distorted image in the other detuned piano, one key at a time. With that as a backdrop, the film's twisted main theme appears in the guise of a fateful-sounding whistler, partnered by piccolo. It is taken up then by electric harpsichord, electric guitar, and sitar.

With such sparse yet vivid instrumental forces on hand (including two dozen strings, a Novachord polyphonic synthesizer, and a Japanese panpipe instrument called the *sho*), Mancini becomes the aural unconscious of this story. It was originally written as a spooky stage play by Frederick Knott (the plot: blind Suzie Hendricks innocently receives a child's doll inside of which drugs are being smuggled, and now the bad guys want to find it), but director Terence Young can be praised for successfully reproducing the gradual sense of constriction in Knott's play—that is, how the tension of the plot follows an inclined plane toward more and tighter suspense, transferring the claustrophobia of the original stage set to the screen, shooting almost the entire film in one basement apartment: the kitchenette area against the street side, the sitting room with a few steps that lead up to the hallway door and the brief passage leading back to the bedroom. It is a one-dimensional space, yet he shoots without awkwardness from natural angles and teaches us how Suzie has learned to navigate its confines. Blinded some months earlier by a crash and fire, rallied and encouraged to be independent by her husband, a somewhat older architectural photographer named Sam (Efrem Zimbalist Jr.), Suzie is about to come under siege alone in her Greenwich Village flat from a trio of wily drug runners—or rather, two small-time crooks over their heads in the drug game (Richard Crenna and Jack Weston) and one sadistic smuggler (Alan Arkin as the heartless "Roat," who seems to take more pleasure in torturing and backstabbing than in any of the financial profits of his trade).

Once Roat has detained Sam, Suzie's husband, who is across town and unable to come to the rescue this time (there is a clear, sincere Mancini melody associated with Sam's warm, safe presence throughout the film and reappearing at the end), he heads for the showdown in her apartment to get the doll back. Suzie senses her vulnerability, being without sight. But she realizes, too, that she can render Roat equally blind if the whole apartment is made dark when he arrives. In a kind of frenzy, she dashes around the place wielding her walking stick toward all the lightbulbs she can find. The rising desperation of the scene is not only described by but also driven by the music cue that Mancini, in his scoring sheets, has called "Bulbous Terror": the Novachord adds a two-note ostinato in 6/8 double time to a mix of broken slashing orchestral chords on piano. At the height of the mayhem (Suzie even breaks out into the building's corridor to smash the bulbs there), three soprano saxes enter along with the *sho* on top like a taunting counterpoint until one final scream from Suzie halts the scherzo at three and a half minutes.

When Roat arrives, he chains the apartment door shut and sprays gasoline over the sitting room just to terrorize Suzie with the scent of it (like the car fire that blinded her). The score goes deep again over shifting strings, using notes from the main theme's first phrase, and at last Suzie gives in, digging out the doll from where she had hidden it. But as Roat tears open the doll's stitching to get at the heroin packs inside, Suzie prepares her own onslaught, gathering a kitchen knife in one hand and a vase full of Sam's photo-developing fluid in the other. She flings the liquid at Roat, dousing and temporarily blinding him, then begins her own assault, lighting matches and throwing them at his flammable head. For a time, this keeps him at bay, but when her last match is spent, there is only the dark standing between them. She cannot tell where he has gone; then suddenly she hears the familiar noise of the refrigerator motor and she realizes the door is ajar, and therein is one bulb she forgot to smash. Roat rouses to his feet with rape and murder on his mind. When Suzie thrusts his gut with the huge kitchen knife, the music score also returns, lunging through the double basses, tremolo strings, and a percussive crash that reverberates alone for a full ten seconds thereafter as Roat collapses. He must be dead.

Suzie screams hysterically for help but cannot unchain the door. She is just working her way across the floor toward the windows when suddenly a form leaps across the screen and grabs her leg (audiences in the 1967 theaters let out a long involuntary scream at this point; theater owners were instructed as part of their distribution contract to seat no new patrons during the film's last ten minutes in order to preserve the fright quotient of these last scenes, of the darkness, of the music, uncompromised). Mancini's score crests here with a Grand Guignol forte. Roat's leap is scored with a sudden yelp by the brass, a violent sweep across the metal strings inside the pianos, and the full string section in primitive harmonies now with two trombones and two bass trombones added over a relentless timpani ostinato, all playing at their loudest, all straining up the scale in pentatonic gradations. Roat, like some deathless zombie, drags himself across the floor while the full orchestra pumps and slurs overlapping harmonies; Suzie is fumbling to find the one plug that will disconnect that refrigerator bulb and make the darkness total again. Again her scream ends the cue before we know the outcome.

We cut outside to the street and hear the siren of a responding police car. Sam rushes in with the officers to the wrecked apartment. Only when we spot Suzie alive in the corner behind the refrigerator door does the score come back in again, this time with muted violins over lower strings in that reassuring song we heard when Sam was home before. The film ends with their embrace, and the melody is now offered as a vocal (Sue Raney) pop song with a light samba beat over the cast recap. Even though the 1960s habit of opening and closing otherwise dramatic films with an exploitable pop song was heavily criticized later (Rod McKuen's likable song "Jean" at the harrowing end of *The Prime of Miss Jean Brodie* [1969] is one example from that same period of an absurd close-out to a strong film), the song that closes *Wait Until Dark* seems to work well—maybe because the audience is so eager for relief after forty minutes of unreleased tension, and maybe because the song in question here has already been referenced throughout the film. Its mild lyric by Jay Livingston and Ray Evans ("Who cares how cold and gray the day may be; / wait until dark and we'll be warm") is just okay, but its subdued presentation at the film's play-out seems wholly satisfying and fitting. *Wait Until Dark* found a huge favorable audience in its day, and Hepburn was nominated for the best actress Oscar. In years to come, several film music textbooks would cite Mancini's music as an ingenious way to score a psychological thriller.

Maddeningly, there was little official attention in those days to what are two of Mancini's best scores: *Wait Until Dark* and *Two for the Road*. No awards, no soundtrack album (until forty years later) of the *Wait Until Dark* music, and only a studio reduction recording of the *Two for the Road* score, minus the participation of Stephane Grappelli. And yet from an overview of Mancini's career, these two efforts represent a definite cadence, a transition from one career period to another—scores that have moved beyond being just a sequence of charismatic pop tunes or isolated descriptive pieces. These were whole, single-vision scores—the one an extended treatment of a single, intelligent, complex melody structure, the other a dark monochromatic thesis on clashing tonalities. Mancini *was* evolving. He had taken Chris's challenges and Donen's initial no to heart, and rather than falling back, he opened up and deepened a bit.

CHAPTER 8

The Break with Blake

Even as Mancini was evolving in his scores for directors like Stanley Donen and Terence Young, Blake Edwards was still making films that required him to retrofit the old multi-themed jazz-pop to their soundtracks. Still, there are quantifiable refinements to the big band blends and scoring details to be noted in the next two Mancini/Edwards projects.

Probably no one cared in 1967 whether Edwards brought back his familiar television detective, Peter Gunn, in any form. In that era of the far more brash and thrilling James Bond craze, with its international intrigue and million-dollar stunts, Gunn's wry local gumshoe must have seemed pretty gauche. And indeed there were a few regrettable aspects to the film called *Gunn*. The overly clever banter between this private eye and the clichéd people in his casebook seemed forced, and several scenes held on too long, waiting for such dialogue to run its course. And yet there was still something about the coolness of the Gunn character (Craig Stevens again), with his expressionless voice and demeanor that now seemed even more engaging (or attractively disengaging); the shadowy lighting scheme (color cinematography by the original black-and-white series cameraman Philip Lathrop); the chain-of-clues story leading from waterfront dives to plush, corrupt boudoirs; and, of course, the easy walking bass line of the jazz-laced scoring that had made the series so distinctive on television nine years earlier. Here, though, Mancini was wonderfully updating his own sound with a series of superb miniatures heard in the background of club scenes or behind dialogue, in restaurants or at Gunn's apartment, but always detached from the story completely—though often with some caveat connection in Mancini's head. Mancini's joy and generosity are infectious—from his fuzz guitar/electric saxophone version of the *Gunn* theme to the new song heard at a modern-day speakeasy, the lightly Latin "I Like the Look" with Leslie Bricusse's lyric; from the vibes' blues "Silver Tears," which we hear under Gunn and Edie's love talk, to the buoyant jazz waltz for eight flutes and four soprano saxes we hear at a dockside diner. There is a chaste country tune, "Theme for Sam," when Gunn discovers in his bed a girl who is somehow connected to his current case, and a swinger tune for twelve flutes as that same girl later sunbathes on Gunn's patio (distracting a traffic chopper overhead).

These are all charming, isolated pieces of soundtrack music that shift intuitively from commentary to background ambiance without conscience or care—young man's music like the old days—and yet the complex layered harmonies (twelve flutes!) and band blends show Mancini's advancement. It was exactly what Edwards had wanted, without knowing how to articulate it. (In the film, he even playfully acknowledges Mancini's ongoing importance to the Gunn universe by placing the composer on screen at one point. As Gunn enters a piano bar, the camera pans to the right past the sleazy clientele until we suddenly notice Henry himself seated at the keyboard playing a jazz interlude of his own creation called "A Lovely Sound" and comically trying to brush away the attentions of two escort beauties who have crowded on either side of his piano bench and are interfering with his playing.) What a pleasure, anyway, to spot each new jazz-ensemble piece within the overly convoluted story and realize Mancini's ambitiousness of harmony and instrumentation anew.

Second of the new Edwards projects was just called *The Party*, a comic diatribe against blowhard Hollywood with its brick-faced executives, dumb blondes, young lushes, opportunists, and hangers-on whose only talent is cocktail chat. All it needed for a soundtrack was cool and classy ambient jazz-pop and maybe a rocker or two. Peter Sellers starred as a sweet-natured but clumsy Indian actor, Hrundi V. Bakshi, who blunders his way through a Hollywood cocktail party, unintentionally wreaking havoc on producers and starlets alike and practically destroying the premises among more of Edwards's typical pratfalls and errant projectiles, liars and lusters, innocents and inebriants, and a final cleansing flood that douses everyone equally. Besides some tasty all-out jazz in the Dizzy Gillespie tradition on the soundtrack, two new pieces reflect Mancini's application of perspective here: one is the film's mock-rock music for the main title (ingeniously Mancini actually writes in some intentional awkward chord changes to this arrangement, mimicking those innumerable rock groups of the love-child 1960s who learned only four chords and could not manage the proper modulations down through a progression to find the tonic/dominant key relationships), and the other is a smooth sophisticated song, "Nothing to Lose," which Bakshi hears a guest (Claudine Longet) singing in one of the upstairs rooms away from all the party noise. This is a close but cooler cousin to "Wait Until Dark," written in the pleasing key of F major, honest, modest, sincere, and satisfying.

Mancini still kept watching for more dramatic film stories on the horizon, though. And while Blake Edwards took a hiatus from work, during which he finalized a divorce from his wife, Pat, and married the already world-famous Julie Andrews, Mancini thought he had found two such films. One was a big-budget period piece from Ben Hecht's memoir set in early twentieth-century Chicago, *Gaily, Gaily* (1969). (For the British release, where the word *gaily* had taken on modern baggage, the film was known as *Chicago, Chicago*.) Its set design gave an accurate representation of life in the big city in those early streetcar days: the political back rooms, criminal back alleys, brothels and proper parlors, ale halls, dance halls, and hash halls near Skid Row. But Beau Bridges's character of Ben was not given enough dimension, let alone trajectory, to carry a whole film, no matter how unique the setting. Narratively, then, Mancini could only spot-check the elements of the plot for us in his music, though he had wanted to dig in deeply to do some compositional storytelling. So there was a rousing tune for honky-tonk piano and banjo called "There's Enough to Go Around"; one energetic tango; and a pure prairie anthem inspired perhaps by the long-past hymns of Stephen Foster's America. The choppy nature of the film kept each of those melodic ideas separate, though, and the project ultimately resisted any kind of cohesive scoring.

The second film, however, did seem to accept narrative music much more readily. *Me, Natalie* was another minor coming-of-age story set in another big-city time tunnel, 1969 Greenwich Village. It starred Oscar winner Patty Duke as a hippie-generation ugly duckling dreaming of love but really needing a dose of self-actualization first and not knowing where to look. Aiming at dramatic cohesion, Mancini chose one overall voice for Natalie and her Village environs: a kind of polite baroque sound with a contemporary overlay of the wandering flower-child folksinger. He put together an ensemble of strings and an equally warm sixteen-voice chorus to represent Natalie and supplemented those with the Baldwin electric harpsichord, electric bass and piano, rock organ, a group of individual winds, and a rhythm section.

Whereas *Two for the Road* had been a romantic story driven by a single marker melody, *Me, Natalie* used two tunes that were actually sung in the film, tunes whose lyrics were provided by a familiar voice from Mancini's Universal musicals: the staff-actor-turned-pop-poet Rod McKuen. The song "We" is the F-major representation of Natalie's romantic idealistic side (with a likable and sincere bridge at its center), while the other song, "Natalie," is the film's dilemma song in E minor that so gently represents the lone woman not yet comfortable with herself. Natalie is sure that her nose is too big and her breasts are too small to ever amount to a worthy human being. In truth, of course, it is her desire that feels too big and her self too small.

In the evolution of Mancini as a melodist, this latter song represents a progress. It is as long-lined as "Two for the Road"; twenty measures make up its first line before beginning a second pass, and it proceeds with several line extensions after that, taking it outside the usual A-B-A thirty-two-bar pop-song formula. It is more like A-B-A-C-A. After "Two for the Road," "Natalie" is the continuation of this "first cadence" as it relates to melody writing; this is Mancini writing very close to the bone, with a control of the melodic line that comes near to the naturalness of speech. ("Here again your dramatic sense has to come in," Mancini said. "You're aiming for more complex and yet still naturalistic structures. Here's Natalie, this kind of sad girl—a pretty girl within an ugly girl—and she needed a melody with that kind of ambiguity to it. The melody line had to be more involved. It has more extensions and turns in it than, say, a simple tune like 'Charade.'") In Mancini's evolution, compare the simple pale tune from those McKuen/Universal days "What's It Gonna Be?" with "Natalie," and you can see the maturation. "Moon River" and "Dear Heart" were simple, too, but not without their sophistications. "Soldier in the Rain," as mentioned earlier, was more like a Satie interlude than a pop tune. "Nothing to Lose" combined a modern feel with a solid, satisfying straightforward tablature. "Two for the Road" was an astro-leap of design, its structure more manifold, its language direct, personal, and expressive. The song "Natalie" now tests those same qualities in yet a more freely intuitive way, still "serving the film first" but using that occasion to evolve Mancini's own voice. Natalie's twenty-something adolescence was well explored by such a song.

For the soundtrack of her many idealistic, comic, brave, and crazy jaunts around the city with friends and dates to parks, clubs, campuses, and student flats, Mancini offers a scat-singing chorus in a happy jazz-baroque vein, using a stop-time meter (the rhythm of the old Charleston dance) in dotted notes, suddenly switching to a fast waltz for four bars, then turning legato for the bridge (with sax, trumpet), then returning to 4/4 time and the modern jazz harmonies of the scat. The richness of that large choral sound is used to best advantage in support of the main theme throughout the film, taking over from the McKuen vocals when the emotion of the scene needs to swell or needs to slow down and ruminate. And because of the way director Fred Coe keeps the music on the soundtrack interacting with the story as much as possible, those choral intrusions seem fairly natural in keeping with Natalie's impulsive, romantic, self-debating spirit.

Perhaps Mancini's sympathies for Natalie Miller were inspired, again, by his own parenting issues at this time; his son, Chris, was about nineteen and approaching Natalie's age and stage. Returned from military school, he had been enrolled in a regular public school, hoping normalcy would work its magic and blend him into the happy mainstream. He should have graduated by now anyway. Mancini took the phone call at home that Chris was being kicked out of the place. Wanting to reach out again, Mancini arranged for Chris's current rock band, the Die Hard Trippers, to record the Rod McKuen garage rocker "Off-Ramp to Nowhere" for one of Natalie's Village club scenes. But it was Chris who decided what to try next: a ranch-styled school in Arizona. There, he suggested, he could hold his own and build an independent ego, not just as someone's son but as his own self—shades of Natalie Miller. He would be moving away from the teenage years by moving away from home. The twins were seventeen; Hank and Ginny were middle-aged veterans. President Richard Nixon had moved into the White House. There was a sense everywhere of "let's see how things will go." At any rate, *Me, Natalie* was not the great narrative score Mancini had been wanting. In some ways it was just an extension of the song score. He still had yet to spread out orchestrally with formal narrative-type scoring. Until that day he turned to two more distractions coming from two completely unexpected sources, activities that had nothing to do with the movies.

꞊ ꞊ ꞊

The first detour, circa 1969, came in the form of an invitation from the board of directors of the Philadelphia Orchestra. At that time the venerable Eugene Ormandy was still its music director and sustainer, if not creator, of what had come to be known in the classical music world as the "Philadelphia Sound"—smoothly blended orchestral sections that maintained their individuality (strings, brass, winds) but when projected out to the round acoustic of the Academy of Music Hall in Philadelphia melted beautifully into a whole. This was particularly satisfying to the ear in the works of full-bodied romantic composers like Tchaikovsky, Sibelius, and Rachmaninoff, but also made the most of ascetic modern and soloistic works. The idea now was to bring a whole new audience into the hall that would match what was being done in Massachusetts with the Boston Pops Orchestra in terms of concerts, recordings, and television. A new Philly pops orchestra could present lighter music, invite guest stars from the popular culture, and gain a portion of that recording market for their endowment. The time seemed right for two reasons: first, the veteran Boston Pops conductor Arthur Fiedler had just moved his guys from RCA Victor to the Deutsche Grammophon label, so RCA was interested in Philly now, and, second, because of Henry Mancini and others, pop orchestral music had been selling a lot of records lately. The board asked Mancini to prepare an inaugural concert for them to premiere their new invention: the Philadelphia Orchestra Pops.

Mancini saw it as a chance to compose some cameo pieces to showcase different sections of the orchestra. The result was five rather platitudinous miniatures (spotlighting the strings section, solo flute, piano, percussion, and violin) and a three-part suite, *Beaver Valley '37* that would evoke his own boyhood memories growing up in West Aliquippa. The suite's first movement, "The River," was a comely and innocent waltz for piano and flute (richly filled out with strings and brass choir) about anyone's wistful youth; the second, a grim processional about the Pennsylvania steel mills; the third, a vigorous tarantella tribute to his own well-remembered Sons of Italy band. Both the RCA recording of these works and the inaugural concert were considered successes, though they were Mancini's only such venture with them, and the Philly Pops itself did not really catch on until the 1980s when pop/jazz pianist/conductor Peter Nero took over as permanent director.

RCA released the Mancini/Philly album on its classical Red Seal label as they had formerly done for the Boston Pops. Mancini himself remained with RCA's black-label pop series, though, still under contract for three or four albums a year. And yet no one could have foreseen what his next album in fulfillment of that contract was about to bring. His second detour, then, an album called *A Warm Shade of Ivory*, was just supposed to be a pleasant, restful record of recent radio hits. The new wrinkle in the whole project was that Mancini was not only arranger/conductor but also piano soloist. In what he called his "one-finger piano style," Mancini rendered simple melody lines with elementary chord fills and a few runs to trace each melody against the soft upholstery of his brass choir, strings, and wordless chorus. "Sensuous, thoughtful, warm" were the adjectives used by some critics judging the album when it came out. But others heard it as Mancini's blandest music ever—destined to be packaged for use in restaurants and elevators all over the country, instant background music, devoid of profile or ambition. Its sleepy meters and pillowlike richness do make one wonder why Mancini was playing into another of the criticisms he had always fought—that his soundtrack albums and even his jazz were too close to processed pop. Now here he was celebrating Muzak by perfecting it. What is remarkable about the whole project, though, is what happened next. His longtime disc producer at RCA, the jovial Texan Joe Reisman, heard that director Franco Zeffirelli was making a new youth-oriented film version of *Romeo and Juliet*, and that composer Nino Rota (who had scored all of Federico Fellini's films and whose theme music for *Boccaccio '70* Mancini had already recorded) was doing the score. They knew that such a story *must* have some sort of exploitable love theme. Reisman bought performance rights and put "Love Theme from *Romeo and Juliet*," also known as "A Time for Us," on the market as a 45-rpm single disc.

The year 1969 was a time of peace and love in pop music. Baby boomer listeners did not much care where their songs originated nor who performed them—they just wanted melody and soft rock. Stevie Wonder's "My Cherie Amour" was big at that time as was Neil Diamond's "Sweet Caroline." For more than a month, the Beatles hit "Get Back" was number one. Now, because some radio disc jockey in Florida began giving exposure to the quiet piano-solo opening of Mancini's recording of Rota's "Love Theme from *Romeo and Juliet*," people started humming along. Before anyone was prepared, the record overtook the Beatles and entered *Billboard*'s top-ten chart on June 7, 1969. For two weeks thereafter, Mancini's single sat at number two, right under the Beatles. Then on June 28 it became the number-one single record in the country and stayed there for two more weeks, a feat not matched even by Mancini's three other monster hits: "Peter Gunn," "Moon River," and "The Pink Panther." This quiet, introverted arrangement of a tune that was not even Mancini's own, and with its soft piano line, mild strummed beat, muted strings and horns behind Rota's mannerly minstrel melody, was unlikely material for such hype in the era of the Vietnam War. Indeed it was an eclectic time: the Rolling Stones were howling out "Honky Tonk Woman" on the same stations that were broadcasting Mancini.

The "Love Theme from *Romeo and Juliet*" single, of course, drove sales of the album, and *A Warm Shade of Ivory* posted the million-record sales mark before the year was out. Mancini would win a Grammy for the single's arrangement, although to be honored for such a workmanlike accomplishment and to be ignored for innovations on the *Gunn* movie soundtrack, albums such as *Mancini '67*, *Mr. Lucky Goes Latin*, and others offers a lesson in how the power of sales overshadows art. For the rest of his career, Mancini had to include Rota's love theme in all of his concert appearances, always having to explain beforehand that he had nothing to do with writing it.

The unfortunate aftermath of that huge career surprise was to encourage him and RCA to embark on a series of similarly meek and subdued piano/orchestra Muzak albums over the next several years and to emphasize Mancini's life as a recording artist independent of his movie-scoring life—and very far afield from his cool-jazz past. Morgan Ames, now a critic for magazines like *High Fidelity*, wrote that these piano/orchestra albums were beautifully arranged but meaningless. Listening today, one is struck by just how slow these album tracks are—there is a dead weight to them that is inexplicable. Everything in pop music was up for grabs, it seemed, as the whole industry was changing, and, at least for the record, Mancini was playing it safe with his piano programs. They sold better than soundtrack albums.

Like it or not, this refocusing of his career onto the recording industry was forcing Mancini to catch up with all the new disc-making, sound-filtering, microphone-dampening, multitracking studio procedures that had taken over the industry of late. One of the chief differences was that these days instead of gathering an orchestra or big band in a studio for a session of, say, three recording dates, rehearsing, adjusting, and laying down final tracks, all under the direction of a single recording engineer who had worked out the microphone balances weeks ahead of time, record producers were working in what was called a "modular" format, each section of the band being laid down on tape on a separate day. Perhaps you record the rhythm section one day, then rewind the tape and overlay the brass parts on the next day, listening through earphones to the previous track while the new one is performed. That afternoon, strings might come in to record their bits in isolation, and so on. These modules would then be assembled and blended into a final version in which it would appear that everyone had played together. Some more subtle kind of acoustic was always lost in this process. The "space" between the sections (where the overtones of, say, the string section somehow influenced the brass, and so forth, as in any sitting orchestra) no longer existed. In the modular format, although the sections appear to play together on the record, to the trained ear and somehow intuitively to any listener, they also sacrifice some warmth, some intangible aural breathing room that affects the final product.

By the early 1970s even Ginny Mancini, who had been an eager and dependable alto in Mancini's chorus for a dozen years, and had sung in countless other people's sessions for longer than that, was saying that it was "no longer fun." What she had loved was singing there in the studio "live" with the other seven or fifteen choristers and the full orchestra. Now, in comparison, recording was a sterile process. The chorus would be brought in and headsets distributed, and they would record their module alone. For Ginny, this was too much like "phoning in" your contribution. She began to semi-retire from the recording industry. Many years later she said:

> Yes, I certainly did miss those days of studio recording—the times I sang with Mel Torme's group and learned so much even during the recording sessions with the singers and the musicians there in the same room. Mel was a wonderful teacher of harmony. You know, there I was singing in the middle of a four-part chord and it was nirvana! Henry's sessions were just as wonderful when they were recorded "live," so to speak, in the studio with everyone present. One of the reasons I stopped singing was that I showed up for one of his dates, and it was about five minutes to eight o'clock, and usually the musicians were already in the room, ready to receive the downbeat. And I said, "Where is everyone?" and he said, "We're just tracking tonight, just laying down the rhythm section." And I said, "You mean to tell me we're not going to rehearse with the whole orchestra?" No, the technology was changing, and everything was being laid down on different tracks at different sessions. So it was no longer fun for me. I think that was the last session I ever did.[2]

Certainly the conciliatory side of Mancini wanted to please the industry, so he learned the modular way of making music in order to survive. That is also why he went along with the bland pop-piano albums for a while. The industry could use them.

But it was into that climate now, with Mancini juggling concert work, those pop recordings, and his truer ambition to move on to more narrative movie scoring, that a personal dilemma cropped up to complicate things even more: a rift between him and the chief proponent of his initial success, Blake Edwards—or, rather, between Blake Edwards and the rest of the world. In just a few months' time, Edwards would break all ties with Mancini, renounce Hollywood altogether, and move to the other side of the globe, leaving Mancini a free agent on *all* fronts, unsure where his next film opportunities might be found and facing the unknown 1970s.

— — —

Sparking the trouble was Edwards's next planned film—a big intentionally old-fashioned musical, *Darling Lili* (1970), for which Edwards's new wife, Julie Andrews, would play a popular British music-hall star, Lili Smith, who is also a German spy of the First World War. Her assignment is to lavish special attention on an American flyer, Maj. William Larrabee (Rock Hudson), which includes backstage passes (in both meanings of the word) to her shows, all the while seeking to get military secrets out of him about bombing runs. In the course of this mission, she naturally falls in love with him and is about to blow her cover.

Johnny Mercer would be brought back to team with Mancini in writing a whole score full of songs that would spoof the music and rhymes of that era. Perhaps it sounded like a fun project to all involved, but it was disastrous planning (or perhaps defiance) on Edwards's part to follow up his recent less-than-successful films with an ultra-conventional screen musical with sing-along songs and a creaking plot. It would be an ill-advised choice today, but it seems downright insane for 1969 at the height of the national political debates over war and racism, the generation-gap chatter, and, on the creative front, the anti-Broadway politics of shows like *Hair* and anti-establishment films like *MASH*, *Midnight Cowboy*, and *Easy Rider*. (Of course, this was also the period of bafflingly old-fashioned movie melodramas like *Airport* and *Love Story* and the aforementioned million-selling piano Muzak, so maybe *Darling Lili*'s backwardness was not alone after all.)

But for whatever reason, Edwards proceeded, though he was becoming gradually wary and suspicious of his sponsoring studio. As always, he attempted to tell his story by straddling several genres. Seen today, the mix of romance, sudden comedy routines, sweet musical numbers, scowling German generals loyal to the kaiser, exciting aerial dogfight footage, and Edwards's own dark undercurrent seems agreeably entertaining. The pace of the two-hour version (there are longer and shorter edits available) is brisk and efficient, and music has a both grounding and propelling influence on the whole. There is, however, no obvious central thrust to the story, no strong sense of viewer commitment. Andrews and Hudson are fine; the spy plot and the humor (via a forever-soused flyer named T. C. who often partners with Larrabee, and two bumbling Clouseau-like investigators trying to catch Lili at her spy game) are fun. But, as in past films, the mixing of story clichés from so many different categories unsettled people in its day so that word-of-mouth reaction to the film was disappointing.

The Mancini/Mercer songs mostly stay out of that controversy. They are simple and flowing (their introductions often overlap a preceding dramatic scene and help keep the film moving along), and of course they are all presented as actual stage performances by Lili. Their musical tone and certainly their lyrics are meant to sound antique ("I'll give you three guesses who loves you") and their onstage quaintness is an effective camouflage for what we know to be Lili's true, traitorous agenda backstage. And yet the songs are *so* unabashed and naïve (including one sung by a class of French schoolchildren that is embarrassingly imitative of Andrews's own lesson song, "Do-Re-Mi," in *The Sound of Music*) that it is hard to believe Edwards is pitching all of this to us seriously. When Paramount Studios could not decide how to market the film to their 1969–1970 audience, they began to demand a lot of cuts. Daily, Edwards found reasons to be furious at them as the film proceeded, and that anger was soon to be spread out toward nearly everyone, including his best collaborator, Mancini.

However, notice should be taken of what Mancini did accomplish on *Darling Lili* as a song writer and scorer. An airy overture of Mancini's period tunes makes way for the film's main song, the one piece that stands outside of the specific setting and time of the story to speak for the composer himself—a chilling waltz with Mercer's title, "Whistling Away the Dark." On screen, in the distance, we see a theatrical followspot making a cameo of Lili's face on stage as she sings the opening line, "Often I think this sad old world is whistling in the dark." The camera approaches her. The tune is a cousin-in-kind of the "Charade" waltz, except that where that was an A-minor music-box song, "Whistling Away the Dark" is in E minor and is also somehow sadder: "Often," says the second pass of Mercer's lyric, "I think my poor old heart has given up for good." Edwards shoots Julie Andrews's complete stage performance of the song as the first scene of his film, keeping the camera close as she sings, sweeping around her as she moves about the boards under dreamy lens flares from the footlights. In the middle of the song, as divided strings take over the tune, she spins in waltzing circles by herself at center stage until the last lyric ("So walk me back home . . . tell me dreams really come true . . . / whistling here in the dark with you."). As she returns to face forward again, the followspot shrinks from her full figure to the tight cameo of her face, and as the song ends, the light goes out. Edwards cuts to an audience applauding. We see a few soldier uniforms in the crowd, revealing the wartime milieu of the story. Air-raid sirens break up the ovation, though; the audience starts to look around, worried. We cut outside the theater to a shot of a German zeppelin on prowl in the skies, and then we cut back inside to the audience beginning to panic. From the stage, Lili calms them by striking up songs that everyone will know, such as "It's a Long Way to Tipperary." Over that singing and the sight of Lili exercising her own special charm and reassuring her public come the film's opening titles and credits.

It was Mancini and Mercer's intention that most of their original songs here "sound like you've heard them before," like old homesick standards. There is a timeless lullaby quality to "The Girl from No Man's Land" (sung as Lili strolls the grounds of an army hospital, serenading wounded troops). Three other songs, while solid and satisfying, are as interchangeable (and intentionally "corny," as Mancini once said) as pub sing-alongs: "Your Good-will Ambassador," "Smile Away," and the title tune. Sometimes these are presented as stage songs, other times with the French accordion and guitar in simple harmonies as ambient music.

But audiences, much less critics, saw little need for this odd throwback film, and the studio apparently saw the problem coming and kept bothering Blake Edwards throughout production with visits, questions, and challenges. Soon they were calling for rewrites. Edwards was growing exasperated and beginning to feel that *Darling Lili* was no longer *his* film. The whole experience was starting to strain his relations with many people in the industry, and he was becoming suspicious of everyone around him. As Mancini later described it, "During filming I would get the strangest visits from studio emissaries asking my opinion on what a particular song should be, if it should be in this scene or that. Being somewhat naïve by nature, I didn't see what they were up to so I would talk to them. . . . Then they went to Blake saying they had talked to me and that I agreed with *them* about the scene. When at last I discovered how I had been used, I resented it deeply."[3]

Edwards was duly offended by it all, believed Mancini had been maneuvering behind his back, and soon refused to talk to him ever again. He finished the film, but then as it flopped, he left Hollywood ("forever," he said), settled with Julie Andrews in Europe, and took no calls from Mancini. All Henry could do at that point was to keep the door open. Without intending it so, Mancini found his career at another crossroads. Suddenly he was a best-selling pop star without a film to score, and he was apparently supposed to forget his fifteen-year association with Blake Edwards. Thus his ongoing career as the preeminent film composer seemed up for renegotiation. The horizon was clear but blank.

Mancini flew off with Ginny to Rio de Janeiro, supposedly to be one of the judges in an international songwriting competition but actually to begin a new phase of his career, which would be characterized by much experimentation and restlessness—but would also dangle in front of him just the sort of scoring opportunities he had been wanting.

CHAPTER 9

Off to See the World

The break in Mancini's work with Blake Edwards was a private event that seemed to put his future career into a state of flux. But he sensed a chance to advance, an opportunity in the making, when a phone call reached him at that songwriting contest in Rio. It sounded like an emergency: Paramount Studios calling. They had been bankrolling a gritty film about the 1876 Irish coal miners' strike in Pennsylvania called *The Molly Maguires* (1970), and the project was in trouble. Although director Martin Ritt had achieved an authentic brooding look to his film through the cinematography of James Wong Howe, it was being judged too monotone and grim. At the same time, the music score that had been received was considered too little, too light, casting the drama into doubt. It was well known that Ritt hated the whole Hollywood tradition of using narrative music in films. He was seeking realism—in acting, in production design, in story presentation. Music, he felt, only interfered with those efforts. Elmer Bernstein's sparse, naturalistic score to Ritt's *Hud* (1963), or Sol Kaplan's laconic chamber music for *The Spy Who Came in from the Cold* (1965), or even Taj Mahal's down-home vocal/guitar contribution to *Sounder* (1972) are but three examples of how Ritt managed to find a small place for music in his films while never giving way to old-fashioned notions of music as "necessary showmanship." Now Paramount executives were telling him that the very minimal Irish-folkish music used in the preview version of *The Molly Maguires* was not working for them; it was not accessible enough, not demonstrative enough to draw the bleak story forward. Broadway composer Charles Strouse, who had done *Bye Bye Birdie* in the 1960s and would do *Annie* in the 1970s, had previously found some success writing a folk-based film soundtrack for 1967's *Bonnie and Clyde*, but his scoring here was seen as too flat.

The studio's thought was that with a little more color in the score, and especially a firmer sense of musical drama, the whole momentum of the film might be lifted—less historical pageant, more entertainment. And from Mancini's point of view this was just the breath of fresh air that this composer-in-transition had wanted. He cut short his Rio trip and returned to California to view the recut film and set to work. The producers may have been seeking to lighten and humanize their film by choosing Mancini, but in accepting the job Mancini was seeking to darken, legitimize, and expand his own portfolio. Indeed, the collision of light and dark—not the only experimental aspect of this score in Mancini's oeuvre—its strict adherence to an ethnic model both harmonically and instrumentally, and the absence of any pop content in its orchestral narrative scoring mark it as a first for him.

Always thinking in melodic terms, even when scoring dramatically, Mancini based *The Molly Maguires* music on one principal theme, which opens the film. We are shown the world of the nineteenth-century coal miner—the coal conveyers, smokestacks, the slag heaps, the gray earth and the dusty sunrise, the mine shafts and soiled workers seated on iron coal cars being slowly drawn out of daylight into the black hole of the pit, now lit only by the miners' headlamps and hand lanterns. This first theme begins with a single harp plucking a steady arpeggio, which then becomes support for the solo recorder presenting the miner's tune. It is painfully simple music owing much to ancient Irish folk music (and for film buffs reminding us of a major-key version of Max Steiner's 1930s Irish theme for *The Informer*). The tune's release is taken by mid-range flutes, bassoon, and brass over a deep string foundation as the camera pans the mine works. The theme is repeated in full by an accordion, and then the second release is handled by a solo bassoon. Throughout the score, harp and flute seem to speak for the idealized Irish workers while the accordion (often in its sinister lowest register) seems to speak of trouble and injustice. At six minutes into the film (and into the scoring) we are seeing some of the workers looking up from their routines, exchanging glances; a few break off from the others. Mancini plants a single chord on the accordion that gets our attention. Quiet timpani adds tension as we see some of these miners stay behind at the end of their shift; they are stringing fuse wires under the coal face and laying bombs there. On the soundtrack now two bassoons introduce the strikers' motif—a clever minor-key mockery of an Irish jig, ominous and threatening violence. It is set against low strings on a counter bass line with a steady, suspenseful tolling meter of the timpani as the bomb setters (we will meet them later) resurface topside and walk nonchalantly with their comrades back toward their homes. We are all awaiting the detonation.

Director Ritt lets them walk a long way in the tranquil morning before we hear the explosions under the earth. A great blast bellows from the mouth of the mine. Here, ten minutes into the film, the main title credits begin. On the soundtrack, lower brass replicate the stark accordion chord we heard before; full strings and flutes sweep up and down the scale like the waves of smoke and fire that we are seeing. For those well versed in the Mancini catalog, it also announces a new concentration: straight dramatic orchestral music that is sensitive to the ethnic lore of the setting, instrumentally distinctive in establishing specific sounds that will become emblematic of the characters, and yet thematic in nature. Thus Mancini is using this urgent assignment (which he probably would not have been offered except under such emergency circumstances) to stake out new territory beyond the pop episodic scores (and records) for which he had become famous.

There are limits and faults to what Mancini contributed here, but his restraint and respect for the characters and milieu of this film showed real prudence. His action music never strives toward Hollywood melodrama, but remains modestly within the range of the ethnic tone he has chosen. And although there is a love theme in the film, it is offered most quietly on a flute and Irish harp, is harmonized by some lovely writing for muted strings (just once), and intrudes upon the otherwise serene soundtrack with only the greatest discretion. That very modesty and thinness in the music score would lead to some criticism in the press about Mancini's soundtrack being stingy and repetitive. And yet the producers, having spent four frenzied weeks hiring Mancini and prodding him to save their overdue production, were really keen on exploiting his scoring wherever they could, indeed sometimes manipulating it without Mancini's permission, repeating certain cues so that there would actually be *more* music than he had contributed.

Following the film's prologue, in which we have been introduced to the miner's life and strife, we cut to the train station, where James McParlan (Richard Harris) disembarks. He appears to be a drifter looking for work but is really a Pinkerton detective working with local police to expose the strikers. He takes a room in the boardinghouse of Mary Raines (Samantha Eggar) and gradually meets and is tested by the Mollys (Sean Connery is their ringleader, Jack Kehoe). In an early pub scene we hear two Irish tunes played by an old deaf fiddler. Mancini will use that strained, un-resonant sound of the fiddle later in his dramatic score. We are twenty minutes into the film before another music cue is heard, a repetition of the harp arpeggio and the accordion establishing the Molly theme as we get to know the reticent people of this muddy makeshift town. Cinematography illuminates the shots with a kind of gloomy glow rather than from direct sources of light. That sense of foreboding and authenticity adds inadvertently to an acceptance of Mancini's monochromatic score as well. Brass and full strings repeat the main theme as McParlan is seen heading off in the early morning for his first day of work. Elegiac and nearly noble views of the silent miners walking through the streets at sunup blend with the bassoon and the low dark tones of the soundtrack orchestra.

There is a two-minute montage of McParlan's first day of work, again without dialogue and narrated only by Mancini's music—violas massed and playing on open strings while violins do a variation of that pub fiddler's tune as we watch the process of mining: the blasting, the picking of the coal from blocks into lumps loaded into the coal cars to be hauled up to the surface. Almost immediately McParlan begins to experience for himself the very injustices that the Mollys are meaning to protest—the docked wages, the unsafe conditions—but he has a job to do spying on them. They establish an uneasy connection at first, and then gradually McParlan works his way into Kehoe's confidence and into the Mollys. He participates in sabotage, though he also succeeds in sabotaging some of the group's more deadly terrorism.

So far the music cues, all related by content and voicing, are presented as clean, separate set pieces. When McParlan improvises a game of soccer with the local kids in the street, piccolo and strings play a happy variant of the pub fiddler's song, and later, when McParlan and Mary linger in each other's company, a new harp arpeggio is introduced and a single flute joins diffidently. In those ways what is really a very short score spreads its influence throughout the film, helps the storytelling, and helps to humanize the not-so-expressive characters. For Mancini, *The Molly Maguires* represented an enlivening experience—the chance to compose a strictly orchestral score, bound by given dramatic and ethnic tonal limits, effective in both its scene setting and storytelling and still melodically driven.

And thus began Mancini's experimental decade, the 1970s, in which he welcomed the widest variety of international, ethnic, historical, and topical projects that would require all manner of music.

- - -

Almost immediately on finishing *The Molly Maguires*, Mancini would receive another surprise call from even further afield, announcing that the great Italian neorealist director Vittorio De Sica and the great producer (and husband to Sophia Loren) Carlo Ponti wanted to work with him. Their film *I Girasoli* (1970), soon to take the American title *Sunflower*, was in trouble—or rather the director and producer were having trouble with each other—and they somehow thought that a big, exploitable, romantic score by someone with the reputation of Mancini might mediate their opposing visions for their film. Mancini initially knew nothing of this feud; he merely relished the chance to write music for a renowned team of filmmakers with a renowned pair of stars (Loren and Marcello Mastroianni)—music that was supposed to evoke both wartime Italian and postwar Russian settings. As it turned out, he was walking into a dispute that even music could not soothe. Even as the film was being made, it began slipping away from its original, laudably simple script. De Sica, famous for several of the greatest films ever made (including *Shoeshine* [1946] and *The Bicycle Thieves* [1948]), with their realistic street-shot style and nonprofessional casts, claimed that his project was being blown up into a big international soap opera by Ponti and his money. "How could you have made this film?" critic Charles Thomas Samuels said to De Sica's face the next year. De Sica explained very patiently, if bitterly, what had happened.

At first the project had been called "Giovanna" and was a very elementary script about a Calabrese woman whose husband had gone to Sweden to work in the mines. When he failed to return, she went in search of him and tracked him to Stockholm, where he had a new wife and child. There was a confrontation; she stumbled off into the world, living like, feeling like, an outcast for the rest of her days. But Ponti and other backers objected to that basic plot. No one, it was said, would ever "abandon" Ms. Loren like that in a movie. The script was rewritten so that the Mastroianni character loses his memory in the war and entirely forgets about his former marriage, so his wife, Giovanna, has to go in search of him. By the time that version was being touted, De Sica wanted to pull out, but as he later said, "So much time had already been spent preparing it. The shooting had started. It was weak of me not to have left."[1] By the time Mancini had his first conference with De Sica and Ponti in the production office in Italy, he said, "I suddenly realized I was caught in the middle of an argument that had been going on since the picture had started. . . . I was trying to find the appropriate dramatic places for music and they were going at each other with me as the battleground."[2] Mancini tried to reassure both of them and tried to convince them that music could blend both the personal elements that De Sica wanted and the epic that Ponti wanted. After all, he badly wanted to score their film—it fit into his new international and outward-bound track, and he would be working with world-famous figures who had requested *his* services.

Mancini wrote with great passion, but because he was usually intuitive in his composing, interpolating even unintentionally the powers or weaknesses of each film, there is a subtle disconnect between what his music seems to intend and what it is actually inspired to express. His *Sunflower* theme, which in Japanese pop music markets would eventually become his most popular tune, even beyond "Moon River" and all the rest, has the ingredients of passion and yearning but also retains a certain secondhand quality, accurately reflecting the awkward pulp-fiction tone of the film. In any case, Mancini was really just following orders, wanting to get on board with the bosses and make an enthusiastic contribution. He recalled, "Well, you know the picture. It's really a big Italian, heartbreaking, chest-thumping kind of thing. And I saw it alongside Ponti in the screening room in Rome, and afterward we were going to lunch and we came out of the theater. I just looked at him and I said 'Puccini?' and he beamed back and said, 'Si!'"[3]

I Girasoli's opening piano (arpeggio in the left hand and the simple melody in the right) makes its semi-tragic statement; moves to the bridge; returns to the chorus on the electric harpsichord; then, again with brass backing in a higher key, to a climax before dropping back in strength and closing with the piano arpeggio—a sad piece, heartsick and unsubtle. There are a few subtle moments in the score, though; notice a descending figure on a distanced, reverberating piano as the camera tilts down from Antonio's (Mastroianni's) picture on the wall to Giovanna sitting alone thinking of him. At least musically the moment is captured perfectly. But more often Mancini takes a heavy symphonic approach. Under a shot of soldiers (Antonio among them) returning from the Russian front, we are jolted by the nearly dirgelike meter of a drum and low piano supporting unison lower strings in a formal "retreat theme" by Mancini that seems to insist on underlining the suffering that is already obvious on screen—big, earnest, plodding music, harmonized in simple parallel unison lines, strings and horns in thirds and hints of a balalaika sound.

The score's best sequence drives a montage of Giovanna's foray to Moscow in search of her man, trudging from one Moscow government office to another, from contact to contact, looking for a lead. On the train she sits alone counting her travel money and thinking about her prospects, and on the soundtrack Mancini's orchestra is heading up the scale, rising in volume and intensity. As the camera pans aside to catch (what else?) a sunflower field flying by the train windows, the film's secondary theme gushes forward at full volume in all of its sort-of-Russianness, and music for a moment rules the screen. Eventually Giovanna does find a former soldier who knows Antonio's story—how he was found half frozen in the snow, dragged to safety, and then nursed by a Russian peasant girl named Masha—so we are introduced to a dark accordion sound (again in a distanced mournful acoustic) playing "Masha's Theme." We know now that Antonio has developed (oh, so melo-dramatically) amnesia; he has forgotten all about his marriage to Giovanna and everything before the war. He and Masha have a child. So when Giovanna comes upon them, she is interrupting their settled life. As she sees him again after so many years and miles, strings struggle through rising phrases up to the *Sunflower* theme. He is trying to remember it all, as that theme soars shamelessly. At the time, no one believed this clichéd story, the performances, or the sad fact that the great De Sica had made *I Girasoli* at all. Happily, De Sica was soon able to redeem himself by financing and producing his last masterpiece, the award-winning *Garden of the Finzi-Continis* (1971).

For Mancini, *I Girasoli* can be considered a success, both in the sense of producing a sweeping love theme in his own personal language and forwarding his current ambitions in an overseas market. Blake Edwards was still not talking to him, but within just a few months he had found new clients of his *own*, navigating Irish, Italian, Russian, and soon Asian tonalities in dramatic period-film scores. Those who said he was limited in his scope to Kennedy-era suburban pop would have to reconsider.

For a few months in 1970 it looked as though he might be back in the awards columns, too, garnering two Oscar nominations for his music to *Darling Lili*, then a third for the score to *Sunflower*. The best film score of that year was probably Jerry Goldsmith's part-martial, part-mystical score to *Patton*, but the award went to the ultra-pop scoring of the tearjerker called *Love Story* by Francis Lai. In any case, Mancini went home empty-handed that night—zero wins for three chances. But he could not regret; there was already another multinational project awaiting his attention. Maybe he was *meant* to evolve in this more orchestral direction and not be known so exclusively for award statuettes and radio-play songs.

James Michener had written a long piece of historical fiction about the domestication of the Hawaiian Islands that was then made into a movie called, simply, *Hawaii* (1966). Walter Mirisch, who had executive-produced

The Pink Panther, had used Elmer Bernstein to score that one. Now Mirisch planned a sequel to carry the story forward into what was essentially the second half of that original book. He hired Mancini for the score to *The Hawaiians* (1970; in some markets the film is titled *Master of the Islands*). Bernstein had found, in his musical research, that there was no indigenous Hawaiian music to draw on; the syrupy steel guitars associated with the hula-dance tourist Hawaii were only a recent aberration. Polynesian music mixed with Guinean tribal rhythms had long ago come together with some strong orientalism from China and Japan to create the music that became associated with the Hawaiian Islands. Bernstein had constructed a compromise for his main theme—a kind of tropical, nautical tune with a balmy surface. He added what he thought of as island percussion and some more delicate sounds—pastorals and lullabies that could have sprung from any culture. Mancini found the same impasse in his research and fell back on the same sort of material for his main theme: a white man's island song, the musical equivalent of a postcard of the horizon from shore.

The script for *The Hawaiians* was split in its loyalties between two subplots—one focusing on the ambitious sea captain Whip Hoxworth, played by Charlton Heston; the other on a Chinese girl, Nyuk Tsin, of the Hakka mountain people smuggled to Hawaii among a boatload of Punti-Chinese laborers, played by the relatively unknown Tina Chen (she had acted one previous role in *Alice's Restaurant* [1969]). Her protector on board ship is Kee Munki, played by Oscar-nominated (for *The Sand Pebbles* [1966]) Mako. He teaches her his own native Punti language along with pidgin English, and once they dock he manages to get both of them jobs at Whip's pineapple plantation. Directed by action specialist Tom Gries, and photographed by Blake Edwards's old buddy from *Peter Gunn*, Philip Lathrop, *The Hawaiians* seems vivid in its introduction to Nyuk's culture and in its depiction of her early relationship with the protective Kee Munki, particularly as Chen and Mako are readily watchable performers. But the film can never quite settle on their story, for it has to keep leaping back to revisit the official world of Hoxworth and its bankable American star. Heston himself admitted that flaw in the script even before they began shooting, confiding in his published journals, "The main problem in *The Hawaiians'* script was that the story is really about Nyuk Tsin. . . . Though I was the top-billed actor in the film my part was less important than hers. In an effort to center the film on my side, the script took the story away from its real core."[+]

That asymmetry is perhaps better addressed and almost remedied in the music score by Mancini, for while his clichéd and rather "touristy" main theme opens the film, the better parts of the score are uttered by a small ensemble of imported Chinese, Japanese, and Javanese instruments. When the music is at its best, these players, confined to melodies that Mancini based on indigenous scales of those three cultures, are set against the softening, somewhat modernizing effect of a western string section. We first hear such an ensemble after the big orchestral main title music that accompanies the sight of a big masthead ship under full sail. Our view moves into the deep hold of that vessel, where Chinese peasant workers and artisans are packed, heading for jobs on the Hawaiian Islands. A low plucking is heard (played on a *chyn*, or "cheng," a seven-stringed Chinese zither that is held flat on the player's lap, plucked and stopped like a guitar). A pick is drawn across the *chyn* strings, creating a slow-motion arpeggio as a hesitant murmuring is heard from a kind of Chinese ocarina (called a *hsun*) in the alto register. We meet Nyuk Tsin and Kee Munki there as their intimate music plays. A small, pure bell-like sound, even finer in tone than a celesta, pings out the four-note introductory phrase that will then become a harmony to the melody we come to associate with Nyuk from now on—an Asiatic tune that will be known as "Auntie's Theme" in the score. (It is later explained that any children born to Nyuk and Munki in this foreign place will actually belong to his true wife back home in China. Nyuk is, therefore, only "Auntie" to them.) Her theme will become the key melody of the film—more convincing, certainly more serious than Hoxworth's island theme. Mancini makes sure that the duet between the *chyn* and the pinging finger-bells playing "Auntie's Theme" is truly transparent so that the amusing English lesson between these two peasant passengers is musically supported but not overwhelmed and not, by any means, caricatured or derided.

It is eventually declared that Nyuk Tsin's official island name, as she arrives and takes up land of her own, will now be "Wu Chow's Auntie," as she has had her first baby with Munki and has agreed to be its surrogate caretaker. Under her "investiture" some narrative scoring sneaks in with a light backing of flute and muted strings playing "Auntie's Theme" softly like a nursery song.

As the multilayered plot proceeds, Mancini supplements his basic "Auntie" scoring and his island music with a few separate but associated themes: a rhythmic marimba-led interlude (darkened with bass flutes and trombones) as Whip sends smuggler agents out in flatboats to snatch a rare pineapple seed plant as a test crop for his own plantation; a heavy orchestral dirge as Munki is exiled to a leper colony on Molokai Island; and, for a beautiful geisha girl who arrives on Whip's plantation looking for work, a delicately sensuous and lovely Japanese air that blends perfectly the pentatonic scale and western harmonies from muted strings. ("Yes, I remember that," Mancini said years later. "I liked that very much—sort of *Madame Butterfly* music."[5]) Heard only twice in the film, pressed into the background, this latter melody, both as a representation of the geisha character and as an individualized statement in Mancini's own language, this piece called "Fumiko" is a good example of taking in ethnic material and making it personal. Indeed, Mancini's score for *The Hawaiians* ranks well among his straight dramatic efforts. Even his "touristy" main island theme can be forgiven eventually, as it is used to represent the white man's view of the islands. (For more substantial island themes from films, consult Bronislau Kaper's *Green Dolphin Street* [1947] or his later *Mutiny on the Bounty* [1962] love theme or Dimitri Tiomkin's *Return to Paradise* [1953]. And of course there is the lovely beach island sound Mancini assembled in his *Driftwood and Dreams* album fourteen years before *The Hawaiians.*) What may keep this score from greater praise is the fact that the various themes are neither varied nor very much integrated. The common scales and sounds do give the score a consistent feel at least. In these experimental 1970s Mancini was still exploring the middle ground between the multi-themed soundtracks for which he was famous and the whole-cloth scores to which he aspired.

— — —

By 1971, having expanded on his pop-Panther, cool-romantic musical reputation by experimenting with all of those exotic tonal outposts and foreign scales, Mancini now took the toughest challenge yet, intentionally leading him as far as possible from the modern American suburban settings of his hits. This would be his most experimental and exigent score ever, written for a Scandinavian psychodrama by Laslo Benedek called *The Night Visitor* (1971), known in its British and European releases as *Salem Come to Supper.*

Not even the shady colors and tonal tension of *Man Afraid*, not even the aural creepiness of autoharps and organ beds in *Experiment in Terror* could prepare us for the disturbing, schizophrenic, and yet carefully controlled sounds of this score. On screen we are immediately introduced to an opaque wintry landscape of blue ice and black underbrush somewhere in Sweden. Ponds, rocky paths, woods, and what look like old fortress ruins are all around us, and moving through the scene at a slow trot, cold and suffering, dressed only in underclothing and boots, is a solitary man. This is Salem (Max Von Sydow). He has found a way to escape at will from the Asylum for the Criminally Insane, where he has been confined for the murder of a farmhand.

His obsession now is to somehow exact revenge on the people who framed him: Ester (Liv Ullman), Dr. Anton (Per Oscarsson), and Salem's former wife, Emmie, who is their maid. Except for the perplexed police inspector (Trevor Howard), who is called in on the case once more people start turning up dead, everyone in this story is either corrupt or aberrant.

The settings are either stark winterscapes or the overheated cottages and cramped rooms of the locals, where even the bungalow doors seem too small and constricted to allow free passage. It is an uncomfortable film about guilt, vengeance, and secrets. For those subjects and those colors, Mancini, who always said he "saw" scores in sounds, compiled a tight, restrictive, neurotic ensemble of just eighteen instruments, allowing just enough shading to tell a story and yet remain monochromatic. The grouping of instruments included twelve woodwinds in threes and five keyboards (electric organ, piano, harpsichord, detuned piano, and detuned harpsichord). Those fleeting moments in *Wait Until Dark* when the regular piano and the off-pitch piano traded notes with each other to a most unsettling effect now were exploited to the fullest, right from the first crackling chord of *The Night Visitor*.

In the beginning, the ensemble's keyboard players drop their hands down on the harpsichords—one a thick C chord against a detuned quarter-tone version of same—and they let the dissonance decay for five seconds before high oboe enters on B with a dramatic descending phrase (B-A-F-E) whose last note hands over to English horn. The chord repeats and the English horn hands over to the bassoon, then in turn to the deep hollow tube of a contrabass clarinet. This melds with bassoon for the final chord of the introduction, whereupon the regular harpsichord begins a simple minor-key outline, the scaffolding of a baroque chaconne in A minor. A high, rather unreal melody comes in now on electric organ, a tune made up of two-note cells, descending half notes held for two beats, creating a troubled hobbling impression, fatalistic and foreboding. Part of whatever power this film has is that although its characters have a modern rural setting around them, the whole district seems to be frozen in the Middle Ages, as though caught in some wicked fairy tale.

Mancini's unforgiving score without themes, with only that flat brooding dynamic and those wounded rhythmic patterns, keeps the dark mood and the psychological oppression uppermost. Medieval modal chords on the harpsichord (A minor is finally reestablished) signal the end of the main title music. The camera begins to move, following Salem through the cold twilight, and the score begins a lopsided meter on the two harpsichords, giving an unbalanced feel to the faltering progress of the piece. Bassoon and contrabass clarinet move underneath in dark, clotted phrases. The sound of a frigid winter wind mixes from the sound-effects track into this orchestration, and an agitated snare drum (the ensemble's eighteenth and only percussion instrument) adds a sense of urgency and distress. A high clarinet/flute duo carries the main line over gloomy piano/harpsichord phrases juxtaposed from below. Contrabass clarinet hands over to the more common range of the regular clarinet and so on up through the ensemble in chromatic steps until Salem reaches the farmhouse that we see lit warmly from within. There the higher notes of the two harpsichords are compared, perfect pitch answered by the detuned pitch of its twin.

With all of this tonal ambiguity, one could suppose that Mancini might be flirting with a formal serial-row style of composition like Arnold Schoenberg, but it is not quite *that* adventuresome a score. One has to possess a few more years of advanced compositional study than Mancini ever had at Juilliard or with Krenek to work out the mathematics and logic of an original twelve-tone row in the serial system of composing. And Mancini, adept and brave as he was (remember the complex jazz harmonies and instrumental blends in the *Gunn* film score), never aspired to that height of academic exercise. *The Night Visitor* music is more properly categorized as aggressively chromatic.

We see the points of light that are cottage windows, then the dark hulk of the farmhouse itself surrounded by white snowy acreage. The score, softening, retreats as Salem sneaks toward the house and enters through an unlocked window. Ester and Anton are talking about their disdain for the bleak countryside, wishing they could move to the city, where he could open a medical practice. A second music cue begins as the couple retires to bed and Salem emerges out of the shadows in an upper room. Contrabass clarinet and bassoon rise in a modal line to a slow reprise of the organ main title motif with harpsichord arpeggio. A single ground note is repeated on the piano as a foundation. Salem has taken a hypodermic needle from the doctor's bag and, inexplicably at this point, left a necktie with which to later implicate Anton in the revenge killing to come. Without being noticed, Salem sneaks back out of that house and heads for a nearby farm. In the cottage there, young Brittany is asleep; the shot of Salem's hand behind her bedroom's lace curtain is scored with a deep organ note as the new ground. Atop it the two pianos, one tuned, one flat, play a mirrored phrase—Salem enters and approaches Brittany's sleeping form on the bed. Harpsichord contributes deep two-note phrases, and then the pianos again, this time in dissonant couplets, trade with the harpsichord. All of these are quiet, clandestine murmurings but brought up on the soundtrack to a close, attentive volume. Brittany wakes to find Salem standing over her. She believed him to still be imprisoned in the asylum. He says only, "I've been thinking about you for a long time." Deep organ notes enter, and as he unbuttons her nightgown and the camera closes in on her face, the two disturbed pianos are joined by the two harpsichords, and we are made to feel the two sides of this confrontation at once—the chaos and terror from her angle and the diabolical resolve from his.

The impressive cast fights to keep this cold, unsympathetic, unrewarding material from freezing us out. Furthermore, the incredible ease with which Salem can come and go from his multi-fastened fortress cell and the absurd sight of him running through the frigid landscape in underclothes from prison to farmhouse and back again (and again) come close to parody. Add to this the plot device, which will become most important, that the doctor's pet parrot was also present at the original farmhand crime scene and everyone seems afraid that the bird will someday "sing" (one of its favorite phrases is "Salem come to supper"), and you have a dangerously farcical scenario, particularly given how deadly serious the whole production wants to be.

Fortunately, with the dissonant tones of his music, Mancini supports and reinforces an admonitory mood. The score's denouement will be tied to that police inspector's last dash from one of the murder scenes back to the asylum, hoping to see if Salem is there. We watch the police cruiser tearing over winding wintry roads and Salem, carrying all of his escape gear, sprinting on foot through the backwoods to resume his cell. In the score an urgently loping rhythm on the harpsichords and piano is pierced by a high oboe/flute duo and then trades off with the low end of the whole ensemble in a kind of passacaglia finale for the eighteen instruments together. Here producer Mel Ferrer has cut Mancini's original composition and crudely repeated some sections in order to blatantly match the action as Salem scales the walls of the fortress; at one point the music is dropped altogether as a shot is inserted of the police cruiser.

By the time the inspector arrives at the asylum, Salem is already tucked innocently in his cot. The long arm of the law seems foiled at that point. But then something emerges from the inner pocket of the jacket Salem had taken from the doctor's house—it is the doctor's missing parrot. Even if it were not taunting him with the phrase "Salem come to supper," its presence would be proof enough that Salem must have been at the doctor's cottage very recently. All Salem can do in response is to laugh crazily. The organ and the harpsichord of the opening main title music reprise over the closing credits and end on the modal medieval chords, which then reduce to a single note and fade.

In one way Mancini was lucky that Ferrer had bought into his cold, sonic concept for this score at all and let it stand. In another way it is maddening that Ferrer felt the need to cut into it at times. But, no matter, *The Night Visitor* seems a successful assignment in this experimental period, even if the film itself was quickly dumped from first-run theaters to be double-billed in the United States with horror films like *Night of the Living Dead*. Like the oriental instrumentation in *The Hawaiians* and the selective ensemble in *The Molly Maguires*, this film's sound was unique, well measured, and smartly applied to its story. Mancini was definitely not pandering to his pop-music audience with scores like those. And his scoring was evolving to the kind of composed-through-narrative style he admired.

― ― ―

There are two more scores in this international experimental phase of Mancini's career—another chance to score a Russian setting, for a film called *The Girl from Petrovka* (1974) with Goldie Hawn and Hal Holbrook, and an unusual adventure about three sailors from a nineteenth-century whaling ship stranded in Eskimo territory, *The White Dawn* (1974). It is interesting to compare Mancini's scoring approach to this later film with that of a dozen years earlier for the exotic setting of *Hatari!* whose entertaining tunefulness was now being replaced by a broader, more consistent, subdued musical-mural approach. As Howard Hawks had brought home from Africa that box of tribal instruments and a recorded chant from the Masai people, so now *The White Dawn* director, Phillip Kaufman, brought back from Baffin Island in the Canadian Arctic Archipelago a few Eskimo-carved pipes and animal-skin drums and a recorded chant of an old Eskimo woman, which Mancini then incorporated into his score.

Without major star power (the irascible Warren Oates, the Emmy- and Oscar-winning Lou Gossett Jr., and the young Timothy Bottoms were all well-known actors but not exactly box-office draws), and with an almost *National Geographic* documentary look to the film (the whites, grays, and silvers of Michael Chapman's Arctic cinematography), both director Kaufman and Paramount Studios began to worry as the footage was being assembled that they might have on their hands too stark, too "cold" a film that would miss the mass audience. It was suggested that an alert music score was needed to encourage the film's acceptance. Producer Marty Ransohoff had wanted to work with Mancini since the mid-1960s, so the deal was struck. *The White Dawn*'s black-and-white prologue ("Based on true events . . .") chronicles the voyage of a grand-masted whaling vessel out of New Bedford, Massachusetts, circa 1896, chasing along the main ice floes after a run of whales in the North Atlantic. One of the smaller harpoon chase boats is wrecked against scatter ice in mad pursuit of a black whale. Its crew is dumped out, and four of them survive.

Mancini's musical setting for the prologue is a grand traditional adventure statement. Four French horns announce the interval of the "heroic fifth" as its first two notes of the six-note whale motif; then a four-part harmony response comes from the tubas and baritone horns. The French horns play the fifth again and invert the second phrase, and the others develop their response. The rest of the orchestra now blends in (full strings, two bassoons, four clarinets, autoharp, one symphonic harp, and one Irish harp, which will develop as a solo voice elsewhere in the score) playing the seafaring theme as we hear the sea captain reading from the ship's log. When a hearty "Thar she blows!" is heard, Mancini's orchestra kicks up to a 12/8 time signature. The tubas and baritone horns go into double time, and strings begin a running figure underneath, everyone in a state of hot pursuit. This music is alternately ecstatic (the seafaring theme at the top of its tilt) and ominous as the small harpoon boat is being dragged by its line, which is now embedded in the whale's hide. Billy (Oates), the profligate third mate, wants to hang on at all costs, but the others fear for their lives. The music is roused, the brass converge from different directions, until all instruments fuse on a final blurred chord as the chase boat smacks into an ice floe, breaks up, and disgorges its crew into the frigid sea.

Although we then cut to color film for the main title sequence, the snowscape is so stark that the whole world seems colorless, even featureless, except for black dots moving across the upper-left corner of the screen. These are the surviving whalers: Billy, the grouchy, greedy old sea dog; Portuguese Black, the harpooner (Gossett); and the young deckhand, Daggett (Bottoms). One other boatman who survived the crash cannot survive the trek through the snow. That leaves three men staggering forward into white oblivion. Mancini's first musical impression of this scene was a striking example of orchestral timbre that perfectly matched the sight of, and effectively suggested the mortal implications of, the human drama on screen. But for reasons that will be explained later, director Kaufman decided not to use it. That original music behind the opening credits began with the high, thin, airy tone of a piccolo playing what sounds like some tribal invocation of nature that works its way down to within the range of a flute, which then takes over the prayerful musical line. A delicate regular meter enters (one repeated note on the harp) like a cautious ticking accompanied by soft harp glissandos. The flute pursues its searching, somewhat mystical line (still more like a question than a theme), and high violins play behind it as a unison perspective. The men struggle on across a vast white obscurity. Then the high treble of the music is answered by deep, rich brass chords—four French horns, four baritone horns, four tubas. Mancini is teaching us to be sensitive both to the stark alien icescape, with its blinding whiteness and thin airlessness, *and* to its bottomless cold, the fathoms of ice underfoot. String harmonies (a total of twelve violins, six violas, six cellos) join the brass choir. All the layers resolve to a single bass note, on top of which only a distant string chord is left as the lost whalers' hopes are fading. There is no break on their horizon, no sign that they are headed in the right direction, no food, and it is *so* cold. The flute plays its invocation again in the quietude and passes it upward to the solo piccolo again. There is a pause, a sweep across the metal strings of an autoharp, and a low recorder plays off the opening motif as the men lie in the snow, resigned. Then they see the first glimpse of an Eskimo watching them from a distance. One high strum on the autoharp leaves a question mark in the air and ends the scene.

Director Kaufman grew impatient with the music cue we have just described and wanted to scrap it. (Kaufman would disturb Mancini again in nine years by prevailing upon composer Bill Conti to pilfer several music cues from *The White Dawn* for use in his Oscar-winning soundtrack to the 1983 film about America's space program, *The Right Stuff*.) At the dubbing sessions for *The White Dawn*'s soundtrack, Kaufman's reported discomfort with the musical setting of the lost sailors trudging through the snow was that it did not sound "dangerous enough." Mancini's musical concept—the piccolo to flute and strings, then the steep dive to the low brass choir—was deemed too descriptive of the natural world and not of the real risk these men were facing and of the strangeness of the surroundings. "Phil and Marty Ransohoff both didn't feel that [what I had written] captured their plight, the bleakness . . . the whole thing about being alone. It was too structured, a little too romanticized; it was a theme."[6] Although Mancini was not often able to sit in on the actual dubbing of one of his scores onto the film stock, the mixing of orchestral tracks with the dialogue and the sound-effects tracks, he *was* present for those sessions.

> And so it just occurred to me, "Wait, let me try this. . . ." I combined some light, ethereal electronic effects that really sound like a signal from another world with an idea that [Hollywood percussionist] Emil Richards had used in my score to *Arabesque* . . . an ordinary rubber ball dropped onto the unstopped

strings of an open piano . . . or swept across a large gong. And it created the weirdest sounds—actually like a whale—you know, the whale's chant. And so we did that and we ran the picture, and we just, at random, put those swipes in against the electronic sounds. And the minute they heard it, they said, "That's it." So my original main title piece went out, and these atonal sounds are what you hear behind the credits now.[7]

Another music cue follows immediately so that if Mancini's original main title music had been used, the film would have opened with a total of three successive cues and eleven minutes of descriptive music. The first shot we see after the main title is of the dog sleds of the local Eskimo tribe come to pick up the wrecked sailors. "What strange wind has brought them to us?" they say, translated for us in subtitles on screen, which will continue throughout the film. The trek across the ice by sled toward the igloo encampment is scored now with the broken rhythm of a large skin drum. Mancini found that since real Eskimo drums have no real resonance, no body, just a skin tied around a hoop, he had special skin drums made for him. These have a hollow urgent sound to them, and the driving tempo that Mancini assigned to them is always changing between three- and four-beat measures. Then, with a dampered piano chord adding in rhythmically, baritone horns carry a legato line over it, and the electronics and gong effect are heard along with the ever-constant drums. A flute/oboe duo repeats the legato line with two bassoons in counterpoint and brass now pairing up with the drum accents. Finally all of these instruments mix in four layers, and everything resolves down to one primitive chord, which fades as we watch the sleds pull into the village.

"That was probably one of the hardest things I have ever encountered," said Mancini. "Just to know what kind of music would satisfy the needs of the locale and the primitive quality of the people. And I was floundering around there until I heard the old lady's song. Phil had recorded her up in Baffin Bay, and when I heard her, that triggered not only that theme, but it sent me in a direction for the other stuff too."[8]

The Eskimos, led by their chief, Sarkak, call these shipwrecked foundlings "half man, half dog," saying they are bad-luck creatures born of the Dog Spirit. Nevertheless, they take them in, nurse them back to essential health, and allow them to hunt and live with the village. The first real music we experience since the rescue scene comes half an hour into the film, accompanying a seal hunt. The Irish harp scribes the simple arpeggio that will counterpoint the theme, which first appears on high, crisp bells, then on successive grades of recorders. It is a major-key folksy chant based on one chord, handed around a number of solo instruments, relieved by a responsive phrase on the oboe and by a rondo passage of different winds running scales, returning quietly to the first theme statement and thence to the receding harp arpeggio to a close 4/4 time with a last bar of 2/4.

During these early hunts Daggett finds one tribal friend of his age, who teaches him their ways; the young deckhand has also begun to notice one girl. Billy spends his time either complaining or scheming to get out of the whaling business and into trading in stolen furs. Mancini gives an inverted version of the main theme to those scenes depicting the whalers' interactions with tribal women—Daggett with one of the chief's wives and Portuguese with a woman the chief has picked for him. Daggett and his woman wander off over a rocky bayside terrain to be alone as the full orchestra introduces a sort of love theme, then moves through an expansive rendering of the familiar Eskimo chant in strong unison strings and complementary brass. As with *The Molly Maguires, The White Dawn* score deals with relatively narrow thematic materials, but its application to the story and the way it embraces the scenes has a tremendously empathic feel to it, the work of a craftsman who has a fondness for the job and who has learned something about strictly narrative scoring along the way. The scoring here proves more interactive with its film than that music for *The Molly Maguires* partly because it is being asked to accompany landscape vistas and more vigorous montage sequences of hunting and tribal migration, a humorous knife-throwing contest, and a mystical native element introduced by that old tribal matriarch who warns everyone that these intruders from the south bring nothing but bad luck. But there is also a sense of Mancini's evolution here, moving on toward more fully integrated dramatic narrative scoring. No awards or press attention came in for this film or its music, not even a soundtrack album was released, but the evolution of Mancini from pop tunesmith to full-service scorer, for anyone willing to examine his catalog, was by now practically complete.

Less satisfying but still in line with Mancini's developmental wave is his last score in this international period: the heavily romanticized pseudo-Russian music, full of strings and balalaikas, to *The Girl from Petrovka*. Robert Ellis Miller was known more as a performer's director than as a striking filmmaker. He coached Alan Arkin to an Oscar nomination for playing a deaf mute in *The Heart Is a Lonely Hunter* (1968) and likewise Tom Conti playing a Scottish rake poet in *Reuben, Reuben* (1983). In *The Girl from Petrovka* he had Hal Holbrook as an American journalist falling in love with the strange waif of a girl he has met through a local Moscow friend, Kostya (Anthony Hopkins). Goldie Hawn, with her small, humorous, infantile face framed by blonde bangs, plays the girl, Oktyabrina, with an unreliable Slavic accent and a sort of underplayed charm (part exuberance, part pout, part naïveté) that can be overemphasized fairly quickly. She is a ballet student and, as written in the script, flighty, playful, soulful, and seductive. Miller stages their bittersweet relationship almost too matter-of-factly so that to register sentiment in the viewer he has to rely on the script to bring her down from buoyant innocence to reckless dissidence, facing a five-year prison term at the hands of the Soviet vice squad.

Mancini, as the sensitive receptor he had always been, instinctively reads both the film's intentions and its shortcomings in his music. He provides a love theme that has both the minor-key yearning of middle-aged Joe Merrick (Holbrook) for this endearing lost girl and the feeling of excessive sentimentality that makes the film not quite convincing to this day. His main theme seems to be trying to manufacture more emotion than it actually contains. It also seems to stray from the Russian setting, sounding more like an Italian serenade than a Russian *narodnaya muzika*, more at home in a piazza than in Red Square. Accepting the sentimental nature of the theme, though, Mancini applies it, exploits it, most effectively.

The score opens with a passing mention of Russian dance music, then shifts into the film's main theme on accordion with unison strings and harmonized horns behind it. We learn from Holbrook's narration as Joe Merrick that he is the Moscow reporter for an American newspaper who has loved and lost this endearing girl, and he wants to tell us about her. The melody is really a slow, voluptuary waltz, indulgent in its reeling phraseology and its octave leap in the middle, visited variously throughout the film as we get to know these characters more personally—at its worst, flooding in with hearts and flowers to generate desperate love; at its best, reiterated tenderly and hesitantly when the characters are trying not to let their emotions show too much.

There is one fascinating musical moment in *The Girl from Petrovka*, though, not related to that love theme. Leonid is a young rehearsal pianist who often plays for Oktyabrina's dance class. His real love is jazz, but since the Soviet ministry had declared American jazz to be decadent, he has to play and compose in secret. He dreams of going to the West someday to study Errol Garner and Fats Waller records. Oktyabrina brings Joe up to a loft apartment, where there is a piano, and there we hear Leonid play a small free-form fifteen-bar jazz piece by Mancini. For Leonid, it is "fresh air from a far country." For us, it is a rare glimpse into Mancini's personal harmonic language when encouraged to draw a direct line from his cool-jazz roots to the post-cool modernisms of the 1970s. "Leonid's Theme" is a piece pulled not so much from the scene contexts as from Mancini's inner ear. It is a carefully worked out piano impromptu. Mancini's hand sketch of it says "Moodily" as a directive. The first bar is a stark, bluesy, almost dissonant chord (two flats) introducing a three-note phrase; the second bar repeats the chord but lets the phrase descend. The third bar, changing to a 3/4 meter, modulates by a run of sixteenth notes to an even colder chord, then back to 4/4, the whole progress being a meditative stroll through some rather dark nightspots of the mind. No regular meter ties these phrases together; it is played *rubato*, full of pauses, speculations, and resignations. The first bar appears again before the end, like a recurring motto that gives the one-minute piece more sense of structure than a mere cocktail improvisation could have.

For Leonid, the piece expresses an advanced knowledge of jazz lineage and a little of his anger at not being able to pursue the music he chooses. Late in the film we see him in some cruise ship's orchestra playing some banal foxtrot. He looks off longingly into the distance, and Mancini's soundtrack plays those first two bars of "Leonid's Theme," which have become a symbol of his yearning. This is the mature Mancini at work at his craft: storyteller of the personal.

And so he had done it, or so Mancini thought: he had expanded his repertoire beyond 1960s jazz-pop, and although none of the international films on which he had been laboring were particularly successful, it was known around town that he *had* worked on them. He had composed seriously in many kinds of ethnic music, and he had scored, in large-scale orchestral terms, purely narrative music. What is more, some pretty prestigious world and domestic filmmakers had hired him. It felt liberating. Perhaps there was some significance, then, that as he returned to home soil he immediately took up a series of Americana scoring assignments whose stories were set in remote or culturally isolated parts of his own country, exploring them as though from an alien altitude.

Actor/director Paul Newman was in charge of one of those films, titled *Sometimes a Great Notion*, set in an Oregon logging camp. The plot from a novel by Ken Kesey presented the Stamper clan—gruff-and-bluster loggers headed by Henry Fonda with Newman as his foreman, Lee Remick as Newman's wife, and Richard Jaeckel and Michael Sarrazin as younger Stampers. They have three weeks to get their logs to market in defiance of a strike to ensure their whole season's income. Newman said he wanted the film's score to resemble the sort of indigenous commercial pop-country music that was already naturally pouring from transistor radios in pickup trucks all over the Pacific Northwest, so Mancini wrote him a wailing, whining country ballad ("All His Children," with lyrics by Alan and Marilyn Bergman) to open the film and to return throughout, alternating with a series of similar tunes scored for steel guitar, harmonica, electric organ, some tenor sax, two trumpets in thirds (which was a familiar pop-country style of that day), and some country fiddling. Music was part of the observed setting rather than a participant in any of the storytelling. Only during one scene does Mancini get to enter the drama. The youngest Stamper, alone with Lee Remick's character, Viv, asks her, more or less, why she puts up with the macho insensitivity and barren isolation of this life, and she tells him the story of her colorless girlhood. Mancini brings in, barely perceptible and not as though from some household radio but from memory itself, two streams of high strings echoing each other in a simple, nostalgic relationship, slowly, floatingly pursuing a tune that we will never hear again nor can truly quite catch this time. Viv wakes, as it were, from the dreaminess of the moment and declares herself satisfied with the life she leads, though because of that enigmatic music we are left to wonder.

Country fiddling figures again, more demonstrably, in another film from this period set in the boondocks at the turn of the last century and called *Oklahoma Crude*. Stanley Kramer directs Faye Dunaway as a fierce-willed woman who has come into possession of a single productive oil well. Jack Palance plays her nemesis, representing ruthless oil barons who want what is hers. George C. Scott is the rapscallion, cantankerous vagabond Cleon, a hired gun she finds to protect her interests. Mancini found that working for late-career Kramer was rather like working for late-career Howard Hawks: his needs from a music score were lightweight, random, and undefined. The main theme here is a bright, fun, but ultimately trivial sort of barn dance—leaping phrases for the country fiddler of the major fifth, then major sixth, and then the same foot-stomping meter he had just written for a countrified TV series of that season called *Cade's County*. In the case of *Oklahoma Crude*, that fiddler is brought back on the soundtrack whenever the story rouses toward comic adventure. Elsewhere a sly, sneaking theme (shades of "Professor Fate's Theme" in *The Great Race*) for baritone horn, harmonica, and altered saloon piano appears whenever Cleon goes into action with his less-than-legal schemes to shut down (at least around this one gusher) "big oil."

Perhaps because these country sounds were already in his head, thanks to all the bucolic plots he had been asked to score in recent months, but perhaps also because the pop-music charts had seen some gains in the popularity of commercial country music through acts like the Nashville

Brass and Charlie Pride, Mancini agreed that his next pop album projects would address that trend. As a result, his next two or three releases as a recording artist featured his sleepy Muzak piano style dragging us through the drabness of hammock tunes like "Take Me Home, Country Roads." Oddly enough, they sold well.

Meanwhile Mancini's film-score agenda stayed with an Americana theme for a while longer. Beginning in 1975 he took on three screen stories set not in remote American territories but in remote times. None of them seemed to need much in the way of whole-cloth narrative scoring, however. George Roy Hill's *The Great Waldo Pepper* was about the early barnstorming days of biplane aviation throughout the Midwest, but all it wanted was a soundtrack consisting of a few circus-band marches and coronet waltzes. On the other hand, the biopic *W. C. Fields and Me*, starring Rod Steiger, took happy advantage of three distinct, but still undeveloped, period themes on its soundtrack mimicking the 1920s–1930s style: one for Depression-era Hollywood (an upbeat flapper piece for pit band and ukulele); one a sympathetic string motif for the girl Carlotta (Valerie Perrine) who put up with Fields's drinking, callous remarks, and inattention because she thought he could help her film career and because she said she had begun to care for him; and one main Fields theme, which is a slow, bluesy clarinet song that pretends to be jovial in an easygoing way and yet is full of regret. As Mancini said, "I always felt W. C. Fields was a very sad character with a lot of self-doubt, despite his arrogance."[9]

Third of these Americana scores was the 1930s throwback music he gave to the Walter Matthau vehicle *Little Miss Marker* (1980), a remake of the 1934 Shirley Temple classic taken from the Damon Runyan story about a gruff, cynical bookie who takes a small girl (Sara Stimson) as collateral (a "marker") on a ten dollar IOU. Here producers were counting on the charm and amusement generated between the little girl's flat, perfunctory way of speaking and Matthau's slow-burn exasperation to spark laughs. But chemistry never materialized, partly because they coached so much stoicism into the child that a real character never emerged and partly, therefore, because Matthau had nothing to "play off of." And yet going a long way to cheer everyone was the "olde curiosity shoppe" score by Mancini. Over main title stop-motion animation of a wooden toy set (cars, carts, shops, cops, pedestrians) of a model Depression-era street, Mancini introduces an energetic shuffle rhythm (bass, syncopated piano, and four-to-the-bar strummed guitar in Kansas City style). Each measure takes one step down the scale, heading back up for the next four, and as the rhythm continues, the squashed novelty voice of a Harmon-muted trumpet comes in with Mancini's quaint, carefree period melody. Tenor sax then improvises on the next chorus, then a jazz violin (remembering Stephane Grappelli's early solos with Django Reinhardt), and then slide trombone before the whole thing is summarized by the full band with particular joy. The enthusiasm of this opening prepares the viewer to expect such pleasure from the film to come that inevitably there will be disappointment in store. Indeed whenever the happy hop of this music comes back, it lifts the film terrifically, yet there is no successful counterpart to it in the film itself. A secondary theme is a slow-stride lazy blues, but it is dangerously similar to the clarinet theme in *W. C. Fields and Me*. At any rate, none of this music really joins or drives the screen story; it is mere accompaniment.

One capper film to this whole travelogue period in Mancini's scoring career, though it actually comes in the middle of this period, is the most unusual assignment he accepted to score the multiple parts of a documentary film called *Visions of Eight*, about the 1972 international Olympic Games. He was being asked to meet with eight world directors whose short films of the recent Olympiad were being collected into a single theatrical release. He tried to propose to each director what he thought music might do for their particular segment. But it was tough to get traction with any of his ideas. Mai Zetterling decided on no music at all for her section on Olympic weight lifters as did Arthur Penn for his slow-motion meditation on pole vaulters. Milos Foreman wanted only Bavarian folk music, a little Debussy, and a little Beethoven for his decathlon tribute. Indeed, for the first thirty-five minutes of *Visions of Eight* there were maybe two minutes of Mancini music (a light pop piece for studio brass with electric organ accents as we tour the buildings and tourist haunts of Olympic Village, then a rendition of his main "Salute to the Olympians"). Finally, in Michael Pfleghar's section on women competitors, music enters the scene—in this case, a surprisingly humorous 7/4-metered jazz-pop piece for flute and saxes with a fast, light tapping rhythm behind it underlining shots of the women track athletes warming up for their sprints and mile runs. Music that follows the race starter's pistol seems misjudged, though, its frantic, frivolous tone almost seeming to ridicule the scene as though the runners were now pawns in some cartoon. And similarly weak is Mancini's reactive music to the segment honoring that year's young girl gymnasts. In 1972's Olympics the all-around point leader was Ludmilla Tourischeva. American audiences watching on television took to her and her pixie grins, and Mancini translated her graceful femininity down to a sentimental piano theme. But as a theme it seems contrived (a ploy to remind people of the "Love Theme from *Romeo and Juliet*"?) and certainly catches none of her manifest skills on the gym floor.

The best segment for Mancini music in *Visions of Eight*, then, turns out to be the Claude Lelouch essay on "The Losers," first looking at unsuccessful boxers, bikers, horsemen, and swimmers, then in a second section watching a series of Olympic wrestlers brought down to the mat by triumphant opponents having to swallow their pride, their hopes, and all that training. Mancini composed a downcast, long-lined Bach-like *lacrimoso*. As Lelouch has cut together five minutes of different wrestlers in pain, disgruntlement, defeat, and humiliation, Mancini's steady, flowing lament continues (clarinet, then oboe, then electric harpsichord solo over strings), not so much in protest as in sympathy. The large string orchestra rises impassioned and contrapuntal as the scene intensifies; one wrestler, in pain and exhausted, tries to stand and limps off beside a medic, who, as the hulking athlete sags and begins to collapse, picks him up in both arms like a pieta and carries him away. And that same music informs the desperate doggedness of the last wrestler, who, having wrecked his knee, keeps getting up, falling, getting back into the match, and falling again. We, like gods slightly elevated over the event, are amazed at such determination. In the end the referee declares the match over, and the winner walks off, arm in arm with the loser, out of the ring, like brothers. Mancini gives a blessing on them both by ending his sad cue with a peaceful major-key chord. It is a sequence that proves that even in such an unfocused period of Mancini's evolution, he could still score to the point if the situation on screen carried its own dramatic possibilities, its own narrative authority. All he wanted was a strong storyteller with whom to collaborate.

And so when a call came in from the great director Alfred Hitchcock's office, asking Mancini about music for his new suspense thriller, to be called *Frenzy* (1975), it felt like a real deliverance. So many of the scores for past Hitchcock films had become famous in their own right. What could Mancini conjure up for him, even beyond his own *Night Visitor* sounds?

Frenzy would be Hitchcock's first film produced in his native London in twenty years. He had just experienced two major film failures, directing *Torn Curtain* (1966) and *Topaz* (1969), each of which had died at the box office and, as examples of the famous "Hitch" style, had felt cranky and phony. It was whispered that his notions about suspense had become old-fashioned and that he could never satisfy the more tightly coiled baby boomer generation. François Truffaut, after his famous series of interviews with Hitchcock was published, talked about the powerful pressures to which Hitch was being subjected to "update" his style and that for once he was allowing studios like Universal to influence him. They told him which stars to hire, which cameramen. They doctored his scripts, and, most forcefully of all, they had rejected out of hand the huge, roaring, "old-fashioned" orchestral score composed for *Torn Curtain* by longtime collaborator Bernard Herrmann. Benny Herrmann had scored all of Hitch's most famous films—*North by Northwest, Vertigo, Psycho*—in his highly personal, stringent, provocative style modeled on Richard Wagner and Anton Webern. His score for *Torn Curtain* was considered too ponderous and oppressive, especially during those days when Mancini's lighter scores were selling thousands of records (and were responsible for selling movie tickets as well), bringing extra publicity to their studios. What they said they wanted was a brighter score for *Torn Curtain*, something with "themes," and Hitch, feeling vulnerable in his own career at that time, caved in. It ended the long association between him and the cantankerous Herrmann. British composer John Addison, famous for rousing patriotic war scores like the music for *Cockleshell Heroes* (1955) and infectious pastiche period scores like *Tom Jones* (1963), did the replacement music for Hitch—with "themes." French composer Maurice Jarre did an obediently glittery score for *Topaz*.

Universal Studios agreed to contract for *Frenzy* only with a list of stipulations attached: Hitchcock would shoot the film in fifty-five days with second-string British actors; it must be done in color—no "artsy" black-and-white; and for the music score they wanted someone exploitable. So in the end Mancini's name had come up not, as he had hoped, because of his recent "serious" work, but because of his previous reputation for lighter "*Charade*-like" suspense music.

In his own autobiography Mancini reports that the discussions between himself and Hitchcock seemed clear—he thought he understood what was wanted. *Frenzy* was the story by Anthony Shaffer of an ordinary Londoner (Barry Foster) who becomes the unwitting suspect in a series of sexually motivated necktie murders across the city and now must clear himself. The opening shot of the film under the main titles is from a helicopter moving down the sunny River Thames through London, floating like a stately royal passage past the Houses of Parliament and the Tower Bridge. Mancini wrote what amounted to a Bachian organ andante, opening in D minor, for organ and an orchestra of strings and brass and expressive of the weight and formality of the gray London landmarks as well as of the slightly suspicious relationship between studio and director. Had Mancini felt freer there would have been more movement and expressivity in the music; as it was, he seems a bit intimidated by the presence (and silence) of Hitchcock on the project and, hoping not to offend, fails to engage him at all. The director came to every recording session of Mancini's score and, though noncommittal, nodded approvingly so that Mancini proceeded piece by piece, still elated by the prospect of having a Hitchcock film on his resume.

But then somewhere between the dubbing sessions (laying the recorded music tracks onto the film and watching them blend with the picture) and Hitchcock's increasingly tense meetings with Universal representatives, Mancini got the word that his score was being phased out and then rejected altogether. Word came down that the music was too dark, too "down." From his own private lair, and still smarting from his rejected score, Herrmann snapped something to the effect that Mancini had given them "pseudo-Herrmann" whereas what Hitchcock had wanted was pseudo-Mancini. Unaware of the studio's desire for a less melodramatic score, Mancini had been working here to further develop his formal orchestral suspense writing with a decidedly British air this time, but it was just what Universal executives did not want.

Crestfallen at the wreckage before him, Mancini was also genuinely puzzled. Hitch had verbally agreed with Mancini's stated approach and then suddenly, apparently, had turned away. For one thing, Mancini believed his score sounded nothing like Herrmann, and, for another, the music that was brought in to replace Mancini by lightweight British composer Ron Goodwin (*Those Magnificent Men in Their Flying Machines* [1965], *Battle of Britain* [1969]) seemed often incongruous with the film itself. That *cannot* be what Hitch had wanted all along, he marveled.

It is strange to see *Frenzy* now, to hear how Goodwin's main title music makes the same stately royal processional approach down the River Thames as Mancini had taken except that it is in a major key (perhaps therefore lighter) and minus an organ. It makes the ongoing footage play rather like a London travelogue. The first music cue after that follows the main character, who has just been fired from his job, down an ordinary working-class street lined with delivery lorries, produce crates, and passersby. Inexplicably the music is bright and glittery, full of trumpets and glockenspiel as though RAF Spitfires were returning triumphantly from the air war over Europe. Was Mancini's scoring rejected for this? According to Goodwin, quoted by his good friend Mancini, Hitchcock had asked him for "sparkling early morning music with no hint of the horrors to come."[10]

Truffaut relates how pale and drawn Hitchcock was before *Frenzy* had its premiere at Cannes, knowing he had been through two failures so recently—

then how rejuvenated and relieved he was when the film won praise.[11] It was that kind of fear that had caused him to bow to the studio's blind vision of a "lighter" score in the first place. The irony was that Mancini was now being second-guessed for being too dark, too symphonic after having been criticized for being too light, too popular before. The *Frenzy* debacle was a painful topic for years to come.

Mancini flew back home to Hollywood and figured he might as well take a call from that other industry that had been such a big part of his resume and that was pursuing him again now: television.

Henry's parents, Quinto and
Anna Mancini (ca. 1920s).

Fishing for compliments from
his critical father. Henry around
age thirteen (ca. 1935).

The young Henry
with his parents
in West Aliquippa,
Pennsylvania.

Portrait of
Mancini's musical
and personal
mentor in
Pittsburgh, Max
Adkins (1939).

Mancini in the
Army Air Corps
band until called
overseas as the
war heats up; photo
taken in France
(ca. 1942–1945).

Wartime winds down.

Mancini's parents at the wedding of Henry and Ginny (Feb. 13, 1947).

Tex Beneke hired Mancini as pianist, then as orchestrator/arranger for his postwar big band, 1947–1952.

Ginny's singing career with the Mello-Larks: Ginny, Bob Smith,
Jack Biermann, Tommy Hamm (ca. 1940s).

With *Peter Gunn* star, Craig Stevens, and costar Lola Albright checking a tune at the piano for use at Gunn's favorite hangout, the jazz club called Mother's (ca. late 1950s).

Where Dad works. The Mancini kids entertain themselves (ca. late 1950s).

Checking the sound against the sense of a score (ca. late 1950s).

With Blake Edwards (ca. 1960s).

By the early 1960s, after hits like the *"Peter Gunn* Theme"
and "Moon River," everyone was trying to get Mancini's attention.

Orderly as always
with deadlines
pinned to the
wall, Mancini
contemplates
his current
assignment
(ca. 1962).

Mancini with Johnny Mercer and producer Martin Jurow
around the time of *Days of Wine and Roses* (1962).

New Year's Eve 1965: Henry, Ginny, Felice, Chris, Monica.

Always a favorite
with Audrey Hepburn;
Mancini visits the set of
Wait Until Dark (1967).

The family, making it through the 1970s: Felice, Henry, Ginny, Monica, Chris.

After Johnny Mercer's passing, Mancini's most rewarding lyricist partner was the British hit maker Leslie Bricusse.

Mancini helped launch Quincy Jones's career in
Hollywood; here with Lionel Ritchie (ca. 1980s).

Film scoring is all about coordination, recording a music cue while the
scene is actually being projected behind the musicians (ca. 1970s).

Blake Edwards brings back Peter Sellers in *Return of the Pink Panther* (1975).

Conducting Julie Andrews in one of his best songs, "It's Easy to Say" (June 10, 1979).

At Edwards's chalet in Gstaad, Switzerland: Leslie Bricusse, Tony Adams, Henry, Ginny, Blake, Julie (Oct. 1993).

Dinner in Malibu, family time (ca. 1980s).

Henry and Ginny, one of Hollywood's rare enduring marriages.

CHAPTER 10

Back to Television?

Like any workingman returning from a business trip overseas, Mancini had a lot of mail, untaken calls, and business proposals waiting for him when he came back from his London debacle. His still strong sense of ambition and the disciplined need to keep busy, an anxiety perhaps inspired by his father's skepticism and his own family responsibilities, kept him searching for new outlets for his music. He also wanted to continue his progress with narrative scoring. Surprisingly, the most cordial offers he was getting now, the jobs with the most leeway for original scoring, were coming from television—TV movies and series pilots that promised to leave him free to score as he pleased. One guy even offered to give Mancini his own TV series on which to discuss and demonstrate film music to a syndicated audience. That was an opposite direction to a "serious" scoring career, but tempting, all the same.

Undertaking the series, to be called *The Mancini Generation*, was a colossal commitment. The music materials were drawn from his whole backlog of arrangements alongside some new charts, but in addition to the musical rehearsals there were camera rehearsals and host-segment preparations all of which were shot together during one four-week period and then sliced up for insertion into the shows. An applause track was piped in to simulate a real audience. Unique to each show was a sequence during which Mancini invited one college student enrolled in a film course at some university across the country to take a past Mancini recording and conceive, shoot, and edit an experimental film based on the music. The short films, then, were shown on the program, and Mancini used the opportunity to push support for film and film-scoring study courses in schools of the future. The effort involved in screening and presenting those films eventually led Mancini to establish a perennial scholarship in his name to aid promising film music students.

The Mancini Generation was eventually seen on 150 stations nationwide and also led to an RCA album sporting the series title, his first jazz-pop album since the 1960s. Together again, for the show and the album, were many of the players from Mancini's band in those days: Dick Nash, Jimmy Rowles (now on keyboards and ARP synthesizer), Victor Feldman on percussion, Bud Brisbois on trumpet. The arrangements were pure swing charts—some aggressive like Basie, some jaunty and humorous with complex wind harmonies or baroque touches, some bluesy and warm. Like each big band album before, Mancini attempted to create a singular sound palette for this one, consciously updating the genre again. Indeed there is a sense of joy in the arrangements and in the choice of band material. Traditionally, swinging tracks like "Eager Beaver," "Killer Joe," or "Swinging Shepherd Blues" are built on sophisticated close harmonies in the brass. The funkier tracks resort to the electric bass and wa-wa guitar effects, but, working together with layered thick brass chords and bass flute-bottomed ensembles, the blend is a happy one. And the album opener, the supercharged theme Mancini wrote for the *Generation* TV series itself, is a good example of his desire to blend a big band tradition with something contemporary. Its main motto is a piercing urgent phrase for two piccolos over a syncopated beat that was half funk, half Charleston, all introduced by a rather startling two-bar run up the chromatic scale on the ARP synthesizer programmed to sound somewhere between a mellow cat's meow and the siren of some emergency vehicle in the city. It was meant to be attention-grabbing, like a fanfare, for Mancini knew that a TV theme must be recognizable and memorable inside of ten seconds. But from today's perspective it is not such an intriguing sound—in fact, we are relieved when it stops.

There lies the one problem with Mancini's relationship to electronics in general during this time and with the *Mancini Generation* album in particular: the incongruity, sometimes even absurdity, of those fledgling synthesizers he chose to apply to his otherwise charismatic arrangements. Always searching for new sounds, he approached the whole range of synths before experience could match ambition. "I think electronics are definitely with us," he said contemporaneously.

There was a tendency in the beginning, especially in TV scoring, to go pretty heavy on it. But I think it's getting back. It's quite interesting. Electronics can be very helpful at times. You just have to know the nature of the sound you want. . . . The hardest thing is to find out what these things can do. So I'm constantly listening and getting demonstrations of the various instruments to find out how I can use them. . . . But then sometimes I listen back to the electronic sounds I used in the beginning, and I wonder, what the hell was that? What was I thinking?[1]

Mancini's daughter Monica later expanded on this subject:

Yeah, in those years a lot of electronics were coming into the scoring business, and he was trying like crazy to keep up with all that stuff. He'd have a guy come over with this whole synth setup, and he was trying to really get into that. But, you know, his heart was really with big orchestras and hiring musicians—having all those guys in the studio and being one of the guys. He loved just hanging with the musicians; there was an energy in the room. With just a couple of guys on synth keyboards to work with, it was all less personal.[2]

One bridge score (released theatrically but done by TV guys) that relies on electronics, has a consistent architecture, but is also in a jazz-pop style was written for the caper film produced by TV executive Norman Lear called *The Thief Who Came to Dinner* (1973). Ryan O'Neal plays an inept computer technician who reformats himself into a jewel thief. Rather than protest the loss of the traditional resonant string bass as the bottom line of all orchestras and the driving force of jazz-pop, and rather than fight the insurgence of the electric bass into pop and multimedia music, here Mancini dedicates a whole score to it and gives it narrative authority. The score sits coolly between funk and pop, between electronics (electric bass, keyboards, organ, and ARP) and a traditional brass/sax band. Its funk bass line is stated as a solo that not merely counterpoints the main theme but also practically represents a mini-melody in itself. Then the quirky sound of the ARP and organ together quote the main tune over that bass line: a minor-key chromatic theme with built-in diminished seventh and leaps of the fifth followed by thick, complex brass harmonies that make up the bridge. There is also a Bacharach-like syncopation to the phraseology of the brass that is a further clue to the unique direction Mancini was trying to explore here. In a sense, this is just another "ethnicity" he was attempting to voice: the 1970s funk movement. He uses the slow-funk bass line both to mark time underneath the movie's main jewel-heist sequence and, as mentioned before, to be a story-leading motto in itself. For the "love interest" character, Laura (Jacqueline Bisset), muted strings and electric Yamaha keyboard play a pleasant passive melody, more like a nice bit of jazz noodling than a real theme.

And all the while in this mid-1970s era, Mancini was using this whole ongoing synthesizer debate as an excuse to help his son become increasingly involved in the music business. Chris was twenty-four by then, fluent on all kinds of guitars, and educating himself to the capabilities of a widening bank of synthesizers. His father hired him, formally, to program both ARP and Moog keyboards on several of his albums and television projects from this period. Their sounds were less eccentric under Chris's programming know-how. With Chris's help, Mancini was able to dash off no less than seven new logo opening themes for TV series using various combinations of acoustic instruments and synthesizers. For a short-lived series based on H. G. Wells's *The Invisible Man*, Mancini's main theme is typical: a double-time tramping ostinato and a legato (*alla breve*) synth melody in minor fifths and sevenths over it. A trilling two-note gesture in the winds hints at the elusive title character.

For the NBC Network News Division he composed two themes. The theme for its coverage of the 1976 presidential elections (Jimmy Carter's year) modeled itself on a colonial-era fife-and-drum minuteman march with two horns carrying the strong patriotic melody. Network executives liked it so much they resurrected it again in four years for their "Decision '80" election coverage (the beginning of Reagan's reign). The other theme for NBC was the logo music for their nightly newscast. There, two sets of rock-synth tom-toms and organ alternate quick figures behind a flugelhorn theme (urgent and fateful sounding in minor sevenths as in the theme to *Hatari!*) that never resolves but merely sets up the real-life drama for the news anchor to deliver each night. Rightfully, Mancini criticized this latter theme, saying that it took too many seconds to state its motto, whereas a TV theme, particularly a news-imperative logo, ought to finish in, at most, two bars (his took six).

And back to entertainment television, it can be said that Mancini never wrote a more jovial, genial TV theme than the up-tempo funk fete for E♭ clarinet, saxes, harmonica, organ, and synths for the syndicated black family sitcom *What's Happening!*—nor a more bluesy torch song than the theme he wrote for the short-lived TV series *The Blue Knight*, about the nightly adventures of a weary, middle-aged cop on the beat. But scoring TV movies, not just series opening themes, was Mancini's main employment during this period. Most distinctive of all, perhaps, was the score he wrote for *The Mon-*

eychangers, a baby boomer mini–soap opera based on a pulp novel by Arthur Hailey set among the elite power players of the banking industry. In it Kirk Douglas and Christopher Plummer play good-versus-evil contenders for the presidency of a conglomerate bank once the current chief has announced his retirement. A small embezzlement scandal, a bank bombing, a cash-strapped, no-confidence run on one of the local branches, wheeling and dealing, and betrayals behind the vault doors and after banker's hours are just some of the subplots in this primetime potboiler. Alex Vandervoort (Douglas's character) has a mentally institutionalized wife and a mistress. Roscoe Heyward (Plummer's character) has a shifty nephew and an unscrupulous personal ambition. The biggest question for any composer would be how to help such purple material retain a little dignity and how to make the banking industry sound exciting as a setting for a six-and-a-half-hour television melodrama broadcast over several nights.

Mancini's main title music for *The Moneychangers* combines electric keyboard, an electric bass, and the active string section playing an accented bass line in D minor (eight to the bar but with an eighth rest and a quarter note to give an unpredictable urgent feeling). Then it introduces the broad, stately melody in strings; switches to 5/8 time in F major; then one bar in 4/4; then 5/8 bars working their way up the scale until they can reconnect with D minor and a final strong restatement of the main theme in the strings (now with complex brass chords sliding in underneath like those chromatic harmonies learned in *The Thief Who Came to Dinner*). Some baroque piccolo trumpet embellishment seems to invoke the banking industry's fastidious obsession with codes, percentages, procedures, and counting—the royal rituals of capitalism. Now, for the next five minutes (and these are long stretches of music considering the quick pulse of television time), as we watch one bank opening for business—the deactivation of the time-lock doors, the introduction of Edwina Darcy (Alexis Smith) as branch manager, the armored car arrival delivering denominations of cash, the daily teller assignments—Mancini can keep that opening counterpoint going and, through use of extensions and inversions, draw the main title's musical material into the storytelling. And his main theme can still soar to the fore whenever some of this early dialogue allows.

With these elements established during the broadcast's first ten minutes, Mancini can now develop a linear score that follows the drama. While the lofty sound of the brass choir may represent the forces of corporate power, those pulsing strings can invigorate the intrigues of the Hailey novel. And meanwhile hard thirds and fourths give the whole score a kind of modal distancing feeling, as though the financial jousts of modern investment banking were not so far removed from the land grabs and tribe takeovers of the white man's treaty days with the American Indians. This is not to say Mancini was thinking of western films when he was writing *The Moneychangers'* counterpoint bass line, but he was at least channeling the same message of warning against the dangers of ruthless ambition and the timeless power of wealth to corrupt.

Muted strings and a soft electric keyboard are assigned the few romantic fireside scenes between Alex and his mistress—a modest theme of pale color that need not be too assertive or memorable. For the young teller Juanita Nunez, a Hispanic single mother, there is a retiring, lightly Latin motif, less a melody than a back harmony. Here Mancini is wisely alert to the fact that a true song or theme would give too much weight to such a minor character, so he provides just coloration for her music that is recognizable but safely assimilated into the rest of the scoring. The same goes for the childlike celesta motif for Alex's visits to his hospitalized wife. Her nervous breakdown has left her fixated on memories of the old days, alternately wistful and hysterical. Her music approaches these visits with a tea-party delicacy. When Alex talks to others about his wife's "hopeless" condition, Mancini's solo French horn harkens back to the lost couple of *The Days of Wine and Roses.* We also hear the solo horn when the outgoing bank president announces to the board that he is dying, that he has no son to whom his bank can be passed, and that he wants the board to choose his successor. Soon there will be an even sadder theme introduced as the misguided Roscoe watches the old president depart but only dreams of his own promotion.

One other major scoring moment in *The Moneychangers* is the march of the auditors. Manager Edwina Dorsey asks for outside experts to examine some staff accounts in her branch, looking for irregularities, and headquarters sends over a whole team of smart-suited, briefcase-toting audit department trouble-shooters who almost seem to march in step through the front doors. The humorous sight of them descending on the bank one morning like ducklings in a row is scored with a gently teasing military march—strings, electric bass, snare drum in dotted rhythms behind flutes and oboes first, then flugelhorns—deflating the self-importance of all bureaucrats and their rigid belief that efficiency is next to godliness. To be fair to the accounting profession, though, we should report that the visit of those auditors *does* turn up some major embezzlement within the bank as well as Roscoe's role in a later cover-up. So Alex Vandervoort gets the board's nod to become president and vows to fund a housing project that will help people like Juanita; meanwhile he decides to move in with his mistress to experience a little happiness while his wife remains hopelessly out of reach.

"Unrepentant melodrama" is the phrase to describe *The Moneychangers*, and yet it remains one of Mancini's most confident and satisfying scores for television film. Such storytelling music may have drawn his attention away from the art of personal melody composing and songwriting, but it had broadened his vocabulary, his awareness, and, importantly, his maturity. Only a few assignments in the next few years would engage that newfound fluency, but all would be influenced by it.

* * *

Two subsequent TV films had more personal scores, their stories being about old age and the life passages for a couple of middle-class American families. Of course this was also a time when the Mancinis were still spending a lot of evenings talking about what to do with their own family passages, specifically Chris's situation. For it was just now that Chris, twenty-six, "informed us," as Mancini would later describe the moment, that he and his girlfriend, Julie, were expecting a baby. The young couple had met when both were attending the Judson School in Arizona, and again, as Mancini tells it, neither of them had yet "established a career."[3] As early as 1974, Mancini had gotten Chris various music-related jobs around Hollywood, but it was not steady work, and with a son on the way, how would Chris navigate fatherhood? He would seem to have no time left for what should have been his main concentration: working out a career path for himself. And because he had grown up somewhat pushed aside by the intense celebrity and success of the Mancini gravy train (even when he had gone along on his father's concert tours to see the world), he had not developed a sense of how to assist himself—except through youthful repudiations like rock music and school rebellion. Now in his twenties, he was still trying to network and lay down a root system. As a talented musician with an insider's experience of the business, he was able to work on other people's albums, with sharp, intelligent rockers like Frank Zappa and sophisticated jazz-funk proponents like Herbie Hancock. And he kept writing his own songs and playing with a series of hometown LA bands. Still as disciplined and orderly as ever, Henry was worried that once the baby (to be christened Christopher Michael) was born, he would not be properly looked after or, conversely, that the child's parents would be professionally handicapped by having to raise a child at this time. Henry and Ginny began talking about a plan to set things right.

By chance, then, those two TV movies that Mancini had decided to score next were both middle-age-transition stories about families at a crossroads. *A Family Upside Down*, dramatizing the midlife couple who have to begin taking care of elderly parents, has a greeting-card sentimentality about it, so much of the scoring is light and obvious. Ted and Emma Long are the elderly couple who, after Ted's heart attack, have to give up their home, her garden, and his freedom and move in with his son. The main selling points of this TV movie are its cast: Fred Astaire and Helen Hayes play the Longs and, of course, lend their roles a whole lifetime worth of conviction, believability, and charisma. The script has them quaintly humming tunes together like "Daisy, Daisy" and "My Ragtime Gal," the latter becoming a quote in the score. Mancini's main theme—always lightly, almost gingerly scored for celesta and oboe against a few strings—is as elementary as one of those parlor songs, as timid as a guilty son visiting his parents' old-age rest home. Sometimes it feels like a nursery waltz, a little embarrassed with itself, other times just polite and deferential. The quick bridge of the tune is taken by the harpsichord-like patch of a Yamaha keyboard.

The film touches just the surface of the generational collision—how the young grandkids have to curtail their energies now that Grandma Emma is living with them, how discouraged old Ted gets when he has to go without her into hospice care. "I wish I was cooking for you again," Emma tells him, but he replies that he can only eat saltless bran mush anyway. The score moves between reprises of the wistfully well-meaning main theme, reminders of "My Ragtime Gal" and some mild wind/strings scene setups and transitions. Ted's own son (Efrem Zimbalist Jr.) observes the irony of the fact that he has to transport his father up the stairs now as his father had once carried him. "It's all turned upside down now," he says, amazed, and it must have brought up memories for Mancini of his own father, who had not been invited into the family household but had lived alone close by in a mobile home community during the early struggling days of Mancini's career in Hollywood. But guilt was a theme too complex for real discussion in a television movie like this one. Ted and Emma, meanwhile, have their own farewells to cope with, leaving the garden of their old home, old friends dying. The film raises but does not linger over these issues. They are quickly countered by a happier picnic scene or some words of encouragement. It would have been wrong of Mancini's score to dig deeper. There is a new theme for the picnic sequence—a light, uncommitted melody with a kind of skipping rhythm and another quoting of "My Ragtime Gal" to reference the old couple's ageless rapport. Once

Ted is forced to install an elevator chair that attaches to the home banister and bears him up the flight of steps without straining his heart and he playfully drives it up and down, Mancini scores him with a winds/strings jazz waltz that sounds like one of those 1950s screen musicals that could have starred Astaire himself.

There are a few darker musical moments: the main theme is played in a minor key by a string trio when Ted protests feeling powerless ("All I can do is watch other people do things") while string tremolos, deep piano chords, and chromatic washes surround the scene of his heart attack. Oboe and clarinet solos temper the incident from being too scary or harsh for primetime TV. And there *was* a certain terror involved in watching these two iconic actors playing fragile old people going through taxing performances that actually *could* exhaust or endanger them. (In reality, Astaire lived another active ten years after winning an Emmy Award for this role, and Hayes worked nearly fifteen years beyond this project, so they were not at all frail, even though the score, as we have said, seemed cautious in their presence.) But probably Mancini was right in the end—he measured the girth and depth of the film by itself, and his music delineated it well enough.

The Best Place to Be starred Donna Reed as a widow whose husband has just died and who now must redefine her own existence and sense of self. Again we have a thin-spirited TV melodrama using an aging veteran star with a script quietly serious about the issues it represents but unprepared to explore them in any fundamental way—these are what are called, for better or worse, "women's magazine stories." Mancini knows outright that the music must be gentle, transparent, and intimate so as not to interfere with the television surface of the film. Nevertheless, here he treats Donna Reed's character, the widow Sheila Callahan née Price, with great respect but also seems to engage her at some personal level with sensitive and sustained music like he had resisted in the previous TV movie. Maybe this one was just easier to score because it was really about old love/new love, not old age/new fears. The two films shared the same glossy style, sharing also Efrem Zimbalist Jr., this time as Sheila's new man.

The opening theme of *The Best Place to Be* is poised between a couple of shifting Yamaha piano chords wanting to resolve but unable to do so. The first strong cue, watching Sheila's husband having an affair shortly before his death, is a long one and modulates non-thematically among poppish chords with Fender Rhodes electronic piano highlights, phrases for solo winds, and the sustained notes of the Yamaha—unresolved chord progressions again, roaming chromatically and pausing and turning.

Sheila receives a visit from the authorities and is told about her husband's passing. She tries to absorb the news and begins, more mechanically than bravely, making all the arrangements that one must at such a time. But it is as we hear her voice-over narration in the aftermath ("Why, why can't I cry?") that the score begins to find its voice. Mancini establishes a kind of piano mantra that appears whenever she is alone and has to find the center of her emotions somewhere in herself. Over this half-troubled, half-consoling mantra figure, flute, then clarinet, then Fender keys, then high strings, precariously perched, play the "lost" theme. It is a moment of real feeling, perhaps because it is not gushing with emotion but holding back in search of calm. That piano mantra is actually just another example of Mancini counter-lines at work supporting a main theme. Without being a theme, Sheila's mantra often speaks for her here. As seriously intended dramatic scoring, Mancini's strings capitulate into his familiar searching, chromatic phraseology; a flute roams up the scale to where the piano mantra enters again as Sheila remembers married life and compares it to her nights alone now. She curses her late husband for his infidelities and for his dying. In these quick voice-over lines, the script is running through all the archetypical therapeutic stages of mourning that a survivor goes through.

Sheila's new beau (Zimbalist) is a journalist who has written a book on the innocent victims of the conflict in Northern Ireland. His work inspires an Irish-flavored theme to appear in the score, while their relationship rates another new tune, whose piano arpeggio outlines each chord in the melody in the manner of a pop romantic concerto. Music is given pride of place in this TV film, mixed well forward and given a chance to be heard. Ultimately Sheila recognizes that the best place to be is centered in herself, neither dependent behind her first husband nor independent in isolation, but interdependent—strong inside but engaged outside as well. Unison strings with keyboard/brass lock in the happy ending curtain-closing chord with perhaps a questioning seventh interval mixed in there, the voice of maturity.

That same maturity, that same evolving variety of tonalities informed the TV score Mancini wrote in 1980 for director Paul Newman's filmed version of the Tony Award/Pulitzer Prize–winning play by Michael Cristofer, *The Shadow Box*, a chamber drama about three couples staying at a country hospice for cancer patients—one working-class pair, one erudite scholar and his alienated wife, and the sad adult daughter of a failing elderly mother. Reading the play and watching it in the theater, Newman could see how the right tonality of music might help such a film in the same way that subtle lighting can help on stage—sometimes spotting a character, sometimes just adding a glow. In each of these couples, one person has come here to die. We get to know them by eavesdropping on their conversations and occasionally by sitting in as one offscreen doctor interviews them for a videotape archive. Cristofer makes no value judgments on the past lives that his characters reveal or on the best ways to face their imminent deaths. The working-class wife avoids talking about her husband's condition; she tells him to quit this place and come back home with her, as though that will change his diagnosis. He is trying to warn her against such wishful thinking, encouraging her instead to live for and appreciate the here and now. Meanwhile, in another hospice cabin, the very articulate chatter of the scholar is being challenged by a visit from his ex-wife. They nag and joke and scold each other—he having used words all his life instead of emotions, she having used drink—when what they both are, especially now, is afraid. Fear is at the heart of the third couple, too—a desperate old woman and her caretaker daughter. Together they maintain the fantasy story that the beloved daughter/sister Claire will be coming home soon, though she has been long dead. Their lament is not of time wasted but of lost times.

There is no opening or closing music in *The Shadow Box*. But Mancini's main theme, encompassing the idea of time, is introduced after a few minutes as the various off-site family members arrive at the hospice for their visits. That music has a regular meter like a grandfather clock, the wistful universal interplay between two chords on the Fender Rhodes, then a tender oboe (perhaps synth-sampled) takes the theme—a tentative melody that seems to hover around, rather than directly address, the subject of death and loss. There is a particular quality, delicate and aloof, to Mancini's whole score here: it seems to enter only when characters cannot find words, in the silences, the gaps between what they meant to say. The Fender Rhodes, the oboe, a small group of other winds, harp, and a few strings are all that Mancini applies to this film. And even when they play, they barely assert themselves—like a good physician's reassurances when a patient is still processing the prognosis. This is what is meant by composer maturity. The whole brief score to *The Shadow Box* is as clean and efficient as the hospice suites where these ordinary people have come to die, but there is some kind of truth in there that keeps the human element alive. Mancini could not have written so knowing a score in earlier days. He had always written honest and earnest music, at his best, but by now he had refined his language down to a few clean strokes, employing both his mature sense of internal continuity and the new tonalities.

— — —

Mancini's biggest television scoring commission ever, though, was certainly the more than two hours of music he would be contributing to a sprawling four-night, ten-hour network miniseries, *The Thorn Birds*. David L. Wolper and Stan Margulies (*Visions of Eight*) were the producers this time, and they would make this the second most-watched such broadcast in TV history, behind their own front-runner of the 1970s, *Roots*. The locale of *The Thorn Birds* was a wide Australian sheep ranch called Drogheda in New South Wales as set forth in Colleen McCullough's original 1977 novel. Described as half soap opera, half Greek tragedy, the story presents the Cleary family, who run Drogheda: matriarch Mary Cleary (played to the limit by veteran Barbara Stanwyck); Paddy (Richard Kiley); and the youngest Cleary daughter, Meggie (Rachel Ward). Into the predictable rhythms of ranch life and the clannish Cleary melodrama comes the district priest, Fr. Ralph de Bricassart (played by the most successful miniseries star of the time, Richard Chamberlain). Father Ralph is immediately enchanted by the child Meggie, and over the years as she grows up he becomes gradually swayed by and obsessed with her. *The Thorn Birds* then becomes the pulp-fiction story of a priest's "forbidden love," or rather his crisis of conscience as his fast-rising career in the church leads toward becoming a cardinal. He starts out merely musing about Meggie—"Why do you tug at my heart so?"—and ends up ten hours later tormented, admitting, "My punishment is never to be certain again that I love God more than you." For all the ranching, the romancing, sin and sacrilege, guilt and gratification its story covers, and while earnest and compelling in a matinee-drama sort of way, *The Thorn Birds* is still formula entertainment. Mancini, perhaps in spite of himself (and for him it was the only job in town right then, so he was treating it very seriously), approached it formulaically. He created a cadre of themes to be closely associated with each major element of the story—a Drogheda theme; a theme for Meggie; one for the oversight authority of the Catholic Church; one for Meggie's beau, Luke (Brian Brown); one for the old age of Mary Cleary; and so forth. And like the drama itself, none of these themes is very sophisticated or deep to ponder.

Mancini's first task was to decide upon the best musical opening to the whole family saga. He was being told by the producers to write some big, expansive orchestral prelude to the score that would be expressive of the endless Australian landscape in ranch country such as this. Mancini went away and wrote a couple of different versions of that extroverted approach, big orchestral declarations, but, returning with the results, he agreed with everyone else that for some reason they did not work. They seemed to have been imported from some other film—too big for television and, in any case, missing the heart of the story. Instinctively, Mancini decided that two hammered dulcimers simply stating the folksy Drogheda theme were all that was really needed to provide the perfect opening for *The Thorn Birds.* Suddenly it all seemed right.

Throughout the series, music is, of course, used to underscore the emotional milestones of the story, but its main job is to escort (in that simple way that television requires) the storytelling on screen. Early shots of the sheep herding are scored not with the opening theme but with almost a square-dance two-step piece, highlighting the action rather than the setting. This piece is heard again later during a sheep-shearing contest. Father Ralph's first sight of the child Meggie is made to seem fateful and magical by the bell-like sound of glockenspiel and flute playing the painfully elementary "Meggie's Theme," a chaste but slightly doleful melody with an awkward sing-song quality to it. (In later years Mancini would exploit this tune in concert, because it was his one recent hit, beyond its actual worth as a stand-alone melody.) Yet when it reappears throughout the TV series as Father Ralph "goes wistful" about his growing love for Meggie, it gives instant recognition and sympathy to their interpersonal history together. Later in a love scene on the sands of Matlock Island, where priest and girl consort, it is featured without interference as a slick pop piano piece. More original are Mancini's gently affectionate cavatina for Meggie's relationship with the ranch hand Luke and the scoring of a runaway grass fire at Drogheda composed in the form of a somber processional at first, the basses then assuming a double-time running figure as the fire line expands.

For Mancini students, some of the purely functional cues heard in *The Thorn Birds* are more interesting than the TV-simple themes themselves: the Himmelhock sequence, where Meggie and Luke set out on what they hope will be their new life on a new ranch, features a striding, halting, rhythmic figure for winds and strings that speaks to both their mood of enterprise and the reality of their inexperience. And Father Ralph's dissertation on the fable of the thorn bird (which sings only as it dies, giving its life for that song, as it were) is scored closely, music rising and falling behind the telling.

The Thorn Birds eventually pulled tremendous viewer numbers, and its score was nominated for, but lost, a television Emmy Award. And because Mancini was between recording contracts, no soundtrack album of this music was issued until years after his death. In any case, it was all fairly simple music, trading depth for breadth, aware that it was all just an epic daydream story anyway. Perhaps it is best to just accept the music's smooth commercial language as a given; then one can settle back to appreciate its various pleasures and the way it graced a few nights of 1983 television.

— — —

Meanwhile, though, in the real world, Henry and Ginny made their decision about how to help son Chris. They decided to sort of adopt their grandson Christopher Michael into their home and into their middle-aged lives while their son searched for his own best place to be. "We redid Felice's bedroom as a nursery and hired a nanny," Mancini wrote in his autobiography. "Suddenly at the age of 52, Ginny and I found ourselves parenting again. It was not easy . . . [but] it was better for everyone. This left Chris and Julie free to work out their lives and at the same time it assured the boy stability and comfort."[+] To raise their grandson as a way to reach out to their own son was an act of love and maturity for Henry and Ginny. But it was also tricky. By that act Mancini was, in a way, reaching past his own son and taking over as perhaps Quinto might have done. So guilt was still an antagonist there.

But it seems other life events were reaching past Mancini, too, during this season of so much television work. He was not destined to remain a TV composer and a stay-at-home granddad forever. Instead, one chance meeting on the beach with Blake Edwards was about to bring a sea change and, as a direct result, a return to the famous—and in some ways confining—world of the Pink Panther.

CHAPTER 11

The Curse of the
Pink Panther

As Mancini describes in his autobiography, he and Ginny had rented a
beach house in Malibu. From the porch one midday he spotted Blake
Edwards walking out by the water. Years had gone by since they had spoken
seriously; Edwards was still embittered over his experience making *Darling
Lili* and still believed that Mancini had somehow sided with the studio to
second-guess him about the film's alleged weaknesses. He distrusted the
whole Hollywood system after that, especially when they recut and botched
his next (non-Mancini) film, *Wild Rovers* (1971). He began casting around
town for any film property he could reliably control. He certainly needed a
hit—even before *Wild Rovers* and *Darling Lili*, his late-1960s films like *The
Party, Gunn,* and the military farce *What Did You Do in the War, Daddy?* had
disappointed investors, and two subsequent titles, *The Carey Treatment* (1972)
and *The Tamarind Seed* (1974), were hardly triumphs. Somewhere in the midst
of all that, Edwards was hearing gossip to the effect that Peter Sellers's
career could certainly use a boost. Although Edwards had never thought of
continuing the Inspector Clouseau character beyond those two films from
ten years back, lately money men were starting to talk about a new deal, a
sequel's sequel. Perhaps it would not hurt for Edwards to return to one of
the big California studios, in this case United Artists, for discussions about
a possible new Clouseau project.

And so it was, in that same spirit of "maybe," that Edwards paused on the beach at Malibu when he saw Henry Mancini coming out of one of those rental houses and approaching him. Perhaps it would not hurt to listen. And Mancini needed to explain: how the *Darling Lili* studio had manipulated them both; how naïvely Mancini had chatted with studio reps about one film sequence or another; and how they had then rushed off tattling to Edwards about Mancini's supposed criticisms and saying that Mancini agreed with *them*, playing the two men off of each other in order to get their own way in the end. "So [on the beach] I got into it with [Blake]," Mancini later wrote, "and told him what had happened. I told him that I had been misquoted and used by the people from Head Office. The last thing I would do to Blake—or any director—is to second-guess him or go behind his back. It is not good professionally or morally. Blake and I straightened things out that day."[1]

Their timing was fortuitous, of course; if there was going to be a new Pink Panther film it had better be able to announce not only the return of "Edwards and Sellers together again" but also another exploitable music score by Mancini. *Return of the Pink Panther* was planned for distribution in 1975, and the public was so very ready to be amused all over again by the Sellers/Clouseau character that the success of that sequel was followed the very next year by *The Pink Panther Strikes Again*. For his part, Edwards brought a new sense of righteous anger that would inform all of his subsequent movies and in particular inflate his Panther slapstick style from the quiet personal absurdist stumblings and bumblings of the early entries to sometimes epic destructions and dismantlements of whole sets in later ones. As the series evolved, what had begun in the first Panther film as a side interest (the subtle eye for physical comedy gags and an ear for Clouseau's dumb deductions and defective detective work) grew in *A Shot in the Dark* to be the subject of the film: Inspector Clouseau and his foolishness. By 1975 Clouseau and Edwards were laboring in a much broader kind of comedy that seemed to prefer bigger falls, more outrageous gaffes, and louder explosions releasing tons of water, and resulting in mass humiliations for everyone around. The effect was often more boorish than humorous. But as it has been said, Edwards believed the best way to update the new Panther films was to upstage the old ones.

For Mancini, the task of scoring a Pink Panther movie had changed, too—the first film scored with that sly, sneaking sax theme and a lot of beguiling, equally sly cocktail music; the second film scored a bit more like a cartoon where the clever, plodding, main mystery theme on that wavering pump organ represented Clouseau's dysfunctional focus on the case at hand. Now with large-scale visual jokes taking up more screen space than the character comedy of Clouseau, the scoring needed to serve two masters: it needed scene-setting background tunes for clubs, discos, and resorts, and, more than ever, it needed bigger descriptive music to bolster the increasingly unrealistic and aggressive plot devices. In the first two films the crimes and gags as depicted were all at least plausible—a suave jewel thief, a love-jealous murderer, cover-ups and alibis and chases—only Clouseau's awkwardness and attempts to regain composure brought the laughs. In the new films the whole milieu seemed absurd. In *Return of the Pink Panther* Clouseau is seen hurtling through the air like a slow-motion kung-fu fighter defying the laws of physics. In *The Pink Panther Strikes Again* some sort of magic evil Panther-pink ray gun is able to make the United Nations building disappear. What had made the early Panther films funny was that Clouseau's pomposity and idiocy were played out in real circumstances. Now it was as if these Clouseau films had assumed the cartoon-crazy comedy style of those opening Panther animations. And in this awkward mix of purpose, Mancini's scoring even appears to break a major tenet of his avowed policy to stay musically silent when Peter Sellers as Clouseau was doing his long physical comedy routines on screen.

Among Mancini's main principles of comedy scoring was that funny music on top of a scene that is already working hard to be funny is redundant. And yet here in *The Pink Panther Strikes Again* we find he has created for the first time in the Panther series a theme for Inspector Clouseau himself. Mancini would say:

> Even in comedy, to me melody is very important, but to write a humorous melody, I've found, is not easy—something that is warm and humorous, but that doesn't say, "Here I am, look at me, I'm funny." I've gotten past playing wrong notes, or consecutive seconds, or anything obvious like that, except in exceptional circumstances where you're trying to exaggerate. But if you can find a simple humorous melody, it can really enhance the humor on screen. So here [in *The Pink Panther Strikes Again*] I did a little theme for Clouseau, a kind of French melody to lay very noncommittally behind some of his routines.[2]

A simpler piece it could not be: a slow 4/4 time with one tuba/trombone duo alternating with two marimba notes in thirds, four to the bar—a kind of oompah rhythm, then a dim-witted melody in A minor played with one finger on the electric keyboard and having a ridiculous tiptoe feeling to it, so intentionally pedantic and naïve that it actually *can* hang back behind the long sequence of Clouseau trying to get across a moat into a castle, dealing with a drawbridge and various swinging ropes, without attempting to catch any of the comic action. Yet even that indirect relationship between humor on screen and a "cute" theme on the soundtrack seems intrusive to us.

Surprisingly, both *Return of the Pink Panther* and *The Pink Panther Strikes Again* proved to be box-office smash hits, at once relieving and dismaying Blake Edwards, who might have wished for such attention paid to his more personal films. The sequels also served to bring back Mancini's "*Pink Panther Theme*" to renewed appreciation. And so, whether he wanted to get away or not, he found that a third Panther sequel, *Revenge of the Pink Panther* (1978), was going to keep him busy for a few weeks longer. This would prove to be the most awkward and arbitrary of the five Sellers/Clouseau comedies (and with the least-specific Mancini music). Because it takes place in the world of international heroin trafficking and mid-1970s nightclubbing, Mancini's update of the opening Panther theme this time sports a funky electric bass line and a shuffle rhythm. Everything in *Revenge of the Pink Panther* seems to be working toward a conclusion of the franchise. The very lack of plot, the lack of new business added to the Clouseau character and his own quieter nature in this film, the bringing on stage of the long-standing Cato character for a final bow, and, lastly, the more modest quality of the music score, all seem preparations for the series winding down. The story and score do head toward one final locale for a heroin crime, Hong Kong. There are comedy chases through the neon streets there, again stressing the styles of silent-film slapstick, slow-motion fights and crashes and multiple dunkings of people into various bodies of water—all the usual Edwards routines.

Mancini's Hong Kong music opens with big Charlie Chan–type chords in swirling strings, then becomes a high-energy Chinese romp. Elsewhere in the score a couple of shallow glamour tunes appear, dedicated to the character of Simone, but they are really just pop piano pieces swamped by electric slide guitars and overly plush string harmonies. Some critics praised Mancini for making these comedy scores into wordless musicals; others accused him of just trying to stock the film's anticipated soundtrack album with amiable tunes. A third interpretation suggests that his new attention to a fairly continuous narrative/ambient track, rather than bringing in a new tune, shows how far he had come from being a one-man-melody juke-box to becoming a film scorer seeking new opportunities for dramatic and descriptive scoring—not eschewing melody but putting it in its place. And that musical discretion extends to this film's last sight of Clouseau walking off down the road, cozily arm in arm with Dyan Cannon, like any normal couple, having solved his case and having been honored by the French government, chatting casually and with no slapstick gag attached. The score simply commiserates with them and lets the story (and apparently the whole Pink Panther franchise) play out with a fitting musical conclusion.

Mancini further developed this broader orchestral approach to comedy scoring in two new non-Edwards caper films from the late 1970s that were reminiscent of *Charade* yet did not rely on multi-melodic soundtracks. They were sophisticated murder mysteries at their core yet with whimsical main characters caught up in the intrigues. One was about murder in the kitchen with Jacqueline Bisset, *Who Is Killing the Great Chefs of Europe?* (1978), and the other was about murder on a runaway train, *Silver Streak* (1977).

Although the comedy/thriller genre of *Silver Streak* is not so far from the Panther films in kind, it seemed to need music scoring that was much more present, full, and active. A film like this relies on plot, and, musically, the train has to be up to speed as soon as it has left the station. Gene Wilder plays George Caldwell, a mild-mannered book editor traveling on the AMRoad line's Silver Streak train from Los Angeles to Chicago, and Jill Clayburgh is Hilly Burns, an art professor's assistant also on board. When her boss, Professor Shreiner, turns up dead, the plot begins. In the days of *Charade*, Mancini had scored using one central theme and then a whole gallery of individual, unrelated novelty pieces, savory dance tunes, and a few static suspense cues. By now, thirteen years later, Mancini's scoring methods are more integrated with the narrative. There is a casual, rather contrived love theme for George and Hilly, and a couple of club-car pieces, but the bulk of the score is a steady chugging rhythm over top of which sits the broader legato melody—a construction similar to *The Moneychangers'* theme. That theme is not only taken through a series of simple scenic alterations during the film but is also used as the basis of a number of solidly symphonic chase cues to propel the runaway train that is hurtling toward the film's climax. Here is functional music that acts both as drive for the action and suspension to stretch the tension, scoring that is not just marking time, as in the days of *Charade*, but is actually composed as an orchestral piece of music in its own right, albeit frantic and impulsive. Mancini is more confident now, certainly, perhaps also feeling more pushed by the orchestral writers around him to write bigger scores, witnessing the rise of John Williams as the composer of several recent symphonically sophisticated and aggressive scores for "disaster films" like *The Poseidon Adventure, The Towering Inferno*, and *Jaws*.

One other confident stroke of the *Silver Streak* score for Mancini is his improved skill at incorporating electronic sounds—keyboards, guitars, and synthesizers—into the standard orchestral blend. By now he is learning how to use the synths and tonal-pitch computers more subtly, more as a flavor than as a novelty, having listened to son Chris and having practiced on his own. This would become particularly important with the introduction of the Richard Pryor character, Grover Muldoon, who comes into the plot to help George solve the murder and dodge the murderer. For these two characters, the streetwise black man and the clueless white guy, Mancini adds some urban rock music for organ, electric bass, and synth keys heard throughout the caper to come. Late in the plot our familiar chugging rhythm, which has been friendly and toddling so far, begins to sound heavy and threatening, more like stalking as the passengers of the *Silver Streak* begin to realize that their train has no engineer (for he has been added to the murder list). The onrushing motion of the orchestra soon coalesces into a steady pounding vivace with brass punches and a driving bass line over shrill, trilling woodwinds as strings rise to meet the final crashing chords when "two hundred tons of locomotive goes smashing through Central Station on its way to Marshall Fields," as the script exclaims. By the fade-out, all crooks have been apprehended, and George and Hilly have become a couple. Electric keyboard and strings render Hilly's theme, still a bit insipid, but at least a pleasing send-off until the main train theme can return, restored to its original carefree chugging meter. Perhaps Mancini did assess this film's needs accurately. Both the sense of locomotion and the sense of predictability are features of the score he provided. It is good fluff that starts to be exciting but always pulls back from the edge, this being just a pleasure trip.

A more circumspect comedy/mystery followed for Mancini and inspired more original musical results while following the same formula of narrative orchestral writing within his melodic style. From the novel *Someone Is Killing the Great Chefs of Europe*, by Nan and Ivan Lyons, Warner Brothers Studios mounted a film version with the slightly more intriguing title, *Who Is Killing the Great Chefs of Europe?* The main character is Max Vandervere (played by Robert Morley), the erudite, caustically articulate, and humongously overweight editor of a gourmet magazine. He navigates his huge bulk like a great barge among the upper crust of London restaurateurs, seemingly always in motion on his way to another surprise visit at some unsuspecting culinary establishment to conduct a review, as ready to insult a chef as savor a sauce, as much cuisine police as cultural watchdog (he once fined a secretary for hiding a jar of peanut butter in her desk), dropping sarcasms, chides, and asides all across the city in his wake.

Mancini's score is perfectly fitted and instantly influential to its film. It opens with a baroque allegro for high piccolo trumpet set against a standard Haydnesque orchestra while on screen behind the main titles we see a series

of elegant dining-table place settings. And just as the lighting of the cande-
labra there signals the entrance of the trumpet, so its extinguishing signals
the end of the opening credits with director Ted Kotcheff's name. Now the
fat, bloated sound of a solo tuba reprises the main theme as we catch our
first sight of the rotund Max strolling through the London streets toward
his office. Our camera view looks up at him to emphasize his corpulence, and
we can hear him puffing to the rhythm of the music.

Once inside his editorial offices, Max launches into his usual tirade of
barbed insults and critiques of the magazine's staff as though he were only
picking up where he left off the day before. He berates one person for using a
paper cup and wrecks another's display idea for a magazine cover because it
features only fruits ("Give me flesh!"). His faithful secretary, Beecham (Eileen
Atkins), follows him throughout the office, scolding him and reminding him
of a doctor's appointment at 11:15. Someone suggests doing a cover story on
what the disciples might have eaten at Jesus's Last Supper, a notion Max
pronounces "macabre." "What next, I wonder," he scoffs, "the Andes plane
crash cookbook?"

Morley's clipped, precise, and witheringly sarcastic delivery of such lines
sets a higher tone of material satire than the script (by Peter Stone, formerly
of *Charade* and *Arabesque*) or director Kotcheff will be able to sustain for very
long in *Great Chefs*, but at least the music score seems equal to that level of
literate wit all the way through. We note that the Max character here provides a centerpiece that those two other scripts lacked, but it also relegates
the young couple in this current story to a secondary role. Jacqueline Bisset
is Natasha, a pastry chef in her own right, the one "normal" character in
the film, through whom we will experience all the eccentric others. Her ex-
husband, still pursuing her, is an American fast-food businessman, Robby
Ross (George Segal). He seems to think it is a good idea to start up a chain of
omelet outlets in London. Apparently, Max knows both Natasha and Robby.
His magazine is covering the menu for some upcoming royal banquet for
which Natasha has agreed to prepare a Bombe Richelieu dessert. Jean-Pierre
Cassel plays the excitable Swiss chef Louis, who is responsible for the baked
pigeon portion of the banquet. In the royal kitchens, an argument breaks out
between Louis and the French chef Auguste, during which various curses
and foodstuffs are flung about to the tune and energy of Mancini's main
theme reprised.

Our first view of Natasha, though—with her fashionably sophisticated
slacks and boots and cap and stole, her confident stride and half smile—is
immediately embraced by Mancini's "Natasha's Theme," a glittering A-minor

andante in which each quarter note of the melody line, starting with E, alternates with the ground note of A as the tune descends over eight bars. The effect is faintly baroque again—a slow-motion toccata. Classical source music is usually playing during scenes set at Max's office or in the restaurants where he continues to devour meals every chance he gets ("This is one of the most intelligent young woodcocks I've ever eaten"). But Mancini's score is never very far from its next cue. There is a long montage showing Natasha as she gradually molds and builds, layers and frosts a trial bombe for the upcoming banquet—the whole process shown in silence against a lush orchestral version of "Natasha's Theme" on the soundtrack, ending with a flutter of woodwinds as the bombe is lit with a kitchen match and everyone applauds.

The first trouble we witness involves Louis, cooking in his own kitchen. He notices a black cat on the premises and gives a look of terror off-screen as we hear Mancini's soundtrack violins playing on the open strings (G-D-A-E), a certain pedal chord that we will come to associate with each subsequent chef murder. Louis's body will be discovered crammed into his own poultry oven. We can surmise that the murderer might be Auguste, with whom we have seen Louis arguing. Max sends Natasha off to Venice to do a magazine article and to keep her safe from the chef killer. There, at the Italian fish market Mancini plays a pert kind of Italian opera intermezzo for two bassoons and pizzicato strings. Natasha arrives at the kitchen of Fausto, the seafood chef she has come to interview, but there again we hear the same rising pedal chord we noticed at Louis's death, electric keyboard and winds rising with the open strings. Fausto will die among his lobsters, drowned in their holding tank. Someone begins to notice that only the famous chefs featured in Max's recent tribute magazine are being targeted by the killer. Natasha bravely carries on with business as usual. A television station back in England invites her to prepare her now-famous bombe on a cooking show (Mancini's TV theme music for this tacky broadcast is comically quaint, like any local TV audio track), and she agrees to go on the air with it even though she is afraid of the exposure.

The *Great Chefs* theme rises again as Robby races to the TV station to warn Natasha that there is real danger: a bomb in her bombe. He believes it may have been Max all along who has been killing the great chefs of Europe, and in the end we find Max sitting forlorn amid a huge restaurant buffet (all you can eat) as though intending to eat himself to death, no longer seeming to care, because he thinks Natasha has been killed. Mancini scores the sad scene with a poignant classical elegy for the full string orchestra as Max sinks lower and finally collapses with his face in the corner of a cream pie.

But just there, high strings and a solo violin, then woodwinds and electric keyboard strike a secondary theme and Beecham steps forward. She will not let her beloved boss take the blame falsely. She confesses that she had committed all the murders, doing away with all the great chefs as her only possible way to keep Max on his diet: only the absence of great meals to be savored will curb a gargantuan appetite like Max's. And with no more truly great chefs left alive . . . As the tragic music cue ends and Beecham has finished her penitence, cradling the collapsed Max in her arms, suddenly he hiccups back to life, sits up, and looks around simply.

The script does not ask how many more days Max may have to live, since he is still calamitously fat, nor does it answer what will become of Miss Beecham's crimes. We see the remarriage of Natasha and Robby, their wedding vows full of silly promises about blending her gourmet career with his fast-food lifestyle. But their kiss signals the welcome return of Mancini's high piccolo trumpet and a full-speed final performance of the main theme, now seeming more joyous and celebratory than ever.

Who Is Killing the Great Chefs of Europe? proved to be Mancini's most naturally musical film in years, and although he never wrote Anglophile music easily or quite convincingly (witness his awkward score to a Peter Sellers remake of *The Prisoner of Zenda* just after *Great Chefs*), this was his most successful entry in that genre.

- - -

Reenter Blake Edwards, finished with his Pink Panther trilogy and finished, it seemed, with his Hollywood studio feuding for a while, genuinely eager to make a new film from scratch. He announced plans for a new non-Panther (or perhaps anti-Panther) project developed from his own screenplay, using his own production company (though to be distributed by Warner Brothers), starring his own wife and about his own issue: the middle-age angst he calls "male menopause," with all of its comic craziness and sentimental longings. The huge success of the resulting film, called *10* (1979), seemed to vindicate his reputation as a major Hollywood force, a victory won on his own terms but also owing a lot to the musical advocacy of Mancini. Edwards was fifty-seven at the time, but we meet his alter ego here, George Webber, a successful Hollywood songwriter, on the occasion of his forty-second birthday party. He is just noticing the onset of middle age ("I feel betrayed!"). His lyricist colleague Hugh (Robert Webber) kids him about it: "After forty, it's all patch, patch, patch." His longtime girlfriend, Samantha ("Sam," played by Julie Andrews), while sympathetic, seems far more mature at thirty-eight than he.

Edwards makes Sam a stage singer, and we see her rehearsing and finally performing in some sort of operetta during the film. She has a young son at home but now seems to be seeing George exclusively. The original choice for the role of George was George Segal, who withdrew at the last moment. Britain's Dudley Moore was signed and proved to be not such an odd choice after all. He had once been part of the famous London stage satirical revue *Beyond the Fringe*, with Peter Cook and Jonathan Miller; he had also proven that he could carry films such as Stanley Donen's *Bedazzled* (1967). More importantly, just a year before *10* he had costarred with Chevy Chase in the hit comedy *Foul Play*, from which a few plot twists and character ploys (as well as character actors) can be seen in this new Edwards movie. As an added bonus, Moore was an accomplished pianist and composer in "real life," so he could sit at the piano as songwriter George Webber and actually be playing, improvising on camera. This is where Mancini comes in, for viewers experience George's discontent and indecision through a particular song he is trying to write throughout the film.

On the day after his birthday party, still feeling the unsettled angst of middle age, George happens to pull up at a traffic light next to a car containing what he describes as a "vision," the most beautiful girl he has ever seen, apparently on her way to her own wedding. His jaw drops at the sight of her; he calls her "an 11 on a scale of 10," and he alters his drive to follow her. Jenny is her name (Bo Derek), a "girl of the age," free-spirited, bound to traditions only for the sake of courtesy, sophisticated about drugs/sex/rock 'n' roll, naïve about commitments/consequences/cooking. At first George just spies on her wedding; then he tries to find out more about her. He manipulates the clergyman who performed the ceremony into divulging her name (but has to endure the pastor's own amateur songwriting demonstration—a hilarious Mancini tango at the parsonage organ—before he can get away). He even sets up an appointment with Jenny's dentist father to learn, through casual conversation at the spit sink, where she will be going on her honeymoon. He follows her to an elegant Mexican ocean resort, desperately admiring her on the beach from a distance, and then invites her out to dinner; she brings him back to her bungalow. Jenny's father knows of George as a composer, though Jenny herself is only familiar with his famous name and the fact that he writes what she calls "elevator music." (The only non-rock music she knows is Ravel's "Bolero," which she claims is a graphic reminder of the pulse and crescendo of sexual intercourse.) With George on edge, sitting beside his dream girl, they chat awkwardly; then Jenny pulls out a joint. She confesses that when she saw him earlier, she thought to herself, "Now, there's a really attractive older man." Both offended and enticed, George considers his options.

Through that kind of material, Edwards is able to explore many of the themes he has been working out in all of his most personal films—gender roles in contemporary society (e.g., George and Sam arguing in bed about the term *broad* for a woman) or the mixing of story genres in a single film (*10* is at once a sex comedy, a relationship drama, a slapstick farce, even in some ways a musical). And yet, in this film more than usual, Edwards seems able to sustain a certain resonance around George's story, following his journey from Tinseltown to Mexico and back, and from boy to man. Dudley Moore, in particular, helps to hold it all together; believable in both the cynical dialogue and the self-deprecating comedy, he is also able to embody George's gradual accumulation of anxiety and, perhaps toward the end, growth. Edwards even gives dimension and sympathy to some minor characters here—for instance, the jilted Mary Lewis (Dee Wallace), whom George meets in the Mexican resort bar and who shares his abandonment blues. "Oh, Sam," George sighs to himself, alone and still half drunk, "come save me." But he never says it to her. In truth, George will not be ready to settle down until he has worked through his doubts, pouts, impulses, and adolescent idealizations of women.

Three Mancini songs represent the conscience of the film *10*. Their lyrics more or less tell the story of George, and the most inspired of the tunes, "It's Easy to Say," is that melody that George is gradually trying to complete as the film goes along. There are only two pieces of conventional narrative scoring in the whole film—one a mock sea chantey for full orchestra as George attempts to rescue Jenny's husband, who has fallen asleep on his surfboard that is drifting out too far into the bay. George rents a skiff and, in spite of warnings for his own safety, manages to catch up to the groom and snatch him from danger (thus gaining access to Jenny). The music recalls, of course, Mancini's arctic whale hunt music from *The White Dawn* on a smaller scale. The other cue is a brief string passage with vibes in a simple fragment of "It's Easy to Say" as Sam finally hears from George in Mexico and then sits alone thinking of him. A muted trombone (throwback to another generation) muses with her.

With so little traditional scoring, however, *10* is influenced greatly by music. The world of rich Hollywood society seems always to be in lounges or theaters, in rehearsal for something, or switching on music at home or in the car. Muzak seems to be a necessary parallel universe they cannot do without. So behind many dialogue scenes the careful listener can hear old Mancini tunes pulled into service. In a coffee shop where George tries to flirt with a waitress, you can hear "Tinpanola" on the overhead speakers. In the lounge of the Mexican resort, a cool-jazz pianist runs through a repertoire that includes Mancini's "Lujon," "Dreamsville," "Mr. Lucky," and "Siesta"—all lush, lilting, compassionate melodies from the 1960s—as well as David Raksin's "Laura." All of these are elevator music to Jenny's generation because they are soft with harmony and nuance rather than heavy with rhythm and obduracy, but they are meaningful to George's generation because they are thoughtful and empathic. So are Mancini's three new songs for this film.

It was brave of Edwards to open his film with the first of these songs, "Don't Call It Love," played on a solo piano as we read white credits on a pure black screen. This tune has the natural world-weary forbearance of a Hoagy Carmichael or Fats Waller classic. Mancini himself plays the chorus just once under the film's opening titles, and then a high Yamaha keyboard harmony comes in for the bridge. It has a perfect been-through-life-already quality with the gait of a slow stroll, reflective and relaxed—therefore a daring way to open a big Hollywood movie. The second new song in *10* is heard when George sets out on his fateful drive, just having argued with Sam, about to spy the perfect "10" dream girl. On the car stereo he plays a song that Samantha has apparently recorded and released as part of her career. It is called "He Pleases Me." The lyrics by Robert Wells, heard as Blake Edwards shows us leisurely shots of George driving through Beverly Hills, describe him perfectly: "He's no more than a man, / nothing special that you'd run to see . . . / he's a child to be sure, at times insecure, / but he pleases me," Sam sings. The melody with counterpoint has a modern, almost industrial feel to it at first, and then relaxes into traditional harmonies. Where it has been placed in the film, it sounds like Sam counseling George from afar.

The main song from *10*, however, is supposed to be coming from inside of George. Wells's lyrics to "It's Easy to Say" proceed fairly awkwardly with a wordy list of the different ways to say "I love you," even as his more famous lyrics for "The Christmas Song (Chestnuts Roasting On an Open Fire)" once advised that "Merry Christmas" has been said so "many times, many ways." But Mancini's melodic structure, preferably without the lyrics, must be considered one of his four or five most intelligent and personal.

As with Mancini's melody for *Days of Wine and Roses*, this one is written in just two long musical sentences, the second of which starts by repeating the first phrase, then offers its changes based on having been through the earlier statement. In this case, lines are much longer; there are extensions and asides as far afield from its opening Cmaj^7 as A minor, the sound of someone beginning to come to terms with the bafflements of life before arriving, not at the original key for the conclusion, but at the lifted, more hopeful and in comparison-of-feeling "wiser" key of Fmaj^7.

The heart of the whole film *10* shows George sitting alone in the piano bar at the Mexican resort, cut off from all three women we have met: Sam out of reach, Jenny out of his league, even the sweet, sad bar girl Mary Lewis out of commission. He carries a mini-recorder over to the grand piano, tape-records a message to Hugh announcing that this is the new melody he has finally finished for which a lyric is needed, and begins to play "It's Easy to Say." Moore's own rubato rendition of the song at the lounge's keyboard, sometimes surging impulsively, sometimes barely touching the keys, giving it a Francis Poulenc–like poignancy, is allowed to play on without interruption. And at the song's last meditative turn, just as George's gaze goes distant and away from the present, Edwards silently cuts to a dreamlike vision of Jenny in all of her bodily perfection and unreachable youth, running along a sunny beach-of-the-mind in slow motion. The cut back to George at the piano for the conclusion of the song is both jarring and true: the birth of his maturity. It is from there that he decides, even though he is handed Jenny on a platter with full sexual favors, to give it all up and go find Sam again.

For Blake Edwards, *10* represented a financial triumph. For Henry Mancini, already primed and focused in his own growth as an orchestral film scorer and as a melodist, *10* represented a strong character study, which his ear could seize and personalize, and the proof that his recent orchestral/narrative forays had not diluted his song art. He was fifty-five now.

Songs would be the major asset of Blake Edwards's even bigger hit film in 1982, *Victor/Victoria*. He had just completed his most wicked, vindictive comedy yet, called *S.O.B.*, aimed squarely at the kind of Hollywood executives who had made him miserable for so long. But its music score had consisted of little more than two contrasting versions of the nursery song "Polly Wolly Doodle" to be sung by Julie Andrews, satirizing the two directions that her personal career could conceivably take—the one light and silly like a TV variety show; the other perverse, growling, electrified, down and dirty. These Mancini arranged in a couple of days, but the whole project, like the whole joke of the film (a producer trying to promote his latest bad-mouthed film by adding porn), seemed pouty and adolescent. It played not like farce but like raging ridicule of all the abuse he had suffered at the hands of major studios. A better way to get back at them would have been to prove *them* out of touch by aiming right past them to the mass audience with another hit like *10* that was both popular and personal. Amazingly enough, the magician Blake Edwards would confound everyone by achieving both of those ends with an even more massive hit film, *Victor/Victoria*, a major musical with stars, period settings, and big staged dance numbers. And here Mancini would be integral.

The tale of Victor and Victoria had been filmed before in 1933 Germany and again in 1935 Britain. It somewhat daringly, but mostly in fun, described the plight of one Victoria Grant, a down-on-her-luck music-hall singer who could only find work in clubs when she pretended to be a male who in turn was dressed as a female impersonator: a woman playing a man trying to play a woman. After his problems with the old-fashioned musical *Darling Lili*, one would think that Blake Edwards might have avoided the notion of producing another period musical. But following Edwards's choices of subject and slant throughout his career, one can sense that *Victor/Victoria* was probably an irresistible project for him as well as the rather blatant fulfillment of his familiar topics: his love of screen farce and classic musicals, and his misfit penchant-cum-obsession with the theme of gender expectations. Whereas that theme had usually been a sidebar in past films, here it is the whole show.

Julie Andrews plays Victoria, who is hoping to find a job in 1934 Paris. She quickly falls in with a sympathetic, witty, and flagrantly gay club performer, Toddy (played with gusto and abandon by Robert Preston), who helps her hatch the outlandish plot to change her musical act to fit the club Chez Lui, which is hiring female impersonators. She is already a knockout singer. What if she performed a strong female repertoire and then at the close of her act whipped off a wig as though she had been a male in drag all along? What a climax, what a coup, Toddy imagines—Victoria could become the toast of the town as Victor. The ploy works, of course, and Edwards's script then focuses on other people's off-center reactions to her/him/her. The Toddy character is always sweet, supportive, and philosophic. Club investor and, perhaps, gangster King Marchand (James Garner) is at first smitten with the girl he sees on stage, then flabbergasted when she is revealed to be a man. He begins to question his own attractions and launches a whole personal investigation, which includes voyeurism (another favorite Edwards theme) and clumsy hired detectives (another) to learn what he is sure is Victor's secret.

Mancini opens the film with the very French sound of an accordion playing the plaintive, rhetorical waltz that will come to be known as the stage song "Crazy World." Though driven and shaped by its flowing 3/4 time, it is a melody line of extensions and pauses, rushes, plateaus, a reconsideration, a climax, and a return, older and wiser, to the almost art-song-like quality of its piano introduction. The excellent lyric by Leslie Bricusse addresses life on behalf of Victoria and us—how life is all a "crazy roller coaster ride, / but I've got my pride, / I won't give in, / even though I know I'll never win." Together, he and Mancini wrote four main songs for the film: "Crazy World," the patter song "You and Me" for Victor and Toddy to sing at the club, the extravagant Spanish choreography number "The Shady Dame from Seville," and the show-stopping "Le Jazz Hot." They also wrote two novelty pieces—Toddy's soft-shoe tune "Gay Paree" and the sassy showgirl tune "Chicago, Illinois."

An example of Mancini's narrative scoring between the songs can be found as Marchand spies on Victoria, certain that she is hiding something. He sneaks into her apartment and hides in her bathroom closet, hoping that her very anatomy will confirm her "her-ness" for him and realign his self-esteem. For that scene of Marchand sneaking around, Mancini scores an adroit trio of clarinets: bass clarinet doing the bass line and two mid-range clarinets filling out the arpeggio. With that as backing, a slide trombone with a cup mute (later bassoon) begins a surly, sarcastic melody reminiscent of Professor Fate's dastardly theme from *The Great Race*. The bridge of this piece (called "Cat and Mouse") features alto clarinet and piano fill in the 1930s style of Bix Beiderbecke's band. Basically, Mancini has created a purely musical sequence out of this purely visual, functional scene, as musically satisfying as any of the other onstage songs in the film. Marchand does see what he came to see—Victor *is* Victoria—and he goes away relieved and repositioned in his relationship with her, though he does not tell her yet what he knows. Now when they kiss, though they have not yet become fully honest with each other, we hear the first quote of that accordion song we heard over the main titles, "Crazy World," whose lyrics, "Crazy world, / full of crazy contradictions like a child . . . / you win my heart with your wicked art" are especially relevant, as all the characters are trying to juggle appearances, expectations, meanings, and definitions that seem to keep changing.

In its unseeing way, the American public approved of the film *Victor/Victoria* as a slightly spicy, slightly spacey entertainment and made it a hit of that season. The eventual soundtrack album sold well (on Polygram/MGM Records, though Mancini saw to it that his old pal Joe Reisman was brought from RCA Victor to produce it). Reviews were almost all positive, and the film gained seven Oscar nominations, including those for Edwards's script and for Andrews's and Preston's roles. It won only for the best song score, Mancini's first Oscar win since the 1960s. "It was an incredibly easy experience working with Hank," Bricusse remembered much later. "I think

I was no more than three weeks door to door with Henry on that one. His way of working was very like his own personality—very easy and laid back. Almost all the songs we wrote came together very quickly. Of course, the fact that, at the time, Hank and Ginny, Evie [Bricusse's wife], and I were spending Christmas with Blake and Julie at their fabulous chalet in Gstaad didn't exactly add any pressure!"[3]

The Oscar was a real boost for Mancini, who, after all, had been doing some of his best work lately. What he was searching for now were more opportunities to compose music that while good for its film was personal in its language. And yet Mancini was aware, too, that the whole film industry was changing again and that the big-ticket film productions had shifted to become the responsibility of the sons and daughters of the baby boomer generation—a technically savvy, possibly nerdy, television-raised, video-crazed gang who constituted a new kind of in-crowd. They seemed to watch only blockbuster fantasies or gothic melodramas, and the generation's directors (Spielberg, Lucas, Coppola, Dante) hired only a chosen few favorite composers to write their scores.

In three smaller projects during this period one can hear Mancini searching for "the personal" in the music he provided but never quite connecting with that new in-crowd. *A Change of Seasons* (1980) starred Bo Derek as a young student pursued by her college professor, played by Anthony Hopkins. There, despite a couple of opportunities for actual orchestral scoring (note one transitional passage for the celeste-like upper registers of an electric keyboard over light strings that sounds like zephyrs of a breezy day bringing a new season), Mancini's scoring gets bogged down in concept before it ever gets started musically. His main melody is a meandering try at a campus folk tune of the then-popular John Denver type, offered first as a wordless song with flugelhorn/sax backing, then with the Bergmans' embarrassing lyrics added ("Where do you catch the bus for tomorrow / 'cause I gotta get out of today"). It is a song trying to work itself out; its modulations are logical but just bored. And what bits of scoring have been built around that theme are truncated and reluctant.

The same elements, same mood and (middle-class) folksy demeanor were put together somewhat more successfully in Mancini's music for Martin Ritt's picaresque film *Back Roads* (1981), starring Sally Fields. Here the story followed the rural travels of a young hooker and a boxer-turned-drifter (Tommy Lee Jones). Immediately more charismatic characters pulled a more memorable main melody out of Mancini: his song (with better Bergmans lyrics) "Ask Me No Questions." After a graceful descending piano introduction in a country style that then provides the backing for the first six bars, Mancini begins his *Back Roads* melody, a casual waltz in B♭ major sung in simple, winsome tones by Sue Raney; amplified harmonica takes over later, backed by muted strings. The whole small score to *Back Roads* benefits from the strength and sincerity of this tune, casting it into fiddle solos, taking its bass line through some electric bass variations, making use of amplified country-and-western guitar. In small segments this scoring does all that director Ritt wanted (or would allow): it provides a backdrop for Sally Fields's wandering experiences, which lead to love and back again but never quite find a compelling story.

The third of these filler film assignments came from the Disney Studios, who were looking around for someone to score their upcoming spy-era family comedy about a dorky but determined comics-page cartoonist named Woody, who assumes the superhero persona of one of his own characters in order to help a beautiful Soviet spy to defect. His cartoon character, his disguise, and the film were to be known as *Condorman* (1981). Car chases, boat races, laser weapons, hydrofoil battles, and a globe-hopping itinerary were the main ingredients here, but no one told Disney that the cold war had not been a hot topic for nearly twenty years, so even at its best this film could never be a proper James Bond send-up. It was more like some amusement park version of Bond. Mancini himself seemed to be parodying not Bond movie music but Batman television music—namely, Neal Hefti's theme for that campy 1965 TV series. Here it translates as a kind of repetitive industrial rhythm with the fanfare phrase at the end of each line sung by a commercial chorus: "Condorman!" It is the job thereafter of the music score to follow Woody across a lot of different locales as he tries to dodge the Soviets, save the girl, and escape detection as the fallible nerd behind the superhero. His globe-trotting score is never serious—it visits all sorts of clichéd musical genres with that same Condorman fanfare: in Moscow we get a minor-key Cossack version, in Istanbul an archetypical Arabic feel, in the Alps an Austrian bier-fest arrangement. More original or independent music, deeper, finer, might have been all wrong for this film, and Mancini understood that the story did not need a self-declarative music score but one that at every turn could pull itself up and say, "Just kidding."

In any case, what Mancini was most concerned with these days was a decreasing list of truly compelling film offers. He was relieved to be liberated from the repetitive and limiting Panther image. He still had whatever new projects Blake Edwards might provide, and there were already two new films with actor/director Paul Newman coming in the next five years, but Mancini found himself, as before in the 1970s, casting around for the most inspiring project from among a shrinking list of offers. These days, even a recent Oscar was no short track to getting the big jobs in town. In the meantime, his family was begging for attention.

CHAPTER 12

Maturity, the Second Cadence

I
t may seem odd to associate "maturity" with the music of Henry Mancini in the second half of the 1970s when clearly all of his most influential work was already past, having been produced between, say, 1958 and 1969. Maturity in this case does not mean a permanent evolution away from jazz-pop and toward exclusively large-scale formal symphonic scoring, although there would be more of that. Maturity now means that Mancini had learned to deal with all kinds of music: to be able to write, in the same year as those resolute songs for *10*, an anti-thematic orchestral score for a thriller film set in the American Southwest that mixes Indian tribal lore, modern political intrigue, and the spooky science of vampire bats—and to "mean" them both.

The thriller was called *Nightwing* (1979), and working with old friends director Arthur Hiller and producer Marty Ransohoff, Mancini concocted a specific orchestral sound for the film's desert setting with its weird winds, searing hot sands, and nocturnal secrets. He had his large string orchestra (sixteen violins, eight violas, eight cellos, eight basses) play the score once through as written, and then, after *detuning* their instruments by the same quarter tone he had used to detune pianos in *Wait Until Dark* and *The Night Visitor*, he had them play it again to overdub many of the same passages. The metal strings of a piano can be off-tuned and set right again without much trouble, but string players were worried they could do some permanent damage to their instruments' soundboard, bridge, or tuning pegs—more likely, they were worried about damage to their ears. Again, the slight "wrongness" of those out-of-tune passages in the score to *Nightwing* proved tremendously effective in building the atmosphere that the film itself was struggling to achieve. Mancini added to that the sound of the Irish harp, not for its ethnic associations this time but for its slightly tart tone. He also added a muted Yamaha upright keyboard, often directed to be played with its pedal down, an action that blurs the notes it strikes into disorderly chords. For the tribal aspect of the film, Mancini used two solo ocarinas, one high, one low, to give a piping flutelike voice—a peace pipe. A large brass section rounded out the orchestra, especially during the film's depiction of tribal rituals and incantations to come.

We can see Mancini's plan for the score all laid out in the film's main title sequence. Purely by the presence of Mancini's music at the opening do we sense the ancient spiritual forces rumored to be at large in the land and of which this bat colony is a harbinger. The Yamaha keyboard plays four groups of descending sixteenth notes that, conversely, rise in five-note pulses while the Irish harp accents in eighth notes underneath. The result, although in regular 4/4 time, gives the impression of mercurial movement, almost fluttering, shimmering, soon backed by eerie sliding strings. As the first sound heard in the film over Arthur Hiller's shots of the Southwest desert rock formations and the silhouette of a lone Indian shaman against the sun, the harmonic ecstasy of this music captures the imagination and sets up a real sense of wonder. A solo ocarina pipes a primitive pentatonic theme obviously representative of the Indian heritage; a lower ocarina will take it over later. Mancini's deep, rich brass choir enters now (six trombones, four French horns, four baritone horns, two tubas, and also two bass clarinets) in stark contrast to the high, weightless sounds we have been hearing. Clusters of brass tones move with a great gravity and mystery in harmonies that are five notes deep, pentatonic again and mixed with the diatonic. The effect is illusive on the surface but carries a deeper portent for those with ears to hear.

In the story, bats have been attacking the residents of this desert out-post—not just ordinary bats, but those with a crazy fearlessness and a lethal bite: vampire bats. As authorities work out a plan to trap the bat colony in their deepest desert cave by pumping in cyanide gas before they wake at sundown, all the familiar scoring elements are in place, the sense of urgency being typified by a rolling arpeggio in the strings and piano. In an extended eight-minute sequence made up of four separate music cues performed without pause under Mancini's collective title "The Circle Is Closed"—three parts and a coda—it is the orchestra that appears to set the pace of the action on screen, and although *Nightwing* never found an audience, then or since, the score's tonal techniques and architectural solidity make it an important stopover for Mancini.

Maturity, then, means variety (being able to score for voice, band, combo, orchestra), but it also means more attention to structure—evolving the capacity to compose, along more narrative lines, storytelling orchestral scores such as *Nightwing*, *The White Dawn*, even *The Moneychangers*. But Mancini's cadence toward maturity is also one of *tonality*, not just in understanding different specific ethnic elements but rather the absorption into his melodic language of, first, pentatonics, then whole-tone scales, then chromatic relationships (those half-step intervals on a piano keyboard that both enrich and dissimulate a musical line in the direction of greater ambiguity). A theme he wrote for the 1975 soap-opera film *Once Is Not Enough* has an almost modal (fourths and sixths) feeling to it that is quite bracing. Similarly, in the beginning of a record album of recital poetry by Australian radio personality John Laws titled "Just You and Me Together, Love," for which Mancini composed an orchestral background, he scored along more such modal lines, giving a tentative exploratory feeling to the music behind the poem "The Scent of Your Nearness," then switching to a chromatic tonality in a waltz for strings and synthesizer behind the verses of a poem called "Closer." There are other tonalities here during the album's transitional passages between Laws's stanzas—alto sax giving rueful voice to a soft-shoe passage accompanying the self-teasing poem about blind dates, "Hair Slicked Down and Awkward Flowers." Then a Fender Rhodes and the Yamaha, playing in chromatic lines, give a chill to a wintry waltz as poet Laws describes every love affair's "Rhythm of Wanting."

Maybe Mancini's best application of those elements comes in 1981, though, and it can be difficult to talk about. Indeed it is a matter of some distress in following the evolutionary trail of Henry Mancini's career that his skillful, discreet, wise, and mature score for the screen version of *Mommie Dearest* (1981), Christina Crawford's infamous memoir about life with her movie-star mother, Joan Crawford, can only be assessed behind that grotesque melodrama on screen.

Crawford had been, of course, one of MGM's major stars of the 1930s and 1940s, second in Hollywood only to Bette Davis over at the Warner Studios. She was renowned for forceful, glamorous, ruthless roles in films like *Grand Hotel* (1932), *The Women* (1939), and, when her star had seemed to dim a bit, for the powerful comeback film *Mildred Pierce* (1945). Late in life she kept working by accepting flamboyant horror-film roles like *Whatever Happened to Baby Jane?* (1962) and *Trog* (1970) just to preserve the limelight.

Daughter Christina's book sensationalized her legacy by alleging that although Crawford's old-fashioned Hollywood flamboyance was real, so was the ruthlessness and, apparently, the horror. The film's first half presents Christina as a prepubescent child, alternately baby-talked and terrorized by her adopted mother, initially anxious and obedient, gradually confused and rebellious, soon zombielike in her reactions to her mother's chaotic, contradictory demands. The second half presents Christina as a young woman, still controlled, reproved, and attacked by her mother, whose career was faltering, but refusing to address her as "Mommie, dearest" as Joan had once insisted.

To dramatize anything from such a book was to risk voyeurism to a provocative degree, whether or not the story it told was accurate. If Joan Crawford was so genuinely schizophrenic, bitter, abusive, promiscuous, lonely, obsessive, and narcissistic, no film view of her story could be less than sleazy. In strutting around her kingdom like a martinet, delivering ultimatums and playing domestic mad scenes to an audience of two every night, Crawford was probably acting some crazy role all the time to keep from having to play herself. What makes this film version of the story so awful that it has become famous as a campy cult-film classic (with Faye Dunaway as Crawford) is that it presents that outrageously theatrical character in a still more exaggerated way, using the worst soap-opera techniques. Say something challenging to Joan, and the filmmakers cut to a close-up of her as she whips her head around to the camera, shocked and offended, and glares at us for just a beat too long, then delivers some over-enunciated line in the manner of a declaration. Run out of dialogue retorts, and Joan pauses, again a beat too long, and grabs her daughter by the neck to begin a hair-pulling catfight on the floor. Every eyebrow raised is magnified and accentuated (and the film pauses to note it); every word Joan utters is delivered by Dunaway as though it were in italics. After a while, you half expect soap-opera organ chords to underline each speech for you. Such a film is both easily mocked and ultimately disheartening.

The two Franks (director Frank Perry and producer Frank Yablans) and the screenplay can be faulted for not giving a point of view to the story, not evaluating Joan, Hollywood, or fame itself in some way but, rather, just depicting the behaviors and the results as though reveling in them. And yet one element of *Mommie Dearest does* seem to carefully and kindly observe and analyze the events and the psychology of these characters, does seem to take them seriously as though looking right past their flamboyance and insincerity to try to understand: only in the music score for this film is there an exploration beneath the surface. Right from the first, Mancini establishes an intimate, thoughtful voice, hushed and confiding and cautionary. In his A-minor main theme is the basic tragedy of that story, hinting at Joan's obsessive/defensive psychology (six of the first ten notes are the same repeated F#) and her quiet constant desperation (as the second phrase of the theme lifts a step and ends on the perch of a high E). The solo alto flute that offers this theme at first suggests intimacy and vulnerability while behind it is the quietly coiled tension of a repetitive two-bar phrase on the muted pedaled Yamaha keyboard: eighth notes in 3/4 time, given an unsteady, disturbed feeling by underlining (doubling) the fifth note of the first group and the fourth note of the second, then alternating them. This sets up a kind of faltering, stammering quality as the basis of the whole main title sequence.

We are watching Joan awakening at 4:00 A.M. to go through an elaborate series of self-punishing morning ablutions in front of lit mirrors and spotless porcelain sinks. She steams her face, then burrows it in ice and oil; she scrubs her hands and elbows with pumice soap and a bristle brush, using nervous compulsive movements; then she takes a scalding shower. And in Mancini's main title music, beyond those first two obsessive phrases, is the compassion he will try to show, not for Crawford's excesses, but for the whole sordid situation—a spiraling redactive phrase back down the scale, releasing (one might say forgiving) some of the tension with chords that connote sorrow. Instrumentally, by now the ensemble has added harp, three bass flutes, two bass clarinets, and muted strings in deep vertical harmonies. Oboe assumes the main theme at bar 35; later clarinet, then C flute, take it over. Joan's shower is portrayed as a self-cleansing of some sort of guilt, so when we see her perfect wardrobe closet, her perfect bedclothes, her perfectly percolating morning coffee, there is a message of imbalance rather than stability, and sad irony rather than order. Two clarinets and two bassoons have taken over the repeated keyboard phrase now, with the other winds in thick chromatic chords (piano and a second harp add lightness and mystery), still exploring the seemingly shifting time signature, rising and falling at the same instant on a journey through the limbo land between the simple A minor where we began and the A major where we are headed. Here at last, as Dunaway wheels around in her makeup chair to face us for the first time, we see her uncanny resemblance to the star we remember as Joan Crawford.

The concept for that opening music came to Mancini partly as an interpretation of the sterile, nervous world he was seeing on screen, with its underlying sadness, and partly as his notion of the old Hollywood (circa 1939) with its mad devotion of money and energy to a manifestly unreal vision of life (a dichotomy that wore down more than one star over the years). That combination of psychiatry and compassion—exactly what this film biography was missing—runs all through Mancini's score for *Mommie Dearest.*

That unsteady meter from the film's opening comes up again during the cruel swimming pool scene where Joan uses her seductive sinister smile to coax her nine-year-old adopted daughter into a race that the child cannot possibly win. Thick, stacked woodwind chords create the impression of something more serious than mere eccentricity at the heart of Joan: three downward steps toward a dark string ground note seem to say that she is genuinely crazy.

When L. B. Mayer charmingly tells Crawford that there will be no renewal of her longtime MGM contract, her devastation leads to a manic episode in which she races home to destroy her own rose garden in a fit of fury. Early prints of the film include Mancini's driving music for that scene—deep piano chords with basses and cellos at a running tempo, then breaking out into staggered rhythms from the whole orchestra, horns mouthing a cry of pain as the garden's centerpiece tree gets axed. Producer Yablans thought it might be the music there that made audiences find the scene so uncomfortably outrageous and Crawford no longer sympathetic as a character—thus, later prints presented the rose garden scene in stark unscored silence.

More Mancini music was axed later during a scene in which Joan sits before her dressing mirror stroking and admiring her legs and her new shoes. He had originally written a twisted, seductive variation on the main theme that again gave a certain perspective to Joan's character, but for some reason the two Franks left it out. Muted strings in elusive harmonies accompany Christina's first fleeting love as a young woman at boarding school in a deeply disguised arrangement of that main theme. Joan is furious that someone else should be coveting her daughter's attention and has her expelled. At home again, Christina finds that Joan is drinking more: one scene of intoxication is scored with the muted strings running through troubled harmonies up an ominous rising line (low strings underneath) until Joan's drunken eye fixes on Christina standing over her. She pauses in a stupor then suddenly lunges at her. Here the main theme plays in the form of a crazy waltz as the two women wrestle on the floor of the Crawford mansion, the whole fight staged like an unbridled pulp melodrama with bigger-than-life slaps, mugging expressions and trembling and shouting denouement lines like "Oh, why did you ever adopt me!" As Mancini has said, he was never able to convince the filmmakers to back his vision for the score, which, as noted earlier, was the only element of the whole project that seemed to understand what Joan or the film was really about. It was not just the tale of a mad woman but a lost woman. The music took the perspective of her troubled, hurt, but forgiving daughter, while the film could not decide on a perspective and so portrayed everything to excess and postponed judgment and perception until, well, never.

- - -

During this same resurgent season when Mancini seemed to have found new life incorporating a new tonality, he looked up from his film work to see the approach of the irrepressible Hollywood conductor and composer Jack Elliott, who wanted to talk about a concert commission. Elliott had been an active music producer for television and occasional movies and, often in conjunction with Allyn Ferguson, had composed much incidental music there. But he was even more enthusiastic about the live music scene in Los Angeles, often facilitating concert events of non-film-related music and carefully grooming aggregations of local musicians, some professional, some student, to give recitals around the West Coast. By the 1980s he had formed what he called the New American Orchestra under his direction and, in order to commission new music, created the nonprofit Foundation for New American Music. The commission was made to Mancini to compose a fifteen-minute concert work for some combination of the sitting eighty-four-piece orchestra that could be presented with other pieces at LA's Dorothy Chandler Pavilion. Mancini accepted mainly because he had a terrific and specific idea. Recalling how many of Mancini's film-scoring concepts had been inspired by the individual sound of particular studio players he had known, he was hearing in his inner ear the tone and approach of one special player of double-reed instruments named Ray Pizzi. They had first worked together as far back as the *Mancini Generation* television series. Pizzi was a quick-witted, red-haired Italian firecracker who had played sax for many prominent bands and had later sought studio work in Hollywood. Recently his specialty, both in film scoring sessions and in side work, had become the bassoon.

Not well represented in films except as a comical voicing, even less in concert music and hardly at all in jazz, the bassoon is certainly one of the most difficult of all instruments to play, because its double reed requires a great deal of breath and sustained pucker pressure to make a sound. Five feet long and with a three-and-a-half-octave range, it is an instrument with a natural humor, a dramatic lower range, and yet a wistful singing tone when allowed to carry a tune. With Jack Elliot's prodding, Mancini composed what he would simply call "Piece for Jazz Bassoon and Orchestra" with Pizzi in mind. There are two extant performance versions: one in a tight concerto form including solo cadenzas (so why not have called it "Concertino for Jazz Bassoon"?) that runs to about twelve minutes, and one at about eighteen minutes with breaks in the middle for extended, unsupported string bass and drum improvisations. At the work's premiere in 1981 Ray Brown handled the bass solos, while in subsequent performances that duty was taken by the electric bass of Abraham Laboriel. Larry Bunker had been the drum soloist originally, later Steve Schaeffer.

After a long evening of polite receptions for the program of new works put together by Elliott, the Pavilion premiere audience seemed to rouse only at the end of the concert as Mancini's new piece excited, charmed, and humored them. Next day the *LA Daily News* called it "clearly the hit of the evening," saying the piece "*swung* from its chimed beginning to its brassy ending."[1] The *LA Times* called Pizzi "perhaps the first serious master in a small field."[2] Variety said "'Piece' closed the evening in spirited fashion, thanks in equal measure to Mancini's composition itself and the hilariously hip execution of bassoonist Pizzi and bassist Brown who dug into their assigned parts with inspired musical punning and delivery."[3]

Dropping the two solo improvs makes the piece eminently performable by any symphony or municipal orchestra whose own resident bassoonist can handle the double-time syncopated scat-playing that Mancini's score requires and the impossibly long breaths and phrasing that will purposely rob him or her of any classical "polish" in the playing, thus encouraging a kind of funky roguishness to the sound. All that is best in Mancini has been referenced in this piece. It has the hard swing of the late big band era; it has Mancini's mature, sophisticated brass harmonies; it has plenty of humor, especially the way Pizzi sells it; and in the midsection it has a moving chromatic tune.

Three clangs of a C chime and the same ground note in the basses open the "Piece for Jazz Bassoon." That C slowly thickens in orchestration and gathers chromatic harmonies, rising in volume as the bassoon enters, scat-playing a sort of preview of the jazz-waltz to come, repeating each phrase quietly like its own echo. Once this long crescendo/intro has done its job of focusing our attention and opening the curtain, a clubbish trio of piano (or electric piano), bass (or electric bass), and brushes on drums is introduced and officially strikes up the jazz-waltz rhythm that supports the main theme. Here the bassoon soloist teaches us the tune—a minor-key swinger in that same tight, darting 3/4 meter, which repeats after four bars an octave higher. Deep stacked chromatic harmonies in the brass relieve the main theme statement with a brief diversion until winds restate it. This all leads to the first highly animated bassoon improvisation (backed by the rhythm trio). Now, energy expended, the orchestra falls out of tempo and into a rubato transitional passage for the strings alone, having the speculative quality of fourths and fifths, then descending more gently, calmly, and becoming at last a bridge that leads into the second major musical subject (the adagio if this were a concertino)—a 4/4 ballad of much feeling, modal cousin of the tune from *Once Is Not Enough* in the bluesy way that it sways between E^7 and $E^{\flat 7}$ chords. Here the bassoon gets to sing with equal parts Gershwin, chamber blues, and torch song. Mancini has shaped its lyrical phrasing to make the most of the wise-ironic personality of the instrument.

The full string orchestra in unison reprises that tune with a genuinely moving simplicity, including the mellow sound of Mancini's trademark brass choir behind it all. Bassoon, in a reflective mood by now, comments on that backdrop, and then everyone settles while high strings seep in like a hot breeze and all becomes calm, coming to rest on the same ground C-major note as had opened the piece (and again one chime marks the spot). A second mallet-against-the-chime holds everyone suspended in midair for the length of one breath.

In the extended version of the piece, this is where the bass or electric bass solos materialize, although the short version, as we have suggested, is cleaner and preferable. It goes right from the second chime at the end of the adagio to strike up the jazz-waltz tempo again for the concluding section (which in a proper concerto could be called the rondo). It is the return of the opening tune and the bassoonist's best chance to wrestle with that diabolically difficult scat-playing again before the full brass force comes in on the tune. Soon joined by the rhythm trio and the furiously circling strings, it builds to a powerful tutti, then comes to a crashing halt on a single unresolved chord. This sets up a silent platform for the bassoonist's last stark solo, which emerges out of the band fracas in the form of an extended coda. This is the most difficult of cadenza playing, syncopations doubling up on themselves, notes in the higher bassoon register next to those in the lower, humorously hectic, leaving the player out of breath but with one last, knowing gesture in store. After all this rough, jazzy, jivey solo-playing, the bassoonist suddenly draws up into a proper, formal symphonic blowing position and, with striking restraint after the struggle, plays one last resolving bar ever so quietly. Mancini underlines this perfectly with the familiar C chime again, whereupon the bassoon dips down two octaves to have the last word for itself.

In the handful of contemporary performances of the piece, audiences invariably erupted in cheers at this conclusion (even though the composition ends pianissimo) for the sheer theatricality of the performance but also for the very real musical satisfaction of the piece. If Mancini had been granted more time, and if his RCA recording contract had still been in force in 1981, he might have worked harder to have it recorded and released as a disc or even performed at, say, Boston Pops events, where pal John Williams had just taken over as permanent conductor after Arthur Fiedler, or by the Cincinnati Pops, whose longtime director Erich Kunzel had always been a Mancini fan. But instead, after a series of successful concerts, the piece seems to have retired from view. Perhaps Mancini felt it had little life of its own apart from the direct participation of its honoree, Ray Pizzi. On the contrary, the piece seems to have great potential for any bassoon specialist with a sense of jazz lilt and the ability to both sing and swing through that odd instrument.

— — —

Two additional film scores demonstrate this sophisticated chromatic language of Mancini's maturity, each intimate and personal and what we can call "truth speaking" scores: one about a father and son, the other about a doctor and patient—one with a jazz combo theme, the other based on a troubled piano waltz.

The jazz score was for Paul Newman's latest film, *Harry and Son* (1984), which he coproduced and cowrote, directed, and starred in. Essentially a two-character play, with Harry being a middle-aged widower whose undiagnosed vascular ailment is causing blur-outs on the job (particularly hazardous since he is the demolition crane operator for a construction company), the film opens without music, just watching Harry swing that huge, lethal wrecking ball into a condemned building. Under the silent opening credits, Newman then intercuts between Harry and his twenty-something son, Howie (Robbie Benson), moving between his job at a car wash and his downtime at the beach (the setting is the Florida coast). Only after the opening credits, about four minutes into the film, as Harry and Howie are heading home from their days, does Mancini's main theme enter for Harry—an alto sax statement in reaction to a bluesy vamp that alternates between Fmaj[7] and Fmin[7]. It is a most philosophic melody, with a sad exhausted feeling in its chromatic downward skids before it starts back upward again, saying more about Harry's character than any of the film's dialogue during this, his last troubled week. "That's just the way things are," Harry is prone to saying about his many disappointments, and the theme Mancini has written for him is the very middle-aged embodiment of that sentiment. A second theme for son Howie is quiet and bookish, often heard on acoustic classical guitar, and seems forgiving of the boy's beach-bum lifestyle as though both Harry and son were victims of the same ebb tide.

If "Harry's Theme" is a blend of past blues and chromatic daring, Mancini's main theme for the other two-character study of the period, Blake Edwards's *The Man Who Loved Women* (1983), was an update of the innocent but rueful merry-go-round waltz he had used so successfully in the past for songs like "Charade" and "Whistling Away the Dark." This one moves down from A minor through chromatic phrases toward edgy diminished chords to an all-the-more-moving A-major resolution at the end. Unlike those other waltzes, here the bass line moves by strict half steps and creates almost dissonant relationships with the simple tune above, minutely suggesting the psychological turmoil of the main character, David (Burt Reynolds), whose conflicted relationship with his seductive mother has brought him into therapy with psychiatrist Marianna (Julie Andrews), whom he immediately casts in a seductive role. As with his psychological interpretation of Joan Crawford in *Mommie Dearest*, Mancini quickly sympathizes with this main character, following that conflicted piano-waltz introduction with a clear, unconditional E-minor bridge seeking resolve.

This is Mancini dealing, in his maturity, with less than compelling films, yet focusing on the humanity in them. These scores are Mancini's condolences toward such sad characters. He is able to write in contemporary adaptations of the traditions he has always known—the jazz blues with a new overlay of chromaticism, the trinket waltz with an aging air of distress about it—*and* keep them relevant and give them great heart. Again, because pop music had moved on from the lyricism and jazz-pop that Mancini represented, neither of the above film scores received any attention at the time, though they still exist for any musicians to explore.

But without big-budget or even mainstream (i.e., shopping mall multiplex theater fare) film jobs coming his way these days, Mancini was settling for these lesser vehicles just to keep working and using them to dig deeper. As he said of hiring on to films like those or *Once Is Not Enough*, "You do these kinds of projects in place of better ones that aren't there at the moment—just to keep in motion, to keep your legs alive."[4] They were mostly satisfying experiences, then, because he had made something of them—he had found his own truths in them and expressed those musically. And yet there was also a sense of being out of the mainstream of Hollywood studio scoring. Scores like those show his discomfort. Once upon a time he was the stylistic leader, the awards king, and the recording industry force to follow. Now he was just a working musician. In the meantime, John Williams's association with Steven Spielberg and George Lucas composing his massive symphonic space scores and "Indiana Jones" marches, the emergence of a new generation of composers getting all the big film assignments (James Horner, Alan Silvestri), and the encroaching influence of foreign-based composers represented at the Academy Awards (Ennio Morricone, Luis Bacalov, Georges Delerue)—all had Mancini looking critically at the state of his own career. He was never so ambitious or self-centered as to worry more about fame than about producing good music, but he *was* aware of trends around him, and each big film assignment that went to someone else made him wonder what he might have done with it.

It was not because they did not like his serious symphonic sound, as evidenced by the reappearance of that cue from *The White Dawn* in Philip Kaufman's *The Right Stuff.* It was rather Mancini's *name* that they did not really associate with the big new productions. And it was as a result of that dilemma—his desire to enter the epic playing field of the Reagan era, and the fact that he specifically wanted to try his hand at a "super space special effects extravaganza" like those for which John Williams had become famous—that, for all the mature and right reasons, Mancini agreed to his next project even though it would lead to a period of endless and ultimately irredeemable frustration.

CHAPTER 13

Frustration

One look at Mancini's handwritten sketches for his score to the large-scale space alien film *Lifeforce* (1985) reveals how important the job was to him, coming at this stage of his career. At last someone was offering him the kind of blockbuster science fiction epic that John Williams, Jerry Goldsmith, and even the young guys like James Horner (*Brainstorm* [1984]) and Alan Silvestri (*The Abyss* [1989]) were getting. With *Lifeforce* he might join the new ruling class of film composers on its own terms. Mancini's conductor sketch sheets of this new score are practically black with notes, dense with determination.

Always precise in his composing sketches, having been a thoughtful orchestrator all through his career, here with this epic he is trying to control with clarity huge symphonic forces (more than one hundred players). He is using ten-staff music paper instead of the usual eight-staff sheets, and he is leaving nothing to be "filled in" later. His handwriting is full of urgent details, alternating time signatures and busy thirty-second-note runs. And whereas contemporary film composers might just summarize the direction of a running figure on the music paper, indicating where it starts and where it needs to end, letting an orchestrator fill in the intervals, Mancini's own vigorous hand has crowded the *Lifeforce* pages with every note of every run, each chord cluster and every *retardando*. What is more, although Mancini was most often a clear, transparent, and linear composer, here he was venturing way out on a limb he had never dared before: thick, vertical, impressionistic music, all texture and color, crescendo and phrasing, steering around and floating above such staples as theme and meter. Not even the avant-garde dissonances of *The Night Visitor* or the dramatic orchestral sections of *The White Dawn, Man Afraid*, or *Wait Until Dark* are predictive of the seemingly "formless" washes of sound that make up the *Lifeforce* score.

In all, Mancini composed nearly ninety minutes of music for the film, to be performed by the same organization that had recorded Williams's *Star Wars* soundtrack, the London Symphony Orchestra. He worked closely with director Tobe Hooper, making sure that his vision for the score was approved ahead of time, remembering the rejection experience of his score for Hitchcock's *Frenzy*. Mancini's concept for *Lifeforce* had been to take this somewhat salacious tale of soul-sucking aliens (its original title was "The Space Vampires") and, through the power of music, turn it into a kind of tone poem. For two weeks he was quite excited about the prospect: the film opened with a twenty-minute sequence completely reliant on music, during which, without dialogue or major sound effects, Earth astronauts searched an ominous alien spacecraft that had been spotted trailing in the wake of Halley's Comet. As these astronauts floated weightless through the shafts and chambers of the massive ghost ship, exploring, wary of it all, the movement on screen was fluid and deliberate, just begging for musical support. Seeing it as a set piece, Mancini began composing as if to a kind of choreography that would develop slowly as the search progressed and build to the revelation at the ship's core: a cache of alien bodies frozen in suspended animation for some dark purpose. At first he experimented with electronic sounds and atmospheres for this scoring; then he gave over completely to the idea of a tour-de-force orchestral ballet in space. His enthusiasm for the challenge is apparent on paper.

But one key element of the whole commission had escaped him: the film was being supervised by Cannon Pictures, part of the infamous movie brokerage firm the Cannon Group. They had made their money by funding quick and cheap genre films on a one-time basis, turning a profit by almost immediately handing them over to their video-release branch. *Death Wish II*, *Salsa*, and *American Ninja* were among its hits in shopping mall cinemas all over the country. Cannon was run by two men, Menahem Golan and Yoram Globus. In the 1970s Golan had been an ambitious producer of independent film projects in Israel, responsible for a few genuinely artful releases such as Moshe Mizrahi's Oscar-nominated *Ani Obev Otach Rosa* (1972) and the even greater film *The House of Chelouche Street* (1974). With Globus his plan was to model their enterprise less like the big studios of the past and more like a modern grocery store chain: open as many units in areas (genres) that seemed promising; scale down the overhead on each venture and move on to the next project; and be consumer oriented rather than product oriented.

By 1984 they were looking for a larger-scale production with which to legitimize themselves with the Spielberg/Lucas generation. They tapped Hooper, who had already made a big independent movie for himself, the horror cult classic *The Texas Chainsaw Massacre* (1974), and had worked his way up to the Spielberg camp directing *Poltergeist* (1982). Word spread that for the latter film Spielberg had moved in on the production stage and codirected when Hooper had become indecisive. Now with *Lifeforce*, Golan and Globus were giving Hooper another chance. The rather long, gushing, overwrought final cut that Hooper delivered to them—fully scored and brimming with apocalyptic special effects (it turns out that those suspended alien bodies come to life and are *not* friendly but are vampirelike sucklings, greedy for the human life force, even if it means coming down to Earth for an ectoplasmic orgy)—did have a kind of sour romanticism to it. But almost at once the American distributor's test audiences reported a problem to the Golan/Globus office: the film had too much "spacey" speculation, not enough horror action. That opening exploration-of-the-alien-ship sequence with all that ambient music was deemed boring and static. That would be the first thing to go. A film these days must open with tension, provocation—not with mere question marks or self-absorbed visual set pieces where music is the only life force. Of course, in a sense they were right, but knowing how much of the action to come was silly and childish, one begins to wonder if the test audiences' complaints were misplaced. At any rate, the new word went out: *Lifeforce* was being chopped down to a more manageable length and into a form where most of the long reflective or descriptive visual sequences would be truncated. Along with them, their music had to go.

The kindest thing to do in such a situation would have been to bring back a reluctant Mancini to do what he would call the "needle and thread" work of cutting down and realigning his score to the new film version. It is said that such an offer was made to Mancini but that by then he was already involved on his next big film job and so could not oblige. More importantly, though, the Cannon Group was just not about the subtle making of films and carefully reshaping them when there were problems; they were about brokering films and moving on to the next deal. As a result, much of Mancini's original scoring for *Lifeforce* was either gutted or scattered. And with his further participation impossible, another composer, Michael Kamen (*Die Hard, The Dead Zone*), was brought in to write connecting music and in other places to provide what was considered more "horror film" scoring aimed at punching up the action and ostensibly pleasing the younger get-to-the-point audience. Kamen wrote what he thought would mesh with Mancini's material. Music editor Robert Hathaway and adviser Jack Fishman also forced some bars of Mancini's original music to bridge gaps in Kamen's slipcover scoring so that the final accounting was a nondescript, self-canceling drone of almost constantly ecstatic music whose internal logic and subtle pulsing drives, so carefully composed by Mancini to match the primordial invaders' progress, now seemed arbitrary, vacuous, and boastful. Much of the score now accompanied scenes and climaxes for which it was never meant. It was like those old patchwork scores at Universal Studios, except never so cunningly applied.

To watch the film today is to inevitably misjudge Mancini's accomplishment there, so little of it is left in place as the film slogs along Earthbound in the London labs and offices of the officials trying to deal with both the alien presence and the resulting panic in the streets. More of Mancini's scoring is used in the standard zombie-stalking sequences, but, as often as not, the editor merely cuts in the climax of a longer music cue where the brass rise in accord with some special effect, yet we never get to hear the development of music that once led up to that fortissimo nor the motif of which it was a fulfillment. Then, just as our ear begins to find a pattern in the music, the editor fades it down and covers the seam with a Kamen transition, which itself is soon obliterated by another orchestral climax lifted from elsewhere in the original score. It is musical and cinematic goulash. The one conventionally melodic piece in the whole score, a propulsive minor-key dance macabre, is left in place at the end of the film even though the original first cut used the impressive authority of this music to open the film instead. But from Mancini's point of view, the score was trashed.

In many ways *Lifeforce* is Mancini's most troubling music. Its tides of cluster chords and pulsing meters and ambient tonalities can either be judged as a bold leap of faith from his melodic linear style into an abstract universe of pure orchestration whose very language is new and whose musical foundation lies much deeper (in tonal and textured logics) than mere surface theme-and-variations procedures. Or they can be called mere orchestral recitative, a whole score made up of transitional phrases, stalls and vamps and rushes that usually bridge between thematic material but this time make up the score itself. The mood is melancholy, with a range on either side of that toward the sinister one way or poignancy to the other. His huge traditional orchestra is supplemented by a women's chorus (and a small men's chorus) fed through a Fairlight sampling synthesizer to give them an eerie unnatural sound during those scenes of the aliens' transformation of souls. With those forces and Tobe Hooper's original crazy concept, Mancini set to work.

Of Mancini's original sketches, the first section, "Space Walk," opens with a ringing upturned declaration from strings and horns, immediately descending in parallel lines down to the root chord, where a searching (faintly Celtic) motif is waiting from oboe and flute. It has a fateful, steady tolling quality to it with a turning figure underneath. As the astronauts approach the alien craft, solo trumpet takes up the motif of being both heroic and stoic toward what they might find. "Entering the Craft" is the second section and opens with low strings and winds sounding like we are about to begin Rachmaninoff's "Isle of the Dead." Two bassoons take up the turning figure, and divided strings enter with a weird Medusa-like incantation of chromatic lines that twine inward until winds and a solo French horn take over. This develops into an unpredictable conversation (full of pauses and interjections) between cellos and synthesizer until it is broken by a string/brass announcement quoting the introduction to "Space Walk." Here the string and brass sections maneuver weightlessly among a series of impressionistic, chromatic chord changes, and, for the first time, the Fairlight-sampled female choir joins in, thickening the harmony with the strings while the usual bassoon/clarinet combo plays a kind of slithering figure.

On seeing the sleeping bodies suspended, batlike, in the alien craft, the brass and string sections together present a stately procession of chords like some massive organ, expressing the gothic mystery of the moment. A quiet atonal elegy for strings, winds, and that solo horn plays as we discover three humanlike forms hanging there among the creatures. These will be used on Earth as predators to collect, like vampires, human energy to refuel the aliens' own life force. In the music we understand something has ended here and something has begun, though we do not know what.

By the close of what was to be that opening twenty-minute "ballet"—covering the discovery of the alien ship, the introduction of the humanoid vampire units and the rescue ship that brings Carlson and trouble down to Earth—Mancini has established his tonal language for the film, and the naturalness with which he moves among these abstract swatches of musical color and texture gives it all a sense of purpose and premeditation, even though the musical material itself seems querulous. Meanwhile the underlying sense of yearning that persists throughout this score seems to suggest that the whole free-ranging compositional process of *Lifeforce* was a kind of catharsis for Mancini, so tidal and important to him at this stage of his career that he actually overrode his usual instinct for careful shape, containment, and control and wrote beyond himself into orchestral and expressive territory of which he was not quite sure nor quite in command. It does have a singular voice and a strong sense of inner personal integrity—and it strives mightily to be of service to its irascible motion picture—but being so far out of contact with Mancini's usual linear language, it remains a speculative musical mural. Mancini later admitted:

> I really enjoyed working on *Lifeforce*, but the whole reason I did the damn thing was that those first fifteen minutes were like a ballet, a big space ballet, and there were going to be other long stretches for music. So I took the job wanting to get into that. But then the front office got in there, and it was much, much too long, and they cut, made mincemeat out of it, and I wasn't able to get back and put the pieces together, the needle-and-thread work. So it turned out a confusion of styles. . . . I haven't seen it since then. I'd like to remember it as it was.[1]

We can think of *Lifeforce* as representing both the climax of the big, descriptive orchestral scores Mancini had been practicing throughout the 1970s and, unfortunately, prophetic of the kind of frustration he would be experiencing in the business more and more as the old formal Hollywood approach to intentional film scoring slowly and painfully gave way to the more generic ambient forms. Film music was "reinventing" itself away from him.

Mancini's next job was very different, although some of the same frustrations would pursue him: a big-budget holiday production with the ignominious title *Santa Claus: The Movie* (1985). To go from scoring a risible space horror film to a risible kid flick about jolly old St. Nick would seem to scribe the line of a career in trouble, being handed assignments from the bottom of the pile. We have seen why Mancini took on the questionable world of *Lifeforce*. At the beginning, *Santa Claus*, too, seemed like it might hold special interest for a composer. It could have turned out to be a future classic seasonal film. The original concept was for the film to be a $50 million screen musical full of active scoring and exploitable songs, and Leslie Bricusse would do the lyrics. Producers Alexander and Ilya Salkind, who had piloted the big *Superman* movies in the 1970s, had first chosen John Williams to score *Santa Claus*, but when he drifted off, Mancini's name came up.

The Salkinds paid only a modest fee for television actor David Huddleston to star as Santa, but they committed $5 million to retain Dudley Moore to costar as Santa's most enterprising helper, an elf named Patch. John Lithgow was cast as a corrupt Manhattan toy manufacturer. But frustration developed around the whole project fairly early on, and the problem again had to do with front-office indecision. From the beginning, Bricusse had lobbied for the concept of framing this film as a major musical, with songs and singers and dancers, that would be about the whole Yuletide tradition as experienced each year in British and American shops and homes and stories. In 1970 Bricusse had written lyrics and music to a big-screen version of Dickens's *A Christmas Carol* called *Scrooge,* and the results had been musically quite pleasing. He could not convince the Salkinds to do the same here. As he would later describe, what he and Mancini did not know at the time was that the Salkinds had received some substantial funding for their Santa film from big corporations in exchange for product placements within the film: from Coca Cola, *Time* magazine, Pabst Blue Ribbon Beer, and McDonald's, whose logos and products would then be featured on screen, and, more important for our discussion, from EMI Music Publishing to feature some soft-rock records within the film soundtrack by contract artists like Sheena Easton and the band Kaja. So the idea of making *Santa Claus* into an original musical was out.

There are five Mancini/Bricusse songs left in the film, but they appear only in passing without introduction and, because they are just faded away on the soundtrack, without endings. Bricusse, naturally, was fed up, his contributions having been savaged. Later he said:

> We wrote seven songs, though you'd never know it now, and we went through enormously complex recording sessions on those songs. For instance, for one song ["Making Toys"] set in Santa's toy factory—the producers spent millions of dollars on a hugely extravagant set and staged a complete number there, timed to a metronome, expecting to fit our as yet unwritten song in later. Then they canceled the song altogether—a very good song, I may say. [Mancini's march melody covers the scene instead without lyrics, a merry successor to his "High Time" march and "March of the Cue Balls."] And the absurd thing is that the producers almost did what the corporate characters in the story, the John Lithgow character, did to the public by cheating them out of what could have been a lovely film.[2]

And yet, because there was so much pictorial scoring in the film—flying sleigh rides, toy factory tours, and modern cityscapes covered with music that was energetic, abundant, and uncontested by dialogue—Mancini's memory of the whole *Santa Claus* experience was inevitably happier than that of Leslie Bricusse. The final film still retains major portions of his buoyant music, played by the full National Philharmonic Orchestra. Nor is the movie, as directed by Jeannot Szwarc, quite the vulgar commercial spectacle it might have been. The problem is that it never *does* find a comfortable zone as it tries to blend a sense of genuine warmth (depicting a truly generous and modest Santa) with a satiric edge lampooning Madison Avenue. Mancini stays away from all that, though, and scores a storybook North Pole using a light-textured but resplendent symphonic sound, often doubling instruments so that chords sound more plush and so that his toylike themes gain in color if not actually in consequence. At times there is a *Nutcracker Suite* feeling to the score—it is *that* bountiful and compassionate. Had the producers decided to stage the film as an official musical, the Mancini/Bricusse songs and carols (preserved on a soundtrack album eventually issued on EMI Records) might have anchored the film into position as a happy classic.

Over the next couple of years Mancini wrote similarly fluent and fun traditional scores with large British-flavored orchestras (think Haydn visiting Victorian England, dining with composer Sir Edward Elgar and Walt Disney) for two London-based pastiches of the Sherlock Holmes legend. One was a fully animated tale, *The Great Mouse Detective* (1986), and the other was a truly droll reimagining of the Arthur Conan Doyle characters called *Without a Clue* (1988), with Ben Kingsley as Dr. Watson (the *real* brains of detection) and Michael Caine as a dimwitted Holmes. But more serious jobs were conspicuously absent.

By 1987 not only were there real career questions for Mancini, having reached the age of sixty-three, but the senior-citizen passages and crises that everyone must face were starting to intrude on the Mancini household. Ginny's energetic mother, Josephine, well into her eighties, was beginning to lose momentum, becoming bedridden and unhappy with the shift from part-time to full-time nursing care. She had been born in Chihuahua, Mexico, but had married an Irishman, John O'Connor, giving Ginny her distinctive split heritage and a dual sense of cultural dignity. And of course in the Mancini house this new attention to geriatric issues was being balanced with the continuing presence of Hank and Ginny's grandson, Christopher, who was between the ages of ten and twelve in those days. Christopher had all the perks of a famous family but perhaps a fair portion of consternation, too, explaining to himself why he was living with grandparents instead of with one of his own split parents. Certainly the dependability and structure of the senior Mancini home, especially at this less dazzling, more workmanlike stage of Henry's career, was helping the boy establish some personal bearings. The strength of his own father's personality and the famous sisterly empathy of two aunts, Felice and Monica, helped as well. Christopher, by all accounts, seemed to bond easily and readily with people. Mancini writes of taking him along on a sightseeing trip to Africa in 1987, where he showed equal fascination with the local Masai tribesmen and the wildlife of the Savannah. On Lake Victoria he landed a forty-six-pound Nile perch while weighing only seventy pounds himself. In a statement that is very telling of the Mancini sense of modesty and plainness, Henry wrote, "It was not a matter of two grandparents taking a boy on a trip. We were just three people on a journey to a far away land."[3]

Others also seemed drawn to young Christopher. When Mancini paired with the great Italian tenor Luciano Pavarotti in arranging and conducting two albums of folksongs and popular arias in 1984 and 1987, Henry, Ginny, and Christopher were invited to the Pavarotti estate in Pesaro, Italy. Mancini wrote later of his memory of Pavarotti and Christopher riding bicycles together around the villa (part of Pavarotti's fitness routine) and of how the world's greatest opera star had helped Christopher with a baby bird he had found separated from its nest. When the bird died and Christopher wrote a note to be buried with it, Pavarotti found a glass jar for a coffin and, together, they laid it to rest "in a place only Christopher knew." Mancini wrote, "Luciano was very taken by this incident."[4]

Sad family news such as Ginny's mother's death in 1986 soon traded with good news as son Chris, doing well with a steady income working with Arista Music Publishing, announced in 1988 that he and his new wife, Analei, were about to have a son and would name him Luca Nicola after his grandfather Henry's middle name. Chris had recently produced his own album on Atlantic Records of radio-ready rock songs called *No Strings*, playing both guitar and keyboards and offering, in his street-hip tenor, original cuts like "City Girl" and "Hurt Again" with a style reminding savvy listeners of other contemporary bands like Journey and Bon Jovi. And although the album got a solid, respectful hearing in its day, its main advantage for Chris Mancini was that it made him some valuable new friends and landed that eventual job at Arista. "It was a great chance for Chris," his father explained, "since he had never had to be anyplace at a given time and do what anyone told him to do. There was an adjustment at first getting used to a structured existence. But once he took hold, his life began to take shape. . . . He began to feel that he could make a difference in his own life and he was well on his way. He had a steady income."[5] As one of Chris's own lyrics had said, "I've decided to keep myself just one step ahead of trouble."

It was in those days of family endings and beginnings that Mancini decided for the first time in a long while to travel back to his childhood home in Pennsylvania and stir some memories. He was already scheduled to conduct the Pittsburgh Symphony over four nights, and it would be only a short drive in a rented Continental from the city out along the Allegheny River back into the hills to West Aliquippa. With him on that trip was jazz columnist and occasional lyric writer Gene Lees, who took notes as they proceeded on through Hank's old streets to see his old high school and his old flat-board house on Beaver Avenue. Later and for the next six months Lees met with Mancini and coaxed out of him and into a pocket recorder Henry's life story, covering his childhood, the war years, the years at Universal Studios, and the remarkable rise of his career through the colorful 1960s and on up. From those notes, Mancini would fashion his autobiography, released by Contemporary Books in 1989 and as a paperback in 2001 by Rowman and Littlefield. The title he chose, *Did They Mention the Music?* referred to the old question around the Universal music department after each new motion picture returned from an audience preview in some small-town theater and the reaction/opinion cards were being reviewed. Altogether this was a season of both reminiscence and reassessment.

CHAPTER 14

Stolen Moments

In that spirit of life appraisal and conciliation, Mancini turned over some of his own music papers and archives to the UCLA collection, at the same time establishing an ongoing scholarship there for students interested in film music composition. He tried to strike up a new recording contract with the Nippon Columbia Company in Japan and released two CDs with the Royal Philharmonic Orchestra (one collecting his neglected film themes and one offering recent pop-rock hits), but although they were well produced, Nippon did not seem to know how to market them. And equally unfairly, he signed up to score Blake Edwards's two most recent farce films, *Blind Date* and *A Fine Mess*, but watched his music cues being dropped one by one in favor of the pop-rock music that Edwards seemed to prefer for his soundtracks these days. It was just the way things were done in the New Hollywood.

Only a few of Mancini's music tracks were retained in Edwards's period-mystery film called *Sunset* (1988), a clever take on one actual historic encounter between the young cowboy movie star Tom Mix and the elderly real-life cowboy Wyatt Earp. Edwards's script had the two characters team up to confront a current-day (circa 1928) murder and a whole lot of Hollywood corruption. All he wanted from Mancini, he thought, were some music cues to illustrate the 1920s movie industry. Interestingly, though, in addition to writing some mock–Hollywood western music, Mancini chose (and Edwards ultimately allowed him) to musically advocate for the two victimized female characters in the story. One is Christine Alperin, wife of the evil studio head, and her theme, carefully confided in the background as she tells Wyatt about her disappointing life, is a 1920s-style coronet blues with a stride piano complement. The other is Cheryl, a young Hollywood hanger-on who turns to Wyatt for protection from the predatory Alperin himself. As Wyatt returns to his bungalow (he is acting as technical adviser on a Tom Mix western film), he finds Cheryl hiding there. The camera, as Wyatt's point of view, slides around the corner of the doorway into his bedroom, and as Cheryl is slowly revealed in his bed, Mancini's second piano piece, "Cheryl's Theme," plays—first the quiet left-hand chords; then the gentle, vulnerable, faintly apprehensive melody in the right hand—as simple and perfect a piano blues as anything he wrote in the old *Peter Gunn* days. Although this music cue is mixed far in the background of the soundtrack, what you can hear lends tremendous sympathy to the "Cheryl moment" along with a good deal of respect to Wyatt and the gentle way he treats her there. It is a touch of class in what turns out to be a rather sordid crime movie, not so much about old Hollywood as about the roots of meanness in any era. But there was Mancini, looking for stolen moments, even in unwelcoming films, for the affirmation of sensitive and personal scoring.

Likewise, when, soon after, Edwards worked with the Disney company for ABC-TV on a family fantasy, *Justin Case*, in which comedian George Carlin played a detective who comes back as a ghost to solve his own murder, although there was little space assigned for descriptive scoring, Mancini was able to combine both some playful, sneaky mystery aspects of the script with a likable theme that stays close to a certain little ostinato of eighth notes split between an electric bass and an ARP snyth forming the counterpoint (with a minor-key Halloweenish tone) to a most simple minor-thirds melody on top for electric alto sax.

He again used computerized harmonies, juxtaposing acoustic instruments, in another television film, *Never Forget*, about the real-life landmark legal case by Mel Marmelstein, who successfully court-challenged a quack "institute" that had publicly disputed the reality of the Nazi Holocaust. Leonard Nimoy leaned far away from his role as *Star Trek*'s Mr. Spock to coproduce and star in this cautionary tale, working with veteran family-film producer Robert B. Radnitz. It would seem a strange assignment for Henry Mancini, who had never worked with Radnitz or Hebraic music before. His score for *Never Forget* hovers nervously around two simple themes, thinking perhaps of the famous Hebraic cello works by Ernst Bloch, scored for synthesized samples of the lower strings, a few winds, and brass. Just as those themes stay close to a conservative harmonic base, the score as a whole seems constricted by the political ramifications of the subject matter and by the one-sidedness of its presentation. Mancini cannot "get inside" anything here. Certainly no music, no film can approach the experience of the Holocaust and pretend to empathize. Certainly there have been enough eyewitness accounts of the concentration camps to render Holocaust denial foolhardy and smacking of ulterior motives. As told to us, the Nazi atrocities are certainly beyond music, even beyond memoir. So in that sense Mancini was wise to under-dramatize. His sad-faced but noncommittal main theme here is really just a stolen moment of solidarity, a gentle condolence that feeds into a handful of scenes.

\- \- \-

The late 1980s were another transitional period in the whole field of film scoring. The intrepid John Williams still ruled with one prestigious assignment after another, prodded by but not dependent on his associations with directors Spielberg and Lucas. Oscar nominations seemed to rain on him for his film scores: *Home Alone, JFK, The Accidental Tourist, Indiana Jones, Empire of the Sun, The Witches of Eastwick*—all big symphonic, even sometimes choral, scores. Other veterans enjoyed renewed success during these years: John Barry's Oscar win for *Dances with Wolves* and Dave Grusin's scores for *The Fabulous Baker Boys, The Firm*, and *The Milagro Beanfield War* (an Oscar winner). The new breed was beginning to take over, though; James Horner wrote blandly but appropriately for *Field of Dreams*, Hans Zimmer similarly for *Rain Man*. Meanwhile, Mancini was scoring three limited-release films: two were occasioned by friend Marty Ransohoff and were made with the burgeoning home video market in mind, and one was for cable television.

Mancini himself thought of them as a late-career triptych, "none of them world-beaters," as he said. Though their settings were very different, their scoring was of a single cloth, using five synthesizer players and a studio ensemble of traditional string players ranging in number from twenty to forty. Well past his early days with the ARP, here Mancini was taking advantage of the subtler range of computer-driven sounds available now; MIDI (musical instrument digital interface) synths, tone generators, samplers and controllers, and EWIs (electronic wind instrument simulators, which, having computer-sampled real flutes or clarinets or whatever, now could reproduce those specific sounds and blow just like them). He was writing for those synthesized sounds and then relying on the real string groupings for warmth, for shading and articulation.

These three films needed only the most basic assistance from ambient scoring; the postproduction schedules were brief, so there was not a lot of freedom to compose. And yet there are personal touches, stolen moments, in each score. One was Michael Crichton's police-boiler *Physical Evidence* (1989), with Burt Reynolds as a disgraced cop trying to clear his own name of the murder of a crime boss who has been harassing him. A night montage of city skyline and waterfront shots opens the film behind the main titles as Mancini's inexplicably friendly and conciliatory first theme is heard on the EWI oboe against a bed of keyboard chords and strings. The octave stretch of the theme's first notes soon settles into a likable, casual melody based on fifths and thirds, perhaps readying us for good-old-boy Joe Paris, whom Burt Reynolds plays. He is trying to learn who killed the mob boss and is joined on the hunt by his newly assigned, newly licensed lawyer, Jenny Hudson (Theresa Russell). Their growing relationship—the gruff, supposedly charismatic ex-cop and the naïve but purportedly sharp attorney—leads to several supposedly clever verbal sparring matches and one love match. It also inspires a second theme from the score, this one more relaxed, always descending and in a conciliatory, sympathetic mood. It is not quite strong enough as a piece to enrich the shallow characters of the story, but it is a welcome aside from the composer to anyone in the audience who may be listening.

A second police-themed film is *Fear*, which received the same configuration of instruments: five synth players and twenty strings. Casey is a woman with reluctant but penetrating psychic powers who seems to share a wavelength with a psychotic serial killer—she can read his thoughts and at times see through his eyes—therefore, she can be quite useful to the police in tracking him down if she is willing to put herself at such risk. Mancini's "stolen moment" here, standing out from the work-a-day suspense score, is surely his intricate, eerie piano waltz, which appears magically as Casey relates a story about her first psychic-awareness experience. Mancini begins "Casey's Theme" with the alternating arpeggiated chords (Amin to A#min) of a 6/8 waltz meter. Then the poignant and disquieting melody begins on an EWI oboe (G drop to C, octave rise to C is the main motive). "That's another example of a tune," said Mancini, "that fights for resolution at every point and keeps slipping away, then makes it, then slips again and keeps being interesting for that reason."[1] As the supporting arpeggios continue to circle, they descend from G# to G, to F, to E, to D#, then ascend to E, only to wind back down to the consonant D# at the end of the phrase, momentarily in the same key as the melody.

Although the chromatic sidestepping can remind one of *Harry and Son*, what this music more fully recalls is some of the scoring behind that poetry album Mancini did with Australia's John Laws, specifically the piece referred to earlier as "a wintry waltz" that accompanies the stanza "The Rhythm of Wanting." There the tune, in E minor, is far simpler and maunders chromatically but less thoughtfully from its revolving base. "Casey's Theme" is perhaps the ideal example of how personally Mancini had taken this chromatic language, producing a magical ambiguous quality yet still carefully disciplining its modal patterns and anchoring the end of each line by the resolution even as the circling arpeggios, like a weirdly lit Ferris wheel, whirl on.

Franklin Schaffner's *Welcome Home* is the third in this unofficial synthesized trilogy of scores. It uses similar synthesizers and forty strings, but for its representative song a standard barn-dance band gathers around singer Willie Nelson. This tune treads the same mile-marked country road as previous Mancini songs "All His Children" and "Ask Me No Questions." The lyrics by the Bergmans picture the unheralded veteran of the Vietnam War coming back stateside, but there are "no parades, no marching bands, no banners catching the breeze." It sounds pretty tame and familiar at first, but by the time of its first reprise in the film it has accumulated some of the authority of a sincere folksong.

Certainly the one regret of all these "stolen moments" in Mancini's recent scoring is that they were such isolated instances—that the films themselves had not asked for, nor made room for, more participatory scoring. They do show that Mancini was ready, willing, and able to score almost any given cinema story with personal and personable music if only the film itself had strong storytelling or characterizations and the director wanted narrative/interpretive music.

In each of those three recent film scores there were stolen moments of music scoring that rang true. Two more late projects offer proof that Mancini's musical and refinement of technique was still progressing. One is the mellow Blake Edwards rumination about kinship and growing old, *That's Life!* (1986), the most adamantly independent of his major films. It depicted a successful architect, Harvey Fairchild, who is so bent out of shape at the thought of turning sixty that he nearly alienates and sabotages his long-lived marriage, career, and extended family. It was for this modest slice-of-life story that Mancini wrote perhaps his last great song, with a lyric by Leslie Bricusse, "Life in a Looking Glass."

Edwards was determined to produce *That's Life!* independently for the then-paltry sum of $1.5 million, using nonunion crew and his own family and friends as the cast (union representatives picketed Edwards's shooting locations and funded full-page press ads protesting the film). He even used his own house, just north of Malibu in Trancas on the Pacific Coast, for shooting. Wife Julie Andrews stars as Gillian Fairchild, a stage and screen singer married to Harvey (Jack Lemmon), the highly stressed, hypochondriac everyman just entering his sixth decade and beginning to lose track of his marbles.

The plot is as simple as a diary; it covers one weekend leading up to Harvey's sixtieth-birthday bash. We first meet Gillian, who has just come from the hospital for a throat biopsy to determine the nature of a lesion there. The situation echoes Andrews's real-life scare of nodules on her vocal chords, the treatment for which so sadly ended her singing career in the 1990s. Gillian tells Harvey nothing about the danger; she resigns to wait, on private pins and needles, until the lab results are ready Monday morning. She returns home to a house full of everyone else's problems, to listen to Harvey's rants about how shallow his clients are, how purposeless his life is, and how old he will soon be.

As the Fairchild offspring and in-laws gather in anticipation of the big party night and each seems to be in the midst of some life crisis, only the calm, reassuring counsel of Gillian provides the eye for each small storm. Edwards asked his cast to improvise much of their dialogue and to play, within a given frame of each scene, something personal. With Lemmon's performance often being over the top of hysteria and chatter, it is Andrews's Gillian who really controls the film—so carefully styled, so pert and alert, so instinctively available to all her family, and so perfect, even in diction. And yet Gillian is actually in hell dreading her medical diagnosis, still unwilling to tell anyone about it.

Inspired, even abashed, by the intimacy of such a film featuring people, even locations, he knew so well, Mancini met *That's Life!* with a fully personal and empathetic score that both harkens back to the nostalgic West Coast Cool jazz chords of his first success and tempers them with his mature sense of the score-as-a-whole voice that pervades the film. Anchoring the score and helping to universalize the Fairchilds for us is Mancini's wise and warm easygoing ballad in B♭, first heard as Gillian returns home alone from the hospital. As a celebrated singer, she is due to begin a long tour in four weeks but is suddenly dealing with this throat irritation. Doctors will determine whether or not she can do the tour, whether or not there is a real health jeopardy for her. Until she knows, she will have to steel herself for the family gathering. This weekend Harvey himself seems to be in some sort of emotional meltdown—at times comical, as when a client comes on to him or as he consults a fortune teller; at times frustrating, as when he visits a priest who happens to be a former college classmate whose favorite part of the Mass is the wine; at times desperate, as when he confesses to Gillian all that he has failed to accomplish in his life. He wanted to become a great architect, but all he does is design show homes for spoiled rich people. He spends his energies at home wringing his hands, lamenting his prospects, and imagining ulcers and heart attacks. At the doctor's office he is told that his health is perfect, that anxiety, aches, and pains are all in his head. He adds the lack of a firm diagnosis to his list of complaints. Narcissism seems to be his biggest infirmity, the American twentieth-century luxury.

Only at the film's conclusion will we hear Mancini's main melody as a song. There is both a wise sophistication and a reassuring nostalgia to this tune, and it shares several features with the song from *10*, as indeed does the film. *That's Life!* gives us Harvey approaching his sixties; *10* gave us George Webber afraid of his forties. Both men are full of self-doubt: George follows a delusion of escape for a while; Harvey panics when all of his previous delusions run out. Both men have the steady standard of Julie Andrews as a mate; both films poke cruel fun at feckless clergy and the landscaping of the wealthy (George's headlong tumble down a hill by his pool; Harvey's troubles with lawn sprinklers). At least narratively, *That's Life!* has been considered, if not a sequel, a companion piece to *10*. Mancini's main songs for the two films seem to acknowledge that bond. For although the song from *10* begins in Cmaj^7 and ends around there while the song from *That's Life!* is in B♭, their first two phrases span the same intervals—a perfect fifth followed by a perfect fifth. Then, whereas the song from *10* strives upward like the yearning character of George before accepting the lessons that his escapade with Jenny have to teach him up to a high E in an A-minor chord, "Life in a Looking Glass" reconciles thoughtfully downward toward a low E after the two first phrases. It is a melody of closure and reconciliation. Its comforting chord changes have that truth-speaking quality of Mancini's best, and heard in the film at various times, often on a mellow guitar/syth, it has the feeling of coming home.

It is part of Edwards's narrative structure here to keep intercutting between Gillian's and Harvey's lives over this weekend, separate and together, then inserting sudden close-ups of the clinic equipment slowly processing Gillian's throat culture. Expressionless lab technicians and sterile machines work through the different stages of medical analysis, and in brief music cues to accompany those lab shots, Mancini uses the hard, impersonal sounds of a synthesizer while a second synth (harpsichord/guitarlike) plays a reflective but suspended, constricted melody line with muted strings and vibes in distant harmony. Each time Edwards cuts back to the progress of the lab, this instrumentation, with its technological coldness and its anxious pedal-point pulse, is instantly evocative. Will Gillian's biopsy be proven benign, or is there more to worry about? She alerts Harvey that she may want to cancel her upcoming tour, but she will not tell him why.

Familiar Mancini jazz-pop pieces accompany the ongoing "normalcy" of Fairchild family life—a baritone sax/strings/vibes combo at the party as the Fairchild family update one another about their far-flung lives, and two old tunes from *The Pink Panther* ("Champagne and Quail" and "Royal Blue") are used behind dinner scenes. But in this film Edwards has enough inner story layers going on to also need a constant, if narrow, stream of narrative scoring by Mancini—for instance, the high unison strings that break off into divided streams with piano obbligato as Gillian drift-dreams away from the dinner-table talk to look deeply at each of the family members there, wondering what the future holds.

Two great weights are lifted from Gillian Fairchild on the night of Harvey's birthday party: First, she is able to confront him about his hysterical behavior of late. She tells him he has three choices: he can continue to sulk about being old and be afraid; he can follow his spiral down to suicide; or he can "look at what you have" and make some use of it. It has been a long time since Harvey had to take back responsibility for how he lives among others and not dwell so much inside his own head. After that chastisement, he seems at first stunned, and then he seems like one who is beginning to waken. Second, Gillian receives the long-awaited news from her doctor (who attends the birthday party) that her biopsy is benign and she can stop worrying.

By casting a veteran of pop song stylists, Tony Bennett, to sing the main song for the end credits of *That's Life!* Mancini and lyricist Leslie Bricusse blended the sound of late middle age into their already nostalgic ballad—the baby boomers becoming seniors. Bricusse has said that he was thinking of one shot from the movie when he wrote these lyrics. It was the moment when Harvey looks at himself in the mirror: "If you look at your life in a looking glass, / you may see some things you don't want to see, / you may see the day your youth slipped away." And that sage, life-summarizing melody of Mancini caps the film with an affirmative grace.

Although not featured in the film's opening credits, Mancini's name is the first end credit to appear as the song begins and Bennett gently sings, "If you look at your life . . ." with that burnished, jazz-inflected, lived-in voice of his. He understands the vocal arc of the melody perfectly, even embellishing a wordless *vocalise* as the song is fading.

— — —

The other late project that Mancini was able to score exactly as he wanted, and with the most intimate expressive results, was occasioned by his ongoing association with Paul Newman. This was a new screen version of Tennessee Williams's *The Glass Menagerie*. Newman's wife, Joanne Woodward, had already played (on stage at the Williamstown and Long Wharf theaters) the role of the faded, frustrated southern belle Amanda Wingfield, whose hubby had worked for the phone company but then "fell in love with long distance" and left her with a disgruntled son, Tom, and a tremblingly shy crippled daughter, Laura. When the chance to preserve Woodward's interpretation of the role on film came up in 1987, John Malkovich was cast as Tom, the play's bitter, museful narrator, and Karen Allen as his reclusive sister, fragile collector of spun-glass animal figurines that are as vulnerable to sudden movement and loud thoughts as she.

Previous film versions of *The Glass Menagerie* included one in 1950 with Jane Wyman and Kirk Douglas, which had a flowing, reverential score by Max Steiner, and a 1973 television production with Katharine Hepburn and Sam Waterston, which used a simple, childlike piano waltz at the beginning and end as almost its entire John Barry score that had worked perfectly. As this new version went before the cameras, Newman himself had only just won an Oscar as best actor in *The Color of Money* (1986), and he took it as a sign that he could try his hand at directing a classic American play. It so happened that two of Newman's past films as director had been about similarly disappointed and oppressed ladies: the unattached schoolteacher in *Rachel, Rachel* (1969) and the greatly encumbered family matriarch in *The Effect of Gamma Rays on Man-in-the-Moon Marigolds* (1972). Both had simple Americana scores; both had starred Woodward; both were natural stepping-stones for her toward this more famous role of Amanda, the abandoned and aging housewife from Blue Mountain, Tennessee, now living in a dusky flat in St. Louis. Tom hates living there but seems impotent to do anything about it, barely hangs on to a warehouse job, writes poetry, dreams of striking out for far-off places, yet stays behind, sarcastically berating his mother and defending his sister, Laura, who spends her days playing old phonograph records and tending her unchanging glass menagerie. Her favorite figurine is the unicorn, the magical one with the forehead horn. It is all Mama Amanda can do, in the middle of this tense depressive household, to keep up a constant stream of chatter about the old days in a tone of voice somewhere between garden party charm and suppressed hysteria.

Mancini's score has two interlocking parts. His main score keeps so quietly behind the characters that it is easy to dismiss how intense is its gaze on them. It is a character score, in kind, and its tone is that of a troubled but wise blues, somehow passed through one of the avant-garde French composers of the 1930s. The other complimentary layer of the score consists of seven carefully configured ballroom blues for an interchanging group of eight players whose sound emanates from the nearby Paradise Dance Hall. The revolving glitter-ball chandelier from that dance hall casts a strange effect of displaced gaiety when it reflects through Amanda's apartment window and across her walls. Barely audible, these blues pieces seem to be coming from much farther away (like twenty years far) than next door. "Time," says Tom the poet in one of his soliloquies to us, "is the longest distance between two places."

John Malkovich's Tom speaks to us in an almost hypnotized, stoned, but also suffering monotone, so burdened with his mother's false cheerfulness and tidy criticisms. And she is just as smothering to the meek Laura, whom she warns to "keep yourself fresh and pretty for any gentleman caller who might stop by" as they used to in the fabled South. There are precious few gentleman callers now in 1930s St. Louis. Amanda still basks in the memory of it, though, not in the schizophrenic way of Williams's heroines in *A Streetcar Named Desire* or *The Eccentricities of a Nightingale* but rather with a desperate kind of wistfulness, which Woodward personifies in her performance. Mancini's score picks up on that quality but then enmeshes it with the near-despondent perspective of Tom.

"Tom's Theme," which both opens the film and lends its dark question mark to several key moments throughout, is far more than just a slow, plodding blues. It is the bleakest piece of music Mancini ever wrote. Two five-bar phrases, minus a grace-note first bar, act as a kind of out-of-tempo prelude to the piece, the first phrase in D minor beginning on G (a descending oboe and clarinet countered by a bassoon's rising line on the bottom). On screen (and this is happening behind the film's main titles) we see Tom walking toward a set of derelict row houses. The light is flat; the streets are gray and empty. At the end of the first phrase of the prelude there is a long pause—Tom, in character, suddenly turns around and looks at us, at the camera, with his weight shifted back on one leg, not exactly observing us nor wanting something from us; we cannot tell what his attitude might be. Then as he turns back and resumes his walk toward the row houses, the music resumes with its second prelude phrase mirroring the first but beginning on F and at the end of which there is another long pause. Tom turns and regards us again. Is he daring us to something? These interruptions in both the action and the music are uniquely tying the score and the scene together, putting us on notice that music hereafter is going to be the offstage voice of the characters, thin and laconic though it will be.

After this second pause Tom turns back away from us again, and Michael Ballhaus's fluid camera follows him up the steps and into one row house. Mancini's main title music now settles into a slow pulselike tempo (piano, few strings, few winds). The soprano sax begins the main melody in a dark A minor with the sobering fourth interval adding an air of disillusionment to the line. The sax begins on a high F♯ that is repeated until it climbs to the higher A in a B♭(♯♮) chord, then plunges, almost swooning, in a classic blues gesture that carries the strong scent of old southern jazz and then walks on slowly through twenty-eight chord changes across twenty-eight bars before repeating the first phrase of the prelude as a conclusion. Thus the same question mark is posed again, unenlightened, which is, of course, Tom's quandary: how can any of us build a sufficient self on the debris of inadequacies, contradictions, and fragilities that we inherit?

Tom delivers his opening soliloquy directly to the camera as he strolls through the abandoned row-house apartment, Tennessee Williams's legendary musicality of language taking over for any soundtrack scoring. We then meet, as though in Tom's memory, the Wingfields. Mancini's ensemble devolves to two clarinets, and we can speculate whether they might represent Tom and his meek needful sister, Tom and his guilt, or even Amanda and her long-lost prime of life as a southern belle. Mancini's opening cue has indeed been bleak in giving voice to these unhappy people and their self-made sorrow, but it has taught us to identify with them, too, out of respect, rather than musically trying to romanticize them. Real blues just tells it like it is.

Amanda's long speech about her Blue Mountain days as a demure and frill-frocked debutante besieged by gentleman callers is scored with one tune borrowed from another composer. The story goes that when Woodward had performed this role on stage, she had used a piece of music by poet/composer Paul Bowles as a backdrop, and now she requested that Mancini incorporate it in *his* scoring for Amanda's two memory speeches. He obliged with solo violin, then bassoon and winds playing this non-Mancini theme, Bowles's "Jonquils."

Amanda is privately horrified at the underhanded way that life has deposited her with her disabled children into this modern underclass existence.

She learns that Laura has not been attending the local business school as everyone supposed but instead, being so shy, has been stealing away for long walks to fill the class time and then heading home each day as though just released from class—a dreadful secret for anyone to keep. To Amanda it is a personal betrayal. (Through the apartment window we can hear the dance hall music, possibly a band rehearsal of an old trumpet blues that seems to dramatize the Amanda/Laura scene in which that secret is revealed.) It is perhaps those two tones of Amanda's voice—one high, constricted, and sweet, the other breathy and scolding—that Mancini was trying to capture by his choice of soprano sax as the main instrument that sounds in Tom's head, often supported by clarinets and bassoon on either side. By contrast, Laura's music, like her collection of figurines, is delicate and weightless (and rather dull and wan) for piano, celesta, and solo flute. It turns like a figurine on a revolving base to a mechanical waltz.

Tom tells how he has been trying to find a gentleman caller to come over for dinner to meet Laura, and we hear "Tom's Theme" varied in its details and driven by a rolling harp figure as though time passing. When he reveals that he has invited a workplace colleague to meet Laura, she panics, and Ballhaus's camera suddenly becomes very agitated, revolves 360 degrees around her, and there is a brief dissonant music cue from the winds, featuring oboe and bassoon. In these small ways the sparse score makes itself known and the evolution of Mancini's scoring abilities is plain—all the way from the 1960s to this subtle, psychological enhancement through music. Newman introduces some temporarily active camera motions and quick cuts as Amanda's spirits rise at the thought of receiving company for dinner, and Mancini's score almost admits a disturbance into its language in the form of a fluttering suspense passage we might compare to the shimmering occult opening of *Nightwing*.

With a dinner guest on the menu, our awareness of "dinner music" drifting in from the apartment's open window increases and we can start to pick out Mancini's various dance hall pieces—a slow tramp blues, a whimpering waltz blues in the Paul Whiteman style, a muted trumpet foxtrot, a tired rumba, that slurred tango, all as background score. The subtle carry-over between, for instance, the sultry soprano sax heard in the adjacent dance band and the same instrument voicing "Tom's Theme" in the foreground dramatic score helps link the whole film—place and time, character and meaning—together. As Newman once wrote: "I always knew that moving the audience was going to be difficult. Henry, through his beautiful score, managed to make my work easy. He has a great sense of place, of locale, and then of what the characters are experiencing there."[2] During Laura's brief evening with that gentleman caller, Mancini lets her theme rally briefly, meekly, before the crass yakety sax and clarinet from the dance hall retake the floor.

The Wingfields' major disappointment to come is, of course, that Tom's pal from work, though perfectly willing to come for dinner, is actually engaged to be married and unavailable for anyone like Laura. Amanda says the situation is all Tom's fault and begins her final berating of him—mother to son. It is Tom's breaking point. He finally leaves home, "attempting to find in motion what was lost in space." He tells us, "I could have stopped, but I was pursued by something." Here Mancini gives us Tom's prelude again. "I may be walking alone in some strange city before I have found companions when all at once my sister touches my shoulder." ("Laura's Theme," played on a broken, barely pitched piano, whispers here.) "Oh, Laura," Tom breathes, "Laura, I am more faithful than I intended to be." Painful as it is, Tom cannot, nor can any of us, separate from the family ties, loyalties, yearnings, and regrets into which he was born and through which anyone grows. Mancini might have scored this play-out with direct expression of that yearning. But by this age and era and in this context he knew what Tennessee Williams was on about here. There could be nothing truer than the soprano sax teaching us Tom's bleak theme one last time—perhaps with a slower piano pulse, a slightly more tender reading of the theme here than before, and the basses fixing a firm period on the bottom of that last chord.

For Mancini, such efficiency of musical language and modesty of means shows that he could have continued to adapt to whatever kinds of films the next generation might have presented to him. But people still mainly thought of him in terms of his first fame—the nostalgic love songs and cool jazz. Thus, it would turn out that his summarizing music for *That's Life* and his disillusioned blues for *The Glass Menagerie* would constitute his last genuinely satisfying theatrical film jobs—the modern film, with its nostalgic score, and the period film, with its fairly modern harmonies. Both were small and thoughtful productions, yet Mancini worked on them as intensely as he had ever scored a blockbuster in the 1960s. If the work was there, Mancini was still ready to consult, but of course most of the film jobs from the late 1980s or early 1990s on were going to others—or if they did come Mancini's way, they came hobbled and compromised.

CHAPTER 15

A Closing Door That Wasn't There Before

I n four upcoming film deals with the New Hollywood, Mancini would feel so betrayed that he would wish seriously to have his name removed from being credited at all. First was the salacious Blake Edwards romp *Skin Deep* (1989) about an alcoholic LA writer who plows his way through a list of sexual encounters (including a famously crude gag about glow-in-the-dark condoms), trying to thwart a bad case of writer's block. Even though the main character, played by John Ritter, has a preference for the songs of Cole Porter, what we got on the soundtrack was another gallery of 1980s pop records, Edwards having jettisoned the brief pop song and other music that Mancini had already written for the film. Mancini wanted out, but the studio insisted on holding him to his onscreen credit: "Original music by . . ."

Next was the Bill Cosby family film *Ghost Dad* (1990), directed by Sidney Poitier. Certainly Poitier, one of the late twentieth century's great film stars, had directed reliable pictures before, and Cosby had been a staple of stand-up comedy and groundbreaking television roles for decades. Who knows where *Ghost Dad* went wrong? After audience previews and one step away from the studio's signing off on it, after it was all scored and promoted, someone decided it had to be revamped. As with *Lifeforce*, by the time these second-guessers had come into the screening room to tear things apart, Mancini had already moved on. No one had much enthusiasm left for this anachronistic film anyway; they were not about to adapt Mancini's existing score recordings, redistribute them throughout the film, and try them in different places to bridge the new gaps and cuts. Forget it. Better to just span the holes with some continuous beats and some imported records by, well, anybody. The denigration was still painful to Mancini months afterward. "The point is that most of the stuff that's in the picture is not mine. The situation had to do with their deciding to use temporary tracks at various places instead of composed music, and I was not comfortable with all that. It was probably the biggest fiasco that I've ever encountered."[1]

The plot for *Ghost Dad*, which is one of the film's systemic problems, probably looked okay on paper. Cosby played an overworked businessman, a widower whose habit had been to narrate bedtime stories into a tape recorder for his young kids to play back at night while he was away. At least he could be present while absent. When suddenly he dies in a taxicab accident, he takes to haunting his household with reassurances and fatherly advice from beyond the grave. But there is another contrivance: somehow in the cosmic scheme of things, he is only allotted a few days to arrange an inheritance that will support his family, some earthly plan to provide for them once he has crossed. The awkward mix of that family warmth through Cosby's humor, the confusing story with its macabre implications, and the self-conscious special effects was something that the producers never managed to clarify. Mancini's instincts were correct from the beginning, though. The score he gave them did not try to underline the already clichéd family life on screen; its main theme derived its form from three layers: synthesizer and bass guitar repeating the basic chord pattern, a funk guitar blended with a double-time rhythm waiting for the main melody, and the tune itself on ARP—an intriguing concoction, illusive and indistinct, with a chromatic outline that keeps shifting.

Slow meanderings and suspensions of this musical material were to underscore a number of dialogue and spooky action scenes, but only a few cues of such scoring are left in the film as it was released. EWI flute and bell-like details still lie behind Dad's tape-recorded good-nights. Soprano sax, passed to alto, plays a mellow theme under the family's first realization that Dad has returned to them as a spirit and that perhaps in this way they are still parented. Strings, on the edge of tenderness, join that moment until a phantom electric organ enters warily, trading phrases with the alto sax. The family urges their ghost dad to communicate directly with them, not just through signs and knockings in the night. As the kids join Dad's efforts to both fix their financial future and keep his ghostliness a secret from society, the score was supposed to mix the fun of pizzicato string writing with EWI bassoon accents for the sneaky aspects of the plot and chromatic descending synth lines attending the special effects and bringing the viewer into the story. Little of that music remains.

There is no telling now how a well-mounted version of this film with a Mancini score would have fared. Instead, the story struggles for a point of view and its score is diced and randomly strewn about, a disembodied ghost in its own right, spotted only briefly as it disappears around another corner.

Ginny recalled, "I just know that Henry became very frustrated with the business in later years, because in some cases there were people making artistic decisions based on no experience at all, and so the whole industry had changed. Just frustrating for him and, I have been told, for many others as well."[2] Daughter Monica concurred, saying, "He obviously wanted to work, to be hired, to be one of the big guys, but here he was, slowly being replaced by younger, less experienced people and for no good reasons."[3] Mancini himself would simply say, "Well, it's just happening too often for my taste."[4]

Ultimately Poitier wrote to Mancini what others have described as "a lovely letter," not exactly apologizing but expressing appreciation that he was really good at what he did and that more attention "should" have been paid to the music during the chaotic process of putting that particular film back together. Technically, Mancini *had* done a fair job of bridging the film's opposing elements—the family context, the phantom fun, the light funk. In other words, the failure of *Ghost Dad* as a score was not because of Mancini's inability to deal with the New Hollywood. And yet it seemed that the same thing, the same kind of score trashing, kept happening.

Blake Edwards again pulled rank with his 1991 comedy *Switch*, another ghostly tale, about a man who dies and returns to life as a woman—Edwards's old favorite gender-bending topic again in yet another guise. But even here, and as he had done so recently with films, Edwards began lopping off whole portions of Mancini's score, including its main title music in favor of an old pop record of the 1960s. Mancini was feeling more than frustrated; he was feeling betrayed. The score for *Switch* had begun in a burst of fresh inspiration, with Mancini taking an old technique and applying it to the new situation: the notion of basing composition on the particular sound of a single instrument and a specific player. Before even starting the music for *Switch*, he could hear in his head the movie's own designer sound. At a cocktail party he had noted a strange violin player who strolled around the room serenading the guests. The feathery, other-worldly sound that this fellow, David Wilson, produced was emanating from his own modified wireless electric violin. His own short-bowed playing style seemed to be in the Grappelli tradition, yet there was that strange disembodied aspect to the tones he was making—that synthesized alienation, much more subtle than would have been possible for the early generation of electric instruments. It was artificial yet alluring and expressive of the devilish pact at the heart of the gender-trade story in *Switch*. Listening today we find Wilson's sound to be rather curt and controlling (hypnotic) in the main title track, with Abe Laboriel's repetitive bass guitar riff behind it, and Mancini's opening theme to be a rather tight, uncomfortable melody of restricted range, a bit glum. Indeed the whole score sounds constrained, harmonically speaking.

You can either blame the draining effects of this recent spate of altered and trashed scores, which would be enough to discourage anyone, or you could notice that Edwards's film was itself struggling to find a heart. Theatrically released but funded by HBO cable TV and headed there anon, *Switch* was meant to be a 1990s update of the 1960s film *Goodbye Charlie*. In this version Amanda was once a gigolo guy who died at the hands of a jealous lover and now is brought back to see life from the woman's perspective. In spite of the comic performance of Ellen Barkin, there is little to grab onto for scoring purposes here. Fifteen, maybe twenty minutes of music at most are what Mancini provided, but once again the powers that be—in this case Edwards himself, negotiating with funders—overruled Mancini right from the start. It is possible that Edwards saw the score's lack of dynamism, the narrowness of the main theme, but if that were true the two men could have worked it out as they always had. The fact remains that Edwards was listening to the New Hollywood. He had his heart set on opening the film with the old pop folksong by Joni Mitchell "Both Sides Now." He and the executives at HBO liked the way the old lyric seemed to speak to the plot of their film—"I've looked at life from both sides now . . . / and still somehow / it's life's illusions I recall." Not even repeated phone calls from Mancini could dissuade Edwards from that idea. What was gained in that clever lyric match hardly outweighed what was lost by jettisoning Mancini's carefully chosen score concept. His original ethereal opening, while not gripping music, did at least set up the occult premise of the film using that electric violin. It would have also created what Mancini always called the "question mark" for the viewer as to what they were about to see. "Both Sides Now" sets up nothing. Thirty minutes go by before the first fragment of Mancini music is heard in the final version of the film: twenty seconds of a complex modal piano solo barely audible during a private fashion-show sequence.

Edwards's script for *Switch* imagines God and Satan in purgatory debating where the deceased soul of Steve Brooks, the aforementioned unrepentant gigolo and boorish misogynist, should be consigned. A supernatural bargain is struck that if Steve returns to earth as a woman and can get one other female to like him, to value him, he will be allowed into heaven. Edwards can explore his frequent gender theme in the form of a fantasy with all the expected gags of trying to adapt a male consciousness to the female body ("I can't think with all this hair on my head") and actually *owning* breasts now—and, of course, trying to walk with dignity in impossibly high heels.

In his book on the films of Blake Edwards, Sam Wasson called the film "a singular accomplishment . . . creating a fully realized slapstick role for a woman."[5] Narratively, though, all of this comedy and any character development plays either without music on the soundtrack or with background pop-rock records. (Music supervisor Tom Bocci adds one of his *own* rock records plus some Lyle Lovett and other selections.) It is only after an hour of screen time that we get the welcome presence of a sympathetic Mancini song—the score's second main theme, "It's All There," played ever so seductively on Wilson's electric violin. We can barely hear it, though, and anyway it is abruptly cut off before its time. Only thrice do we hear a piece of Mancini's intended main title music: once as Satan visits Amanda and tells her the time for the switch-and-redemption is up; then again when Amanda learns she is pregnant by her earthly boyfriend and tells him she wants to keep the baby, that it is a miracle "to have a life growing inside of you" (the ethereal violin plays that occult minor-key theme again, giving weight to the scene and to Mancini's argument that he should have been allowed to use it where the film began); and then just twenty seconds more are heard on a very willowy-sounding synth guitar as Amanda gives birth. The gracious ending that Edwards gives to *Switch* is to have Amanda bear a baby girl and then die in childbirth in order to return to purgatory, there to be judged finally worthy of heaven, since she has indeed won the affection of one female on earth: her infant daughter, who truly loves her for her own self.

Whereas Mancini had seemed infuriated by the whole experience of *Ghost Dad*, he seemed merely bewildered over what had become of his score to *Switch*. Unlike the other Edwards bedroom comedies from which Mancini's music had been, to varying degrees, expunged, *Switch* had a forthright story to tell and needed (he thought) solid narrative scoring. But starting with the film's opening credits, pop records took over. That was the real "switch."

Mancini already knew that his next film score would have to be built around someone else's prepaid pop tune. But he took the job anyway, just because it was offered by old friend director Arthur Hiller. *Married to It* (1991) may have been someone's idea of a 1990s version of the 1980s hit *The Big Chill*, wherein an ensemble of former college radicals from the 1960s gathered to catch up on old times and to see where their dreams have gone. As a scoring assignment, the whole project begins with that same insult: the main title sequence is once again taken away from Mancini and given over to a pop-folk record by (again) Joni Mitchell called "The Circle Game." Indeed, Hiller uses Mancini's scoring only to cover a couple of montage sequences in the film—a synthesized combo of EWI flute and Clavinet keys backed by a drum machine, all doing a minor-key quasi-baroque interlude as we watch three couples go about their middle-class lives and chatter on about modern suburban life. "The Circle Game" is reprised at a PTA school assembly for the film's close when everyone gathers to celebrate the future generation, who, God willing, will improve on the self-indulgent mess boomers have made. Mancini tries to brighten the tune by giving it to two recorders over a smooth synth backdrop, later with a solo pan flute sound, all aiming at the innocent classroom atmosphere that we all think we remember from our own past. Well intentioned and performed, *Married to It* was just too transparently trying to be a 1990s manifesto for the middle class and went straight from short theater runs to home video, barely leaving a footnote and barely taking up a week of Mancini's time.

By now Mancini's yearning for reprieve from that pinched prosaic kind of scoring—having to fight for every thirty-second cue of synthesized filler, working for those New Hollywood committees that made films by compromise and that certainly had no commitment to the value of a narrative music score—can be felt in the last two pop music albums he would record in 1992 under his aforementioned renewed RCA contract: two programs of old, old songs from the so-called Great American Songbook. His relief can be heard in the thickly lush, almost mossy orchestrations with which he dressed these songs, as though he were luxuriating in the chance to write orchestrally again and to wander the gratifying chord changes and structures of those classic melodies—to be melodic again after all these dry, begrudging electronic "units" of scoring.

For a time Mancini worked with Leslie Bricusse again on an animated update of the old MGM cartoon antagonists *Tom and Jerry* (1992). Along with six songs for the characters to sing, there was a lot of busy music meant to chase the action on screen. Indeed, for the first ten minutes of the film there is no dialogue at all and Mancini's scoring micromanages the storytelling all by itself, handily. His idea for a main theme (which covers the main title animation showing our two heroes in a series of the old, familiar slapstick sight gags) begins with a drum machine that whacks out a hard two-beat; then a couple of harp glissandos sweep past, then flourishes from the National Philharmonic wind section, then a boogie-woogie beat takes hold (low winds and a rhythm piano, somewhere between "Baby Elephant Walk" and "What's Happening!") and the theme starts on an E♭ clarinet. It is a melody based in a wagging tritone with a couple of bent blues notes along the line. Sax takes over for the clarinet the second time around, and a honky-tonk piano does the bridge. It all has a touch of the slovenly swagger attributed to Tom the cartoon cat. Working from his decades of experience, Mancini's orchestra runs, falls, builds, gasps, and scampers in perfect collaboration with the screen. But it was hardly a prestige assignment.

By this point the one most egregious insult left to be leveled at Mancini to cap all the rest would have been if Edwards were to try to resurrect the Pink Panther series again this late in the game, and then to any degree discount Mancini's music in it. In 1993 Edwards did return to the franchise. Of course, Clouseau had died with Sellers, but what if he had produced a son who had many of Clouseau's exasperating qualities? Italian comic actor Roberto Benigni (*Johnny Stecchino*) was tapped for the role, and the plot would have him ineptly, clumsily, but with boundless enthusiasm, trying to solve the kidnapping of an Arab princess. Edwards's optimism for the project extended to rehiring several familiar faces from the original Panther films: Herbert Lom as Inspector (now Commissioner) Dreyfus; Burt Kwok as Cato; even Claudia Cardinale, once a princess, now Maria Gambrelli, Clouseau's mistress and now mother of Jacques (Benigni). And to complete the reunion, he did invite that one final alumnus, Mancini, actually putting him on screen as Bobby McFerrin's scat-singing version of the "*Pink Panther* Theme" is heard at the film's opening: he hands off his baton to the animated panther. There were comic possibilities in the whole setup, but critics quickly caught onto the strain of the whole project. While praising Benigni's energy, they bemoaned that it all felt like a retread, a sequel of a sequel without its own jurisdiction and with too many misfired gags. Mancini's music, likewise, could find little to grab onto of the color or sense of fun that the Pink Panther franchise once represented. Music was no longer very important in any Blake Edwards film anyway. Mancini's end-credit instrumental version of the main theme is particularly satisfying, though, recorded in July 1993 with much of the same London crew as had been doing his recent RCA/BMG albums and with Phil Todd happily taking the tenor-sax solo part that Plas Johnson had originated thirty years earlier.

While this would prove to be Blake Edwards's last film project before retiring, Roberto Benigni would go on to redeem his career with his own Italian comedy, *Life Is Beautiful*, about a father who tries to encourage his young son by playing the clown even though they are confined to a Nazi concentration camp. He would win the best actor Oscar for that role in 1998. Mancini, however, would not get the same chance for redemption. *Son of the Pink Panther* would be his last feature film score. More work was still to come—three charity projects and a sabbatical from screenwriting to help Blake Edwards chase his dream of producing a Broadway show. But this film's closing animation of the panther and the figure of Clouseau Jr. chasing each other off into cartoon infinity has an unhappy resonance to it now alongside Mancini's story.

Almost to Broadway

For thirteen years since Blake Edwards's successful experience with Julie Andrews on the film *Victor/Victoria*, he had been renewing the theatrical rights to the property, the story and characters, at considerable expense. His longtime producer and partner Tony Adams was urging him to do something with it or cut it loose. One idea was to take its song-and-dance aspects to Broadway. But for Edwards to suddenly tackle the wholly untried medium of the stage musical at the age of seventy-one seemed perilous and slightly mad. On the other hand, what a vehicle it would be for Julie Andrews. Now age fifty-eight, she had been looking to achieve her own return to musical theater, where she had begun her career. She would be sixty by the time any serious plans could be realized, so there was not a lot of time to waste if they really wanted to do this thing. But first Edwards, Adams, and choreographer Rob Marshall would have to cobble together some kind of a show. Edwards started writing the musical's "book," and of course Mancini and Leslie Bricusse would try to revisit the same story they had tackled in 1982 and come up with Broadway-styled songs.

One must pause here for a moment, though, to consider that Mancini and Bricusse had actually tried to write a stage musical together once before in 1978 based on the George Bernard Shaw play *Major Barbara*, about a high-society wag who joins the Salvation Army. The writers would be Jerome Lawrence and Robert E. Lee, already famous for their play *Inherit the Wind*, and the production would star Julie Andrews, who, according to Bricusse, would have been at the peak of her powers in a role she was born to play. Sadly, some fifteen original songs hung in the balance as the Shaw estate began to haggle with the fledgling show's producer over how the Shaw material would be handled—whether the original lines that were cleared for stage dialogue could also be used as lyrics in prospective songs and how those rights might be negotiated.

Mancini had been tempted even before that to write a stage musical. He had thought there were great stage-song possibilities in the Antoine de Saint-Exupery allegory "The Little Prince," and he began thinking about it in the late 1960s, but the rights to that material were going to be likewise difficult to negotiate, and before long, lawyers made everyone miserable. So it was not for lack of trying that Mancini had never written an official Broadway score. For a while it looked like *Major Barbara* would be the answer. His melodies for that score draw on various stage-musical traditions. There are vaudevillian soft-shoe numbers ("Everybody Loves You") reminding one of *Darling Lili*'s quaint music-hall tunes; "The Sin Business" echoes Mancini's insouciant clarinet theme from the film *W. C. Fields and Me* with stepped-up energy; and they both recall show tunes from Broadway composer/producer Vincent Youmans's day. There are Richard Rodgers–like soliloquies that had been composed to Bricusse's set-lyrics, adding musical extensions, holds, and changing tempos to accommodate the virtuosity of the words while trying not to sacrifice compositional sense. In Broadway musical theater of the 1970s, Stephen Sondheim raised this latter style to high pop art, using composition and stage conceptualization well beyond Mancini's level.

Even so, there were two excellent songs in the projected score for *Major Barbara* that are important to any survey of Mancini's evolution as a composer. "Insanity" may be Mancini's most Sondheimian song, a finely crafted, lilting waltz that sways back and forth between Cmaj^7 and F^6 chords before nonchalantly flowing elsewhere around Bricusse's scolding lyrics: "Insanity—/ though man worships his Savior, his behavior is odd; / he will happily murder and maim in the name of his god," or "We keep pets and kill children; / we make war to keep peace. What's our modern ideal of a civilized life? Ancient Greece!" Mancini's clever workmanship, lifting those two chords up to land on A♭maj^7 with the line "It's perfectly plain: we're insane," smoothly whirls the waltz off into the next phrase with a bemused inevitability and a touch of sorrow. Almost as successful and more adventurous is "Do I Laugh or Do I Cry?" which begins in very dark chromatics descending from B minor through sevenths and ninths to A minor during the song's first words: "The moment had to come, / something in life, that blinding blow, / something you prayed you'd never know, / crushing you, mangling you, stifling you, strangling you." What then proceeds in a number of line extensions is an easy tune that is perfectly shaped and clearly intentioned but might not have made the most consequential Broadway song when heard from the back row of an expectant full house. It was reflective and inwardly aimed, not ideal qualities for the Great White Way. But as an indication of Mancini working his way back into thoughtful melody writing at that time, it is an important and sincere trial. In the end these songs were never tried on the stage, never edited by Mancini or rethought, never critiqued by others. They remained markers on the shelf, as the Shaw estate decided to keep control and Mancini/ Bricusse decided not to wait around. By 1979 the deal was dead, the option was retired, and the songs for *Major Barbara* were forgotten. But Mancini took the lessons learned there and brought them forward now to the 1990s.

For his plan to put *Victor/Victoria* on the stage, Blake Edwards wanted to reprise two (eventually five) of the songs from the original film, but Mancini/ Bricusse still faced a challenge: this time they were not writing for a fixed, finished film scene but rather for a so-far-unfinished stage play. Having to address the same story they had already "musicalized" years ago was an additional complication. It is disturbing to read of the seemingly wayward, arbitrary, cranky way in which Edwards set about the task of translating the film into a credible Broadway show in the crucial months before try-out performances could commence. But perhaps only free-flowing creative types would understand how these things come together—not by legal-pad lists and typed outlines but by scraps of paper, phone chat, arguments, pouts, apologies, and suppositions. Of course, the director's famous spats with Hollywood preceded him to New York, and there was a coalition of Broadway insiders always suspicious of any California poser, predicting—even hoping—he would fail. (Even on the occasion of Edwards's death in December 2010 at the age of eighty-eight, obituaries continued to criticize his boldness in ever having tried to take on Broadway.)

By some reports Edwards had already invested $2 million of his own money, much of it going into the complicated pre-opening auditions and rehearsals, during which he hoped to attract other investors while gradually learning the language of the stage. As Philip Weiss wrote in a *New York Times* profile, "Now and then around the rehearsal space I hear mutterings from company members about whether Edwards can make the transition [from movies to stage]. He's a film director who is used to building a story with cuts. But in theater you can never split the focus. One day I hear someone say, 'Let's try that shot again.'" Weiss reported being dismayed by the faltering, stumbling slowness of Edwards's rehearsal process: "Who can understand Edwards' methods? He fusses endlessly over one-liners and ignores larger problems. There is a great hole in the first act." Yet he also wrote, "[Edwards] mixes machismo and confession in a way I find beguiling."[1]

Victor/Victoria was supposed to go into previews in the spring of 1995 with a Broadway opening soon after. But so many things were out of shape. And yet in reporting all of these delays and quandaries, haggles and hopes, one is really just postponing the inevitable subject of this chapter—and the real reason for the delays and for its ultimate weaknesses as a show: the sudden and quite unexpected health crisis of its composer.

\- \- \-

Ever since Edwards had told the team that *Victor/Victoria* was definitely going to be a Broadway reality, once funding was finally set, and once Andrews was committed, Mancini and Bricusse had been chipping away at the fledgling score one or two songs at a time in between other jobs. "It was not necessarily the way Hank and I liked to work," Bricusse confirmed later. "Usually when I'm involved with a show my modus operandi is to immerse myself in the characters and the story, whatever the setting, and write in one uninterrupted, sustained effort. This was undeniably much harder, just sort of visiting the project at wildly irregular intervals in a very unsatisfying stop-start process."[2]

As the production started to come together in late 1993 and Edwards and Andrews could see that it was going to happen after all, the team set a completion date: Bricusse and his wife, Evie; Henry and Ginny; Blake and (when she could) Julie would gather as before at the Edwards's home in the mountains above Gstaad, Switzerland, for one all-out push to finalize the score and the book. The month of February 1994 had been cleared on everyone's schedule. Mancini had two concerts to conduct mid-month, but for those he would be gone only three days. Otherwise they were committed to write a show. "From February first till finished," Bricusse proclaimed and it was agreed.

For two weeks composer and lyricist living under the same roof were able to make more strides than the past year had seen. Decisions such as what kinds of songs were needed (even though the script was still sketchy), the variety of meter and mood, intros and ostinatos, all came out of those sessions—the raw material for songs that would be more carefully constructed and refined later. By some accounts they had pieces of twenty-five songs by the middle of February, though only the strongest would be developed, and of course only the ones that fit dramatically into the final show would be used.

The unrelieved focus of the work, with no screen characters to reference but only pages and pages of lyrics tied to theoretical stage action and characters, was rewarding but demanding. At the same time, the effort to find a fresh perspective on a story they had already scored a dozen years ago was beginning to wear on Mancini. Ominously, when he felt exhausted these days, there seemed to be no bouncing back. Sleep was not restorative. Still strong in that sense of personal self-discipline that had been a hallmark of his career, he was nevertheless beginning to sense a real constitutional weakness in his energy levels; even his breathing was being affected. By the time he was feeling lightheaded to the point of fainting, he resolved to consult his doctor back in the States to see about a new health regimen. With Ginny, he flew back to California intending to resume *Victor/Victoria* soon. While he fulfilled those concert dates, Ginny busied herself with long-standing preparations for Henry's seventieth-birthday bash in April to be held at UCLA's Pauley Pavilion, inviting three thousand guests, a band, and a list of celebrities. Ginny was still the ultimate event producer.

Mancini was examined by the family physician once the last concert was completed on February 18. The most immediate jeopardy to his well-being was the discovery of blood clots that had lodged in the lungs and had led to his fatigue and breathlessness. He was hospitalized for a few days and sent home. The physician spoke to Ginny alone about the other crisis: Mancini had an inoperable cancer of the pancreas, which was affecting his liver. To Ginny the doctor confessed that pancreatic is among the most virulent forms of cancer and that Mancini had only months to live. To Henry he explained how serious the situation was without actually calling it terminal. With only a little research, Mancini could have known that his affliction was the fourth leading cause of cancer death in the United States in those days. Even with therapy, the survival rate was something like 5 percent. One of the problems is that there are no definitive symptoms until it is too late. Certainly early detection and a new surgical procedure called "the Whipple," developed in the years since Mancini's death, have improved patients' outlooks once a heavy regimen of chemotherapy and radiation therapies is completed.

But in 1994 Mancini's condition was conclusive. Some very difficult phone calls back to Blake and Julie, Leslie and Evie in Gstaad altered the whole future of *Victor/Victoria*. Mancini began taking a prescribed, if doubtful, cocktail of medications and resolved, in his public statements if not in his midnight mind, to battle his cancer back into remission. He also resolved to continue work, through phone and fax, with Bricusse on the remaining songs for the new show. Bricusse later confessed:

The great shock of receiving that news was that if I'd had to pick three people that I knew in the world who would live to a great age, Henry would have been at the top of the list. He was so laid-back and easygoing and unspoiled. Nothing ever ruffled him. I remember once he was recording at CTS Studios in London, conducting one of the rehearsal arrangements that had been done for him early in the *Victor/Victoria* film sessions with Julie doing "The Shady Dame from Saville," and it was clearly not right. And Henry calmly said, "We'll have to hold it here," and he proceeded to reorchestrate the number right there and then with the musicians. He reassembled the entire piece in, like, twenty-five minutes and had them play it again. And of course he had completely turned it around into something quite wonderful from what had been a total shambles. Unflappable, he was. So how could he now be dangerously ill? That's a shock.[3]

Work, Mancini declared, was therapy. The news spread everywhere that this famous baby boomer music man was ill. On a segment of the ABC-TV magazine show *20/20*, asked about how he was coping with his illness, he said:

Something hit me about two months ago—cancer . . . and it changed my whole work attitude. I used to get depressed about the dumbest things but now this—something has just ripped that whole [mind-set] right off my head . . . [now] I feel very much at peace for some reason. The outcome? I'm not going to fight it. I don't want to call it a psychic experience because it's not that. It is a real cleansing—less buzzing around in your head of things to do and to think about. There is more focus now and, geez, I've been trying to do that for forty years in this business.[4]

Monica and Felice did not necessarily like that line "I'm not going to fight it." They got on the phone researching all sorts of south-of-the-border clinics and cures the American Medical Association might not approve of but that were rumored to be effective. None seemed serious, though. It was left to Chris to give the benediction that trumped all of those frantic last-hour efforts. On national television, he simply said, "We really are just dedicating ourselves to giving our father the best of ourselves right now."[5] About all of those phone calls to "alternative medicine" shops, Monica said, "It's hard to sit still when you think that there is something that can be done. In a weird way it's a wonderful way of giving back. You never know what you can do for a parent or how you can give back anything close to what they've given you."[6] And Felice, who had once written an appreciative poem about her parents that her father had set to music, called "Sometimes," was saying, "It's time to take care of Dad."[7] Mancini, still trying to fathom it all, said,

"What matters most is my family and friends. That's it. Regardless of what happens, things have never been better in my life. I am very much at peace."[8]

To entertainment historian Leonard Maltin, Mancini gave perhaps his last interview on the back patio of his house, thanking the Hollywood musicians for all of their generosity and friendship during these rough times and attributing to the memory of his mother, way back there along the Allegheny River, any sense of peacefulness and "good vibes" he was able to draw on now. In one way he could rationalize all of this sudden press attention not as a farewell but as a nod to his seventieth birthday coming on April 16—with Ginny's high-profile party set for the nineteenth.

All three thousand friends gathered, contributing $2 million to Henry's Young Musician's Fund, to the UCLA Center for the Performing Arts, and to the L.A. County High School for the Arts. John Williams conducted a Hollywood pickup orchestra featuring many of Mancini's familiar sidemen and sidewomen and a few young musicians whom the fund had helped. Quincy Jones spoke about Mancini's support when he had been trying to get jobs as a film composer, then conducted the "*Peter Gunn* Theme." Andy Williams sang "Moon River," and Julie Andrews sang "Two for the Road." Blake Edwards talked about their long relationship. Luciano Pavarotti, with no easy commute all the way from Italy, offered his vigorous and prolonged bear hug and sang, with a Verdi influence, "Happy Birthday to You." "My *grande amico*," he called the guest of honor. At the close, with a hand microphone from the auditorium floor, Mancini spoke a few words of appreciation, seemingly aimed at putting all the guests at ease. He spoke about wanting to see the beginning of the millennium with his grandson and his family and closed with, "Let's get to the year 2000 and we'll worry from there."[9] It was the last time he would face an audience.

At the very end he wrote a few letters, including a collective message to all the union musicians he had employed over the years, telling them to watch their health and saying, "In three months I'll be out of here." He also wrote a note to Army Archerd, the *Daily Variety* columnist who had reported the news of Mancini's illness: "I would like to thank you warmly for the way you handled the story of my recent problem. If I seemed confused in talking with you, please forgive me. I have never gone through anything like this before. You were patient and knew instinctively what had to be done."[10]

On the morning after Mancini's passing, June 14, 1994, the major newspapers ran his picture over headlines such as "Some of America's favorite music" (*New York Times*) and "A river of classics flowed from music man Mancini" (*USA Today*). And yet they devoted a lot more front-page space to stories proving that the world had become a pretty unpleasant place and that perhaps it was a pretty good time to go. Mancini's obituary notice sat there alongside news of the O. J. Simpson murder case; the terrorist bomb blast in the basement parking garage of Manhattan's World Trade Center; the FBI storming of a religious cult compound in Waco, Texas, that killed eighty; and President Clinton's missile attacks against Iraq. For the Mancini family, it seemed that the whole world around them was shaking—not only in the recent deaths of Audrey Hepburn and close friends Helen Hayes and Alexis Smith, but also in the literal sense, as a rare 6.7-magnitude earthquake rocked their Los Angeles neighborhood. Four hundred homes were destroyed and sixty-six people were killed under collapsed freeways and condos. At sea, people were just learning the term El Niño to describe the peculiarly warm Pacific Ocean current that was wreaking havoc on West Coast climates. Blake Edwards began telling people how his mischievous pet cat seemed to look at him now with a strange expression as though channeling Hank.

Perhaps the best tribute comes from Leslie Bricusse, who wrote simply, "At UCLA's Pauley Pavilion, Henry made a quiet but moving speech and took his final bows like the modest man he was. As it says in his most beloved song, he *crossed in style*."[11]

— — —

Back in Gstaad, though, there was another crisis: the still-disassembled, distraught, and heavily invested production team of Broadway-bound *Victor/ Victoria*. What to do without a composer?

It is true that Edwards, Andrews, and Bricusse had a sheath of pre-liminary songs ready to try out for the show, but as anyone in the business knows, there are many steps between ideas for songs and finished stageable music, between conceptualization from an ivory tower in the Swiss Alps and the putting together of a living, talking, dancing, singing stage show that works. Others have chronicled the bumpy, painful process by which this show approached its first performances in Boston, Seattle, and Minneapolis, particularly Philip Weiss in the *New York Times*. Edwards had smoothed the gags on stage into their most comfortable places within the play—some of them lifted from the film; others, like the vaudeville routine of five people sneaking in and out through doorways somehow never aware of one another, newly staged—but he did not yet have a dramatically valid musical comedy. The songs were a problem.

It became clear to Julie Andrews and producer Tony Adams first, then reluctantly to Blake Edwards, that as the show was coming together there were no anchor songs that would send people out of the theater singing, none that would vocalize the climax of the play. "Crazy World" was never meant to be belted by any singer—never meant to bring down the curtain, let alone bring down the house. Its lilting piano introduction and extended reflective melody lines are the features of an intricate movie song. The familiar "Le Jazz Hot" was doing its job as a Broadway bouncer, and a new song, "Paris by Night," was doing its job tying the characters to the setting and to the 1930s milieu, but they did not advance the story line. The star power and charisma of Julie Andrews would bring the people in, but without a cohesive score they would not leave happy.

Daughter Monica has expressed more confidence in her father's unused songs for the musical:

> Obviously if Dad were alive, when any show is mounted and then goes into tryouts and you see what the problems are, you fix them. But Dad just wasn't there to fix them, and certainly he would have been right in there rewriting and doing changes, so it was very difficult when they started dropping pieces of his stuff from the show because they were perceived not to work for one reason or another. Because there were a lot of good numbers that I feel were really strong in the show that were really good "Broadway styled" songs that never were taken into account when critics wrote that Mancini wasn't a stage composer. One song called "This Is Not Going to Change My Life" was supposed to be an opening number and had been kept in right up until the final tryouts, then was dropped. I thought it set up the whole show beautifully. And some ballads, too, that were sacrificed for the flow of the plot. But that was frustrating to see.[12]

It was the sensible, theater-savvy, and sympathetic Leslie Bricusse who knew the terrible truth: they needed to bring in another composer to add the pivotal songs that their show still lacked. Bricusse could conceivably have supplied the music and lyrics himself, having done so for the aforementioned music film *Scrooge* and others. Instead he suggested Frank Wildhorn, a young New York composer with whom he was also currently working on a big new musical version of *Dr. Jekyll and Mr. Hyde*. Wildhorn, with a Broadway musical style somewhere between Jerry Herman and Andrew Lloyd Webber, was brought in to meet Edwards's team, and within days they were working on three songs deemed necessary to plug the holes of *Victor/Victoria*.

Unfortunately, with great integrity and great loyalty to the whole project, Wildhorn took his cue from the ailing songs of Mancini, and that decision led him down the same pale path. The difference was that Wildhorn's songs were more cognizant of the need for simple, sellable melody, and, as a result, they hammer home their elementary hook phrases with a kind of desperation that further loosens the rivets holding the show's credibility together. "Trust Me," the new song through which Toddy explains his plans of passing off Victoria as a female impersonator, begs for a memorable melody but instead falls halfway between the old Hollywood hoofer tune "That's Entertainment" and the background music from some circus tumbler act.

Wildhorn's second-act opener (lyrics are still by Bricusse), "Louie Says," intends to compare the French Revolution era's treatment of over-powdered but powerless women with their emerging roles in the *Victor/Victoria* period. Bricusse and Mancini had already written the finger-snapping tune called "Attitude" for that spot, but while that Fosse-like number had its charm, it was not aggressive enough to open the second act, and its lyric about "living life with flair" was not working. Bricusse's new lyric goes right to the point. But Wildhorn's setting makes it into a worn chorus-line anthem reminiscent of Herman's "It's Today" from his 1960s musical *Mame*. It off-balanced the Edwards show yet a little more.

By this point, with no joyous show-stopping songs beyond "Le Jazz Hot," and with Andrews having to speak-sing a lot of the difficult prosaic lyrics set against wandering melody lines, *Victor/Victoria*'s score was proving to be nearly invisible. The one service for which Edwards and company were most thankful to Wildhorn was his creation of a climactic torch song sung directly to the audience through which Andrews, in her strongest mid-range voice, could sell the evening's message of tolerance and gender equality. It is a rather artificial avowal, since the whole show never aspires to any real depth of insight or dramatic psychology—it was never an "issue play." Nevertheless, when Victoria finally begins to shed her several false fronts and reveal her true identity near the very end, Wildhorn, Bricusse, and Edwards presume to make her speak on behalf of the entire gay community. The song was "Living in the Shadows," and it did at least generate the nightly cheers and stomping feet that Edwards had been seeking. Wildhorn's melody was painfully simple, though—a minor-key pop tune emotionally and texturally modeled on another gay liberation Broadway anthem, Jerry Herman's climax to the show *La Cage aux Folles*, and alarmingly similar, to the point of paraphrase, to Mancini's own "Meggie's Theme" from *The Thorn Birds*.

No matter. They had their capper song to replace the (once again) reflective song that Mancini had planned for that spot, "I Know Where I'm Going," whose lyric (again) was not issue-specific enough but instead spoke in generalities like "being a woman is wonderful / and it's all I want to be" and whose melody sounded like filler chords of some rehearsal pianist. Surely

Mancini at that time, unknowingly unwell, was still writing what he considered template songs to be edited, molded, and recast at the next working sessions. He might never have got it right; he might never have perfected the Broadway style and made it his own (though he did beautifully well in those aborted *Major Barbara* songs), but the fact is we cannot tell regarding *Victor/Victoria*. What we have here is something more than first-draft songs but something less than a presentable score. As the unforgiving *New Yorker* magazine wrote at the time of *Victor/Victoria* on Broadway, "This will be the test: can a Broadway musical make it without a score?"[13]

———

So in Mancini's absence the final tally of *Victor/Victoria*'s music stood at six new Mancini/Bricusse songs, five old songs from the 1982 film, and three new Wildhorn/Bricusse ones. Of the new Mancini material, highlights are those atmospheric seventh and ninth chords in the well-constructed "Paris by Night" and the complicated soliloquy for King Marchand early in act 2 as he experiences doubts about his attraction to Victor/Victoria. By all anecdotal accounts the show proved to be an early smash when it finally opened on Broadway on October 25, 1995, at the Marquis Theater. *Newsday* wrote, "Julie Andrews, 60, who returned to Broadway last night in her first musical in 35 years is absolutely her wonderful self." But then, "The show, which arrives with a fifteen million dollar advance sale and an equally hefty, if negative, advance word, turns out to be a slick familiar good-natured entertainment, full of smart sets and fancy costumes and sexual politics . . . and unfulfilling songs of such cloying banality that we imagine Andrews wincing along with us."[14] The *Hollywood Reporter*'s wandering critic, Robert Osborne, a chronicler like Maltin rather than a true critic, wrote from the road, "As for me, I'd jump at the chance to see 'Victor/Victoria' again and immediately; not only for Andrews, but also to get another look at the sensational 'Le Jazz Hot' number in Act One. It is a show only a Grinch could fail to enjoy."[15]

Grinches who searched their opening-night impressions for some memory of the Mancini/Bricusse songs found little to praise, but that, anyway, was a surface view. Vincent Canby in the *New York Times* called the show "big and patchy." He, too, singled out "Le Jazz Hot" as the show's centerpiece, calling "King's Dilemma" less a song than a rueful talk number and described the first-act closer, "Crazy World," as "gently mournful." His main critique after worshipful praise of Andrews and the "first rate cast" was that "Edwards has found no theatrical equivalent to movie close-ups." In all, he praised the package with many moments "hard to beat." He called the show's message "a rather tepid gesture on behalf of gay liberation" and called Mancini's score "not great" overall.[16] Still, his front-page ruminations were intriguing enough to sustain heavy ticket sales for eight planned months to come.

And yet from an honest distance, audiences were left with the memory of *Victor/Victoria* as an idea that was just a bit too forced—trying to make a screenplay into a three-dimensional stage show; trying to resuscitate past movie characters into embraceable stage presences; trying to make a sheath of prenatal songs carry a still-shifting play. The fits were not tight; the separate parts clanked.

From Mancini's corner, these songs cannot be properly judged in the natural evolution of his music. They were reactive to a project in progress— they speak to the tentative nature of Blake Edwards in an unfamiliar medium, and Mancini never signed off on them. It is wrong to say that he had the wrong kind of talent for stage songs, because he had written good theatrical songs for years, ever since *Darling Lili*. Because of the swiftness with which he passed from health and productivity to mortal illness, these *Victor/Victoria* songs represent nothing so much as drafts. It is tempting to predict better results had he been asked to write songs for some other stage story rather than this been-there gender farce. If it had been a modern chamber story about relationships, would music like that in *The Shadow Box* have come out? If it had been about a young, picaresque Americana hero, would new *Back Roads* ballads have emerged, or would a ghost story on stage have inspired more music like the aborted melodies from *Ghost Dad*? Were there more poignant and elusive tunes in him like "Soldier in the Rain" if the story on stage had inspired them? A more basic point, though, is that no one, save Edwards, would have offered him the chance to do a musical in the 1990s, and with the generosity of that offer, they all did what they could.

It is worth noting here that the other major project interrupted by Mancini's passing, besides his continuing schedule of concert appearances, was the upcoming Tim Burton film *Ed Wood* (1994), starring Johnny Depp as that eccentric true-life helmer of several of the worst films ever made. Back in the 1950s Wood tried desperately, pathetically—and in Burton's version, charmingly—to make some independent films, to join the ranks of Hollywood horror and sci-fi exploitation moviemakers, but had to be content with local sponsors, used equipment, and has-been talents to get anything shot at all. Then in one surprising period he crossed paths with the semi-retired drug-addicted star of the classic *Dracula* (1931), Bela Lugosi, and together they made a few scenes for a future Ed Wood flick. Burton's telling of Wood's life in vintage black-and-white footage captured, more importantly, the tragic character of Lugosi through an Oscar-winning performance by Martin Landau, all surrounded by a compelling 1950s Tinseltown feel. That is the reason Burton initially had wanted Mancini when he thought of trying to reproduce the Universal Studios type of melodramatic scoring of that drive-in monster-movie era. But time ran out for Mancini, and Burton's movie succeeded without him (to a score by Howard Shore).

Daughter Monica recalled, "Yes, Dad was very excited about doing that one. He had gotten a new agent, and he was starting to get a lot of very hip film jobs coming up, but because of his commitment to *Victor/Victoria* he had had to turn down quite a few just to get the thing done. But it had looked as though he would be able to do *Ed Wood*, and Tim Burton had picked him specifically. Then it just wasn't to be."[17]

— — —

The final two projects on Mancini's itinerary during his last days were for charity, and it takes some detective work to discover them, but they are worth a look. The stand-alone song "With Love," with a lyric by Will Jennings, was written (and recorded as a promo tape by Monica) just a couple of months before Mancini's death. He was taking time away from the concentrated tension of the Broadway work to fulfill a promise to his friend Rich Warren, whose Beverly Hills coalition of pediatric AIDS awareness groups was looking for a sort of anthem for the 1990s. The previous decade's AIDS warriors had used the Burt Bacharach song "That's What Friends Are For" from the film *Night Shift* (1982) for a signature theme. Mancini had pledged to write one for the new decade. His connection with the producing agency in this case, the Songs of All Nations program at All Nations Music, was part of his and Ginny's general Democratic Party nod to social reforms with the more specific goal here being "to honor those in the television industry who have made great strides in responsible programming in the area of AIDS awareness and education." Monica sang the song at an Emmy-sponsored gala two years after her father's death, but her original full-voice performance, accompanied by her father in his last trip to a studio, is the version presented on that promo disc and tape.

Without referring to the epidemic of AIDS-related illnesses, the lyric simply charts the stages in everyone's life where love in all of its forms contributes to being able to survive the bad times and appreciate the good. It begins with an uplifting, alternating vamp and then flows through a series of cadences where every phrase starts a hook but none repeats. It is as if the entire song were one continuous bridge on a single strung sentence until it finally lands at the feet of a repeated interval of the fifth offering the title as a kind of exhortation. Any weakness of "With Love" is all bound up in its strengths; there is something less organic about such a long-lined melody made up of hook phrases. And yet there is passion and sincerity in the song, too, which begs to be belted. As Mancini ballads go, it has a rather tense awareness that it is his last, and yet it also has an outreaching spirit that can transfer to any singer—the very kind of crescendo song that *Victor/Victoria* had needed to bring its final Broadway curtain down.

As Monica related, though, by now the effort to record even a single demo tape like this was draining for the composer:

> Dad realized that if he was ever going to fulfill this promise to Rich Warren he had better just get it done. He didn't feel like it, but he didn't want to farm it out to someone else either, so he had Mom book a studio, and the day after his big UCLA birthday tribute we went and did it. But it was hard; we had to help him off the couch to get to the piano, and his playing was just exhausted. Listening to some of the old CDs lately, I have forgotten what a tasty piano player he was, but then to see him sit at this keyboard just sort of plunking out these notes, well, it was really sad. But we got it done and he fulfilled his promise to that particular charity, and everyone was truly happy with the piece.[18]

Ginny Mancini's position on the board of directors of author/therapist Leo Buscaglia's Felice Foundation occasioned Mancini's final film score, *A Memory for Tino*. It was an in-kind charitable contribution on Mancini's part to score this thirty-minute feel-good film aimed at classrooms and at Buscaglia's own seminars around the country. This was the story of a ten-year-old boy who discovers in his mysterious elderly neighbor Mrs. Sunday, formerly known as The Witch, an individual with a welcoming nature, an interesting past, and free cookies. Buscaglia's obviously sentimental message was aimed at families and classrooms of kids, encouraging them to bridge the gap between the geriatric generation and "everyone else" and to realize, à la "With Love," that all differences and barriers are artificial. As in Buscaglia's books and seminars, love is the answer to everything, and everyone has something to give. Here he worked with producer David Kirsch to bring together a small assembly of Hollywood professionals in the film industry for "donation of equipment and technical services" to get his little film made. Director Larry Herbst, a graduate of the University of Southern California film school, was able to script and helm the project, so even its sweet message was offered with an easygoing touch, the performers encouraged to throw off their lines as simply and naturally as possible. Susan Sullivan (*Falcon Crest*) was brought in to appear briefly as Tino's mother, and the rest were drawn from the current day-player casting lists. Mancini contributed a score consisting of twelve cues dedicated to the main premise of the story as described in Buscaglia's own proposal that "the most we can give to anyone and the easiest thing we have to give is our time. A boy and an old woman with nearly nothing in common share their time and it makes a memorable friendship."

Of course, no one knew that time was running short for Mancini, but he had committed two weeks to compose and record the *Tino* score, and he treated it like any other film. In size and urgency it was like a television score to him, and the whole project does come off as a fairly smart, modest after-school special with a minimum of artificial sweetener and low-key performances from the kids—Jon Paul Nicoll as Tino and Scott Hao Nguyen as his skeptical pal, who thinks being friends with an eighty-six-year-old neighbor is creepy.

Mancini's score for *A Memory for Tino* is of no evolutionary importance, but it is interesting to note that its untroubled theme for Tino is based on an introductory phrase (two intervals of a fourth, one step apart) that harkens all the way back to the 1957 theme he wrote for the Chieko character in *Joe Butterfly*, though the harmonies then were pentatonic to coincide with his idea of Japanese tonality and the development of the tune then went along those lines. For Tino, that same phrase passes onto a simple suburban tonic line for a closely matched trio of flute, oboe, and bassoon over the Fender Rhodes sustained chords. To go with the energy of the handheld camera following the boys at play, Tino's theme is first heard as a light jazzy waltz. Mancini then acknowledges, by a darkening and slowing of the waltz, the precipitating event of the story: when the boys' Frisbee flies foul onto the mysterious old lady's porch. A tension motif (bassoon, flute, and guitar patch) denotes the danger Tino perceives. Up close, though, Mrs. Sunday does not seem dangerous or scary. By now Tino's theme has calmed down from the spring waltz to just a pleasant 4/4 homely tune. Its gentle strummed-guitar backing encourages a homegrown quality like the score to *The Thorn Birds*, but the occasional use of vibes (or a vibelike sampler) and soprano sax solos gives it the modern nod that it needs, showing that even though this is just a short film, just for charity, and just about kids, Mancini did not condescend to it. He wrote simply, clearly, quickly, and not deeply but with complete respect for the people who had put their own efforts and money into this project—and for the people who would watch it.

As the film ends, and just before the calm, reassuring reprise of Tino's theme by unison winds, the producers of *A Memory for Tino* have inserted a final silent graphic card on screen that reads, "This film is dedicated to the memory of the composer Henry Mancini, who gave and gave and gave . . ."

So ends Mancini's career as a film composer.

CHAPTER 17

Looking Back, Looking On

In the end, Henry Mancini should be remembered for three contributions to popular culture: first the reinventing, the freshening of film scoring in the 1960s. Before that a formal European symphonic style of music had served generations of movie soundtracks in the 1930s and 1940s until composers like Alex North and Elmer Bernstein brought city jazz and Leonard Rosenman and David Raksin brought atonal and chromatic styles to Hollywood in the 1950s. None of that music seemed quite right for the free-spirited, forward-looking, optimistic baby boomer stories and movie stars that followed. For that young Kennedy-era generation, Mancini offered his own bright and clear sophisticated style—as clean and courteous as mainstream pop, but as cool and knowing as modern jazz. His second contribution was his repackaging of the melodic material from those colorful scores into jazz-pop record albums for home listening (coinciding with the invention of the stereo vinyl disc and high-fidelity recording techniques) that put his memorable tunes and orchestral inventiveness directly into people's lives and gave him, unlike past film composers, fame under his own name. That also had the effect of making people notice for the first time multimedia music (film and TV scoring, even music in advertising) for the big cultural influence it would become. Third was his reintroduction of lyricism into popular music—of carefully composed, personally expressive, harmonically interesting melody writing (only sometimes meant to be sung songs) that had flourished once, then dried up in the 1950s when a cold war reigned between capitalism and communism as between one war-torn generation and their anxious offspring. For that period, rock 'n' roll was seized as an instrument of protest—or rather of release. But 1960s pop wanted more harmony, more melodic movement to speak to the baby boomers' growing sense of conscience, emotionalism, and commitment. The music of the Beatles, Burt Bacharach, Michel Legrand, and Henry Mancini fit in there. Of those influences, Mancini was perhaps the broadest, if also the most traditional, because his own influences reached furthest back.

His melodic writing was unique, though, characterized by a sense of empathy (the egalitarian impulse), optimism, self-effacing humor, yet a shared modern sense of being alone. This particularly appealed to baby boomers who were just starting out on their own, not quite sure their parents did not prefer the triumph of the war years to the doubts of raising a family. Mancini music spoke to all of that. "Lujon" is a perfect statement of it all, as is "Dreamsville," as is "It's Easy to Say."

Leslie Bricusse had this to say about Mancini and his songwriting:

> Very few movie composers are great melody writers, and Hank was prime among them. John Williams, John Barry, and Burt Bacharach share this gift, which is why this quartet has assembled well over a dozen Oscars from some eighty nominations! I could only name Gershwin and Rodgers and Porter as composers whose music was as easily identifiable as Henry's. I think that's the mark of a truly specific and special talent, which causes us to say, "Only Mancini could have done that." I'm thinking of the humor of his jazz patterns and the rhythms underneath them. Just delicious! You smile as they start, like at the opening of the *"Pink Panther* Theme"—it couldn't be anybody else. And then I love when his tunes go into those strange little melancholy side-waters where he sometimes sends them. I love that about "Two for the Road." I think a good thing to do with a Mancini ballad, if you are lucky enough to be writing lyrics for him (or even if you are just listening), is to try and pick a moment in your own life when you've felt a particular feeling that would apply to that theme. It makes it very personal. I've done that more than once.[1]

And Mancini's voice, as a genuinely self-expressive and honest melodist, was matched by—no, surpassed by—his skills as an orchestrator and arranger. Although he used melody structure as self-confession and sometimes those tunes became songs, he was even more a first-rate arranger in the jazz-pop field, a brilliant balancer of brass with winds and of blends within sections. He was a superb harmonizer of strings and a natural architect in turning melodies into satisfying and colorful, often joyous or moving or meaningful, orchestral miniatures.

The previous chapters have explored the lesser-known music of Mancini with special emphasis on the orchestral scores, the song craft, the arranging, and how it all served as personal expression. By 1967 he was beginning to score films with a more narrative orchestral language rather than relying on melody, color, and jazz alone. In the 1970s he experimented with ethnic and atonal compositional voicings, although he never abandoned the importance of melody and indeed was able to incorporate each ethnic dialect into his own personal melodic voice so that it was still Mancini music. Yet he never cut ties with his jazz-pop roots, producing a series of band albums and allowing those traditions to influence the arrangements of his movie theme albums as well.

The steady evolution of Mancini traces a path from the 1970s into the mellow 1980s and to his ultimate maturity—the freedom to score at one moment a dense, impressionistic symphonic score like *Lifeforce*; an astringent, troubled one like *Mommie Dearest*; a chromatic jazz one like *Harry and Son*; then a lavish kiddie concert like *Santa Claus*; a polite piece of Brit wit like *Who Is Killing the Great Chefs* . . . ; and then to write a bluesy career-summary song like "Life in the Looking Glass." No matter that few of those films were hits, that the recording industry lost interest in him, or that his best later songs were done too late to be the crowd favorites they might have become in an earlier era. For that *other* crowd—posterity—and for those who watch the arts outside of trends, Mancini's evolution has been a gratifying procession of work in progress.

It is hard to tell by the sad sequence of trivial films Mancini had to score in the last ten years of his life how far he would have been able to push his evolution as a film scorer. In the end it is safe to say that he had "filled out his card," fulfilled all of his potential. Purists will rightfully place his songwriting legacy a bit outside the pantheon of absolute greats like George Gershwin, Cole Porter, and Harold Arlen. And they will be careful to define his film scoring career somewhat aside from the milieu of screen classicist composers like Bernard Herrmann and Miklos Rozsa, less technically ambitious than Jerry Goldsmith, Alex North, or Hugo Friedhofer. In composition studies, music theory and counterpoint, and in mastery of the literature, contemporaries like Laurence Rosenthal or Sir Richard Rodney Bennett were simply on a different level altogether from Mancini. He could not compete. (But none of them could have written "Dreamsville" either.)

Of his closer colleagues it can be said that he had a wider orchestral and melodic language than John Barry in Britain, more expressive technique than Lalo Schifrin in Hollywood, a parallel but melodically and stylistically richer output than Ennio Morricone. His former employee John Williams copied him early on as a movie comedy scorer and then showed his "sorcerer's apprentice" impatience by enlarging and advancing his symphonic style in the late 1960s through TV scores like *Heidi* and his theatrical breakthrough music to *The Reivers* (1969). Soon he was writing all of those huge, busy "disaster film" scores climaxing with *Jaws* and effectively shrugging off the Mancini legacy with his own massive success, producing music that surpassed his mentor in size, complexity, and visibility. By the 1980s Mancini was envying *him*.

Still, through all those (perhaps unfair) comparisons, Mancini's evolution displays a deepening expressivity—both in how he approached the small film jobs he got and in his melodic growth. His early success took hold with people, not just because he was reinventing the film-score genre into pop styles but also because his themes and settings were so directly personal, so honest. It was as though he were speaking to you, picking up on a conversation you had been sharing all along. "Moon River" was our sense of ongoing yearning, "Charade" our rolling background of worry. And those songs without words were just as expressive. "My Friend Andamo" just sounds like everyone's feelings about camaraderie. "The Sound of Silver" sounds like some simple familiar truth that we all know, that we can sleep on—so do "Nothing to Lose," "The Soft Touch," and "Blue Satin." Themes like "Natalie," "Mommie Dearest," "Hatari!" and "Sunflower" begin to admit that all might not be well, while "Two for the Road" and "Lujon" reassure us that things do not *need* to be resolved before we can proceed, that our strength comes from self-understanding. "It's Easy to Say" re-argues the losses, yearnings, and scares of life and reassures with a new modest confidence what the composer has learned over time: that we are all in this together and that each makes his or her own peace with it. The chromatic jazzy tunes of the 1980s, from *Harry and Son* or *The Man Who Loved Women*, show Mancini's willingness to step a bit further away from the baby boomer comfort zone to explore the unknowns and contradictions of late life. The bleak opening music of *The Glass Menagerie* and the brief discreet entrances of each music cue therein, like *The Shadow Box*, prove that Mancini was certainly aware of despair. The waltz from *Fear*, ominous and possibly sinister, still empathetic, is the "truth-speaking" waltz of the New Millennium life. But those scores—like *Lifeforce* in its original form, with its own forlorn undercurrent—only make his reassuring melodies, his humor, and his wistfully lovely background tunes, which most people have never even noticed, all the more poignant. (Has anyone ever noticed the gentle sympathy of the little piece called "Theme for Losers" in *Me, Natalie*, in which Jimmy Rowles barely touches the piano keys to offer the melody, then muted strings enter with the deepest humility on the second phrase? It is a totally unimportant track and yet so moving. "Cheryl's Theme" is another.) To such an evolutionary succession as that, the late song from *That's Life!* is just a final toast.

That kind of directly personal expressivity in Mancini's best work is what makes him finally worth appreciation and what makes his evolution interesting. Whether in the obvious pleasure he took with skillful arrangements or in the most intimate chord changes of a simple melody, in knowing when to restate a melody to capture an important moment at the end of a film or when to grin, Mancini was a personal writer. He was not only important to the baby boomers who were looking for emotional connections but also valuable to subsequent generations for all the same reasons: as a rare rampart of lyricism and good humor, optimism, ingenuous sexiness, and a wistful reminder that we are all in this Dreamsville together.

Maybe for all of those qualities, Mancini's music will, in its own cool way (as sheet music for any performer to discover, in his own recordings, or as back-scoring for old films and television), keep reaching out, find the next generation, and the next and the next. Here is something fresh, they will think, and it will turn their heads.

Appendix

Scores for Motion Pictures

As described in this text, Mancini worked on many motion picture scores at Universal Studios between 1952 and 1958 as a staff composer. These were most often partial scores to which he contributed only a limited number of music cues in collaboration with other staff composers. These "patchwork scores" were then credited on screen under the name of the music department head: "Music Supervision by Joseph Gershenson." These included Mancini's first arranging duties for films like *Meet Danny Wilson*, his first narrative scoring duties (*Lost in Alaska*), his first movie songs for films like *Six Bridges to Cross* and *Foxfire*, his first movie musicals (*Rock Pretty Baby*), and his first Academy Award nomination for music arranging/scoring (*The Glenn Miller Story*). The list of his film titles while at Universal, including short films and some films that merely tracked in music cues he had already written for previous titles, amount to more than 160 and are enumerated in other archives. Below is a listing of film scores for which Mancini was the main credited composer. (Television scores are listed in the next section.)

1957	*Man Afraid*
	Rock Pretty Baby
	Damn Citizen
	Summer Love
1958	*Touch of Evil*
	Voice in the Mirror

1960	*High Time*
	The Great Impostor
1961	*Breakfast at Tiffany's*
	Bachelor in Paradise
	Hatari!
1962	*Experiment in Terror*
	Mr. Hobbs Takes a Vacation
	Days of Wine and Roses
1963	*Man's Favorite Sport*
	Soldier in the Rain
	Charade
1964	*The Pink Panther*
	A Shot in the Dark
	Dear Heart
1965	*The Great Race*
1966	*Moment to Moment*
	What Did You Do in the War, Daddy?
	Arabesque
1967	*Two for the Road*
	Gunn
	Wait Until Dark
1968	*The Party*
1969	*Me, Natalie*
	Gaily, Gaily (aka *Chicago, Chicago*)
1970	*Darling Lili*
	The Molly Maguires
	The Hawaiians (aka *Master of the Islands*)
	I Girasoli (aka *Sunflower*)
1971	*The Night Visitor* (aka *Salem Come to Supper*)
	Sometimes a Great Notion (aka *Never Give an Inch*)
1972	*The Thief Who Came to Dinner*
1973	*Oklahoma Crude*
	Visions of Eight
1974	*The White Dawn*
	99 & 44/100% Dead
	The Girl from Petrovka
1975	*The Great Waldo Pepper*
	Return of the Pink Panther
	Once Is Not Enough
1976	*W. C. Fields and Me*
	The Pink Panther Strikes Again
	Angela (not released until 1984)

1977	*Alex and the Gypsy*
	Silver Streak
1978	*House Calls*
	Revenge of the Pink Panther
	Who Is Killing the Great Chefs of Europe?
1979	*The Prisoner of Zenda*
	Nightwing
	10
1980	*Little Miss Marker*
	A Change of Seasons
1981	*Back Roads*
	S.O.B.
	Condorman
	Mommie Dearest
1982	*Victor/Victoria*
	Trail of the Pink Panther
1983	*Second Thoughts*
	Curse of the Pink Panther
	Better Late Than Never (aka *Whose Little Girl Are You?*)
	The Man Who Loved Women
1984	*Harry & Son*
1985	*Lifeforce*
	Santa Claus: The Movie
1986	*The Great Mouse Detective* (aka *The Adventures of the Great Mouse Detective*)
	A Fine Mess
	That's Life!
1987	*The Glass Menagerie*
1988	*Sunset*
	Without a Clue
1989	*Physical Evidence*
	Welcome Home
1990	*Ghost Dad*
	Fear
1991	*Switch*
	Married to It
1992	*Tom and Jerry*
1993	*Son of the Pink Panther*

Scores for Television

1958–61	*Peter Gunn* (theme and scores)
1959–60	*Mr. Lucky* (theme and scores)
1962	*Man of the World* (TV series theme)
1963–64	*The Richard Boone Show* (TV anthology series theme)
1964	"Carol for Another Christmas" (theme and score)
1971–77	*NBC Mystery Movie* (TV anthology series theme)
1971–73	*The Curiosity Shop* (TV series theme)
1971–72	*Cade's County* (TV series theme)
1971	"Festival at Ford's Theater" (TV arts special theme)
1972	*The Mancini Generation* (theme, charts, host)
1975	*The Blue Knight* (TV movie score)
1975–76	*The Invisible Man* (TV series theme)
1976	"NBC News Election Coverage" (theme)
1976	*The Moneychangers* (TV miniseries score)
1976–79	*What's Happening!* (TV series theme)
1977	*Kingston Confidential* (TV series theme)
1977	*Sanford Arms* (TV series theme)
1977–78	*NBC Nightly News* (theme)
1978	*A Family Upside Down* (TV movie score)
1979	*The Best Place to Be* (TV movie score)
1979	*Co-Ed Fever* (TV series theme)
1980	*The Shadow Box* (TV movie score)
1982–90	*Newhart* (TV series theme)
1982–87	*Remington Steele* (TV series themes)
1982–86	*Ripley's Believe It or Not* (TV series theme)
1983	*The Thorn Birds* (TV miniseries score)
1983–88	*Hotel* (TV series theme)
1987	*If It's Tuesday This Must Be Belgium* (TV movie score)
1988	*Justin Case* (TV movie score)
1988	*Late Night with David Letterman* ("Viewer Mail" theme)
1989	"Mother, Mother" (TV/charity seminar score)
1989	*Peter Gunn* (TV movie score)
1990	*The New Tic-Tac-Dough* (TV series theme)
1991	*Never Forget* (TV movie score)
1994	*A Memory for Tino* (TV/charity seminar short film score)

Record Albums

(Not including posthumous releases, such as limited pressings of *Wait Until Dark*, *The Hawaiians*, etc.; repackaging of previous material; or foreign pressings duplicating domestic releases)

FILM SCORES

(whether released as soundtracks or as rearranged "Music from . . ." discs)

Touch of Evil (6/58)
Music from Peter Gunn (1/59)
More Music from Peter Gunn (6/59)
Music from Mr. Lucky (2/60)
Music from High Time (10/60)
Music from Breakfast at Tiffany's (9/61)
Music from Experiment in Terror (4/62)
Music from Hatari! (6/62)
Music from Charade (11/63)
Music from The Pink Panther (4/64)
Music from The Great Race (9/65)
Music from Arabesque (7/66)
Music from What Did You Do in the War, Daddy? (8/66)
Music from Two for the Road (5/67)
Music from Gunn (7/67)
Music from The Party (4/68)
Me, Natalie (9/69)
Gaily, Gaily (11/69)
The Molly Maguires (3/70)
Sunflower (I Girasoli) (7/70)
Music from The Hawaiians (7/70)
Sometimes a Great Notion (12/71)
The Night Visitor (Salem Come to Supper) (1/71; released 7/77)
The Thief Who Came to Dinner (4/73)
Oklahoma Crude (7/73)
Visions of Eight (7/73)
Music from The Great Waldo Pepper (4/75)
Music from Return of the Pink Panther (5/75)
W. C. Fields and Me (5/76)
Music from The Pink Panther Strikes Again (11/76)
Music from Revenge of the Pink Panther (8/78)
Who Is Killing the Great Chefs of Europe? (11/78)
Music from 10 (10/79)
Music from Trail of the Pink Panther (11/82)

Lifeforce (7/85)
Music from Santa Claus: The Movie (11/85)
The Great Mouse Detective (1/86 released in 3/92)
The Glass Menagerie (10/87)
Switch (4/91)
Tom and Jerry (2/93)
Music from Son of the Pink Panther (4/94)

ORCHESTRAL FILM THEMES ALBUMS
Our Man in Hollywood (9/62)
The Second Time Around (1/66—budget label)
Mancini Plays Mancini (11/67—budget label)
Theme from Z and Other Film Themes (4/70)
Mancini Plays the Theme from Love Story (12/70)
Big Screen Little Screen (1/72)
Hangin' Out (9/74)
Cop Show Themes (9/76)
Mancini's Angels (4/77)
The Theme Scene (4/78)
Premiere Pops (7/88)
Mostly Monsters, Murders, and Mysteries (9/90)

ORCHESTRAL POPS ALBUMS
Driftwood and Dreams (9/57)
The Mancini Touch (1/60)
Mr. Lucky Goes Latin (3/61)
The Latin Sound of Henry Mancini (6/65)
Music of Hawaii (11/66)
A Warm Shade of Ivory (3/69)
Six Hours Past Sunset (10/69)
Mancini Country (11/70)
Country Gentleman (1/74)
Symphonic Soul (9/75)
As Time Goes By (4/92)

BIG BAND JAZZ-POP ALBUMS
The Blues and the Beat (8/60)
Combo! (3/61)
Uniquely Mancini (6/63)
Mancini '67 (2/67)
The Big Latin Band (8/68)
The Mancini Generation (9/72)

POP CHORAL ALBUMS

Dear Heart and Other Songs about Love (1/65)

The Academy Award Songs (2/66)

A Merry Mancini Christmas (9/66)

MUSICALS

Rock Pretty Baby (6/56)

Summer Love (5/58)

Darling Lili (7/70)

Just You and Me Together Love (10/77)

Victor/Victoria (4/82)

CONCERT SUITES/MEDLEYS

Sousa in Stereo (10/58)

March Step in Stereo (9/59)

The Concert Sound of Henry Mancini (7/64)

Encore! (11/67)

Debut! The Philadelphia Pops (9/69)

Mancini Concert (7/71)

A Concert of Film Music: The London Symphony Orchestra (4/76)

Mancini Rocks the Pops (10/89)

Cinema Italiano: Music of Morricone & Rota (4/91)

Top Hat: Music for Astaire (9/92)

ALBUM ARRANGEMENTS FOR OTHER PERFORMERS

Edie Adams Sings (3/59)

Dreamsville (Edie Adams, vocals) (6/59)

Artie Kane Plays Organ! (1/72)

Brass on Ivory (Doc Severinson, trumpet) (4/72)

Swinging Screen Scene (Artie Kane, keyboards) (10/72)

Brass, Ivory, and Strings (Doc Severinson, trumpet) (3/73)

Mama (Luciano Pavarotti vocals) (6/84)

The Hollywood Musicals (Johnny Mathis, vocals) (10/86)

Volare (Luciano Pavarotti, vocals) (10/87)

Notes

Chapter 1. Allegheny River Launch

1. Henry Mancini and Gene Lees, *Did They Mention the Music?* (Chicago: Contemporary Books, 1989), 10.
2. Ibid., 4.
3. Ibid., 17.
4. Ibid., 21.
5. Ibid., 25.
6. Ibid., 28.
7. George T. Simon, *The Big Bands* (New York: Macmillan, 1967), 364.
8. Mancini and Lees, *Did They Mention the Music?* 33.
9. Ibid., 34.
10. Ibid., 35.

Chapter 2. Not Quite Jazz

1. Mancini and Lees, *Did They Mention the Music?* 46.
2. Ibid., 48.
3. Ibid., 58.
4. Interview with Henry Mancini, April 8, 1992.
5. Mancini and Lees, *Did They Mention the Music?* 60.

Chapter 3. The Music Factory

1. Interview with Henry Mancini, August 18, 1976.
2. Ibid.

3. Ibid.

4. Ibid.

Chapter 4. Big Screen, Little Screen

1. Mancini and Lees, *Did They Mention the Music?* 92.

2. Ibid., 95.

3. Interview with Henry Mancini, April 1, 1992.

4. Morgan Ames, online correspondence with author, October 20, 2010.

5. Henry Mancini, *Sounds and Scores: A Practical Guide to Professional Orchestration* (Northridge, Calif.: Northridge Music, 1962), 2.

6. Ibid., 145–48.

7. Ibid., 25.

8. Ibid., 61.

9. Ibid., 106.

10. Ibid., 110.

11. Interview with Ginny Mancini, February 21, 1995.

12. Interview with Henry Mancini, April 21, 1992.

13. Irwin Bazelon, *Knowing the Score: Notes on Film Music* (New York: Van Nostrand Reinhold, 1975), 126.

Chapter 5. Blake Edwards and the High Times

1. Interview with Henry Mancini, April 21, 1992.

2. Ibid., October 15, 1976, and April 8, 1992.

3. Ibid., May 5, 1992.

4. Ibid., April 21, 1992, and August 18, 1976.

5. Ibid., October 15, 1976.

6. Ibid.

7. Ibid., August 18, 1976.

Chapter 6. Career Crescendos

1. Richard M. Sudhalter, *Stardust Melody* (New York: Oxford University Press, 2002), 313–14.

2. Todd McCarthy, *Howard Hawks* (New York: Grove Press, 1997), 589–90.

3. Mancini and Lees, *Did They Mention the Music?* 108.

4. Interview with Monica Mancini, December 2, 1995.

5. Interview with Stanley Donen, April 2, 1999.

6. Mervyn Cooke, *A History of Film Music* (Cambridge, UK: Cambridge University Press, 2008), 224.

7. Interview with Henry Mancini, April 21, 1992.

Chapter 7. First Cadence

1. Mancini and Lees, *Did They Mention the Music?* 133.
2. Ibid., 131.
3. Ibid.
4. Interview with Henry Mancini, April 8, 1992.
5. Mancini and Lees, *Did They Mention the Music?* 132.
6. Ibid., 126.
7. Interview with Henry Mancini, August 18, 1976.
8. Ibid., October 15, 1976.
9. Ibid., April 3, 1992.
10. Interview with Leslie Bricusse, January 16, 1995.
11. Bazelon, *Knowing the Score*, 154.
12. Interview with Henry Mancini, August 18, 1976.

Chapter 8. The Break with Blake

1. Interview with Henry Mancini, May 5, 1992.
2. Interview with Ginny Mancini, February 21, 1995.
3. Mancini and Lees, *Did They Mention the Music?* 168–69.

Chapter 9. Off to See the World

1. Charles Thomas Samuels, *Encountering Directors* (New York: G. P. Putnam's Sons, 1972), 158–59.
2. Mancini and Lees, *Did They Mention the Music?* 160.
3. Interview with Henry Mancini, October 15, 1976.
4. Charlton Heston, *The Actor's Life* (New York: Simon and Schuster, 1979), 308.
5. Interview with Henry Mancini, May 5, 1992.
6. Ibid., April 3, 1992.
7. Ibid.
8. Ibid.
9. Ibid., April 21, 1992.
10. Ibid.
11. François Truffaut, *Hitchcock*, rev. ed. (New York: Simon and Schuster, 1983), 338–39.

Chapter 10. Back to Television?

1. Interview with Henry Mancini, May 5, 1992.
2. Interview with Monica Mancini, December 2, 1995.
3. Mancini and Lees, *Did They Mention the Music?* 201.
4. Ibid.

Chapter 11. The Curse of the Pink Panther

1. Mancini and Lees, *Did They Mention the Music?* 168–69.
2. Interview with Henry Mancini, August 18, 1976.
3. Interview with Leslie Bricusse, January 16, 1995.

Chapter 12. Maturity, the Second Cadence

1. James Liska, Theater Review, *Los Angeles Daily News*, January 16, 1981.
2. Leonard Feather, *Los Angeles Times*, January 16, 1981.
3. Kirk, Legit Theater Review, *Daily Variety*, January 16, 1981.
4. Interview with Henry Mancini, October 15, 1976.

Chapter 13. Frustration

1. Interview with Henry Mancini, April 3, 1992.
2. Interview with Leslie Bricusse, January 16, 1995.
3. Mancini and Lees, *Did They Mention the Music?* 207.
4. Ibid., 202–3.
5. Ibid., 207.

Chapter 14. Stolen Moments

1. Interview with Henry Mancini, April 21, 1992.
2. Paul Newman writing on the disc liner of the film soundtrack to *The Glass Menagerie.*

Chapter 15. A Closing Door That Wasn't There Before

1. Interview with Henry Mancini, May 5, 1992.
2. Interview with Ginny Mancini, February 21, 1995.
3. Interview with Monica Mancini, December 2, 1995.
4. Interview with Henry Mancini, May 5, 1992.
5. Sam Wasson, *A Splurch in the Kisser: The Movies of Blake Edwards* (Middletown, Conn.: Wesleyan University Press, 2009), 298.

Chapter 16. Almost to Broadway

1. Philip Weiss, "Return of the Punk Panther," *New York Times*, October 1, 1995.
2. Interview with Leslie Bricusse, January 16, 1995.
3. Ibid.
4. "A Family's Love," ABC-TV, *20/20* broadcast, May 27, 1994.
5. Ibid.
6. Ibid.
7. Ibid.
8. Ibid.

9. Betty Goodwin, "Music Man: 4,000 Admirers Turn Out to Mark Henry Mancini's 70th Birthday," *LA Times*, April 21, 1994.

10. Army Archerd, "Mancini's Music Will Live On," *Daily Variety*, June 14, 1994.

11. Henry Mancini and Leslie Bricusse, *The Henry Mancini and Leslie Bricusse Songbook*, edited by Milton Okun (Port Chester, N.Y.: Cherry Lane Music Co., 1996), 8.

12. Interview with Monica Mancini, December 2, 1995.

13. "Theater: Now Playing," blurb review, *New Yorker*, June 1995.

14. Linda Winer, "A Starlit Recycled Gender Bender," *Newsday*, October 26, 1995.

15. Robert Osborne, "Rambling Reporter," Theater Review, *Hollywood Reporter*, November 1, 1995.

16. Vincent Canby, "Julie Andrews Is Back in Drag," *New York Times*, October 26, 1995.

17. Interview with Monica Mancini, December 2, 1995.

18. Ibid.

Chapter 17. Looking Back, Looking On

1. Interview with Leslie Bricusse, January 16, 1995.

Bibliography

Books

Bazelon, Irwin. *Knowing the Score: Notes on Film Music.* New York: Van Nostrand Reinhold, 1975.

Brady, Frank. *Citizen Welles.* New York: Anchor/Doubleday, 1989.

Brown, Royal S. *Overtones and Undertones: Reading Film Music.* Berkeley: University of California Press, 1994.

Burlingame, Jon. *TV's Biggest Hits.* New York: Schirmer Books, 1996.

———. *Sound and Vision: 60 Years of Motion Picture Soundtracks.* New York: Billboard Books, 2000.

Cooke, Mervyn. *A History of Film Music.* Cambridge, UK: Cambridge University Press, 2008.

———. *The Hollywood Film Music Reader.* Oxford: University of Oxford Press, 2010.

Darby, William, and Jack Du Bois. *American Film Music.* Jefferson, N.C.: McFarland, 1990.

Heston, Charlton. *The Actor's Life.* New York: Simon and Schuster, 1979.

Hubbert, Julie. *Celluloid Symphonies: Texts and Contexts in Film Music History.* Berkeley: University of California Press, 2011.

Karlin, Fred, and Rayburn Wright. *On the Track: A Guide to Contemporary Film Scoring.* New York: Schirmer Books, 1990.

Lebrecht, Norman. *The Companion to 20th Century Music.* New York: Simon and Schuster, 1992.

Mancini, Henry. *Sounds and Scores: A Practical Guide to Orchestration.* Northridge, Calif.: Northridge Music, 1962.

Mancini, Henry, and Gene Lees. *Did They Mention the Music?* Chicago: Contemporary Books, 1989.

Mancini, Henry, and Leslie Bricusse. *The Henry Mancini and Leslie Bricusse Songbook.* Ed. Milton Okun. Port Chester, N.Y.: Cherry Lane Music Co., 1996.

McCarthy, Todd. *Howard Hawks.* New York: Grove Press, 1997.

Palmer, Christopher. *The Composer in Hollywood.* London: Marion Boyars, 1990.

Samuels, Charles Thomas. *Encountering Directors.* New York: G. P. Putnam's Sons, 1972.

Simon, George T. *The Big Bands.* New York: Macmillan, 1967.

Sudhalter, Richard M. *Stardust Melody.* New York: Oxford University Press, 2002.

Thomas, Tony. *Music for the Movies.* New York: A. S. Barnes, 1973.

————. *Film Score: The Art and Craft of Movie Music.* Burbank, Calif.: Riverwood Press, 1991.

Truffaut, Francois. *Hitchcock*, rev. ed. New York: Simon and Schuster, 1983.

Wasson, Sam. *A Splurch in the Kisser: The Movies of Blake Edwards.* Middletown, Conn.: Wesleyan University Press, 2009.

Author-Conducted Telephone Interviews

Henry Mancini: August 18, 1976; October 15, 1976; April 1, 3, 8, 21, 1992; May 5, 1992.
Ginny Mancini: February 21, 1995.
Monica Mancini: December 2, 1995.
Leslie Bricusse: January 16, 1995.
Stanley Donen: April 2, 1999.
John Williams: January, 15, 1976.
Elmer Bernstein: January 18, 1979.
Morgan Ames: October 20, 2010 (online).

Disc Recording Liner Notes

Quincy Jones writing on the disc liner of the film soundtrack to *The Pawnbroker* (Mercury Records, SR61011), 1964.

Henry Mancini writing on the disc liner of his music to accompany the poetry of John Laws, *Just You and Me Together Love* (RCA-AFL-12362), 1977.

Paul Newman writing on the disc liner of the film soundtrack to *The Glass Menagerie* (MCA Records, MCA-6222).

Luciano Pavarotti writing on the disc liner of his vocal album *Mama* (London Records 4119591), 1984.

Periodicals

Archerd, Army. "Mancini's Music Will Live On." *Daily Variety*, June 14, 1994.
Burlingame, Jon. "The Music Man." *Los Angeles Times*, April 12, 2004.
Canby, Vincent. "Julie Andrews Is Back in Drag." *New York Times*, October 26, 1995.
Feather, Leonard. *Los Angeles Times*, January 16, 1981.

Goodwin, Betty. "Music Man: 4,000 Admirers Turn Out to Mark Henry Mancini's 70th Birthday." *LA Times*, April 21, 1994.

Kirk. Legit Theater Review. *Daily Variety*, January 16, 1981.

Liska, James, Theater Review. *Los Angeles Daily News*, January 16, 1981.

New Yorker. "Theater: Now Playing" (blurb review), June 1995.

Osborne, Robert. "Rambling Reporter." Theater Review. *Hollywood Reporter*, November 1, 1995.

Powers, James. "Dialogue on Film: Henry Mancini." *American Film Institute Journal* 3, no. 3. (January 1974).

Sarris, Andrew. "Bitter Essence of Blake Edwards." *Village Voice*, May 5, 1987, 59, 99.

Sandler, Adam. "MCA Tunes in Mancini." *Daily Variety*, May 12, 1998.

Simons, Tad. "Victor/Victoria." Legit Theater Review. *Daily Variety*, June 14, 1995.

Weiss, Philip. "Return of the Punk Panther." *New York Times*, October 1, 1995.

Winer, Linda. "A Starlit Recycled Gender Bender." *Newsday*, October 26, 1995.

Index

Music in American Life

America's Music: From the Pilgrims to the Present (rev. 3d ed.)   *Gilbert Chase*

Secular Music in Colonial Annapolis: The Tuesday Club, 1745–56
   John Barry Talley

Bibliographical Handbook of American Music   *D. W. Krummel*

Goin' to Kansas City   *Nathan W. Pearson Jr.*

"Susanna," "Jeanie," and "The Old Folks at Home": The Songs of
   Stephen C. Foster from His Time to Ours (2d ed.)   *William W. Austin*

Songprints: The Musical Experience of Five Shoshone Women   *Judith Vander*

"Happy in the Service of the Lord": Afro-American Gospel Quartets
   in Memphis   *Kip Lornell*

Paul Hindemith in the United States   *Luther Noss*

"My Song Is My Weapon": People's Songs, American Communism,
   and the Politics of Culture, 1930–50   *Robbie Lieberman*

Chosen Voices: The Story of the American Cantorate   *Mark Slobin*

Theodore Thomas: America's Conductor and Builder of Orchestras,
   1835–1905   *Ezra Schabas*

"The Whorehouse Bells Were Ringing" and Other Songs Cowboys Sing
   Collected and edited by Guy Logsdon

Crazeology: The Autobiography of a Chicago Jazzman   *Bud Freeman,
   as told to Robert Wolf*

Discoursing Sweet Music: Brass Bands and Community Life in
   Turn-of-the-Century Pennsylvania   *Kenneth Kreitner*

Mormonism and Music: A History   *Michael Hicks*

Voices of the Jazz Age: Profiles of Eight Vintage Jazzmen   *Chip Deffaa*

Pickin' on Peachtree: A History of Country Music in Atlanta, Georgia
   Wayne W. Daniel

Bitter Music: Collected Journals, Essays, Introductions, and Librettos
   Harry Partch; edited by Thomas McGeary

Ethnic Music on Records: A Discography of Ethnic Recordings Produced
   in the United States, 1893 to 1942   *Richard K. Spottswood*

Downhome Blues Lyrics: An Anthology from the Post–World War II Era
   Jeff Todd Titon

Ellington: The Early Years   *Mark Tucker*

Chicago Soul   *Robert Pruter*

That Half-Barbaric Twang: The Banjo in American Popular Culture
   Karen Linn

Hot Man: The Life of Art Hodes   *Art Hodes and Chadwick Hansen*

The Erotic Muse: American Bawdy Songs (2d ed.)   *Ed Cray*

Barrio Rhythm: Mexican American Music in Los Angeles   *Steven Loza*

The Creation of Jazz: Music, Race, and Culture in Urban America
   Burton W. Peretti

Charles Martin Loeffler: A Life Apart in Music   *Ellen Knight*

Tito Puente and the Making of Latin Music   *Steven Loza*

Juilliard: A History   *Andrea Olmstead*

Understanding Charles Seeger, Pioneer in American Musicology
    Edited by Bell Yung and Helen Rees

Mountains of Music: West Virginia Traditional Music from *Goldenseal*
    Edited by John Lilly

Alice Tully: An Intimate Portrait   *Albert Fuller*

A Blues Life   *Henry Townsend, as told to Bill Greensmith*

Long Steel Rail: The Railroad in American Folksong (2d ed.)   *Norm Cohen*

The Golden Age of Gospel   *Text by Horace Clarence Boyer;*
    photography by Lloyd Yearwood

Aaron Copland: The Life and Work of an Uncommon Man   *Howard Pollack*

Louis Moreau Gottschalk   *S. Frederick Starr*

Race, Rock, and Elvis   *Michael T. Bertrand*

Theremin: Ether Music and Espionage   *Albert Glinsky*

Poetry and Violence: The Ballad Tradition of Mexico's Costa Chica
    John H. McDowell

The Bill Monroe Reader   *Edited by Tom Ewing*

Music in Lubavitcher Life   *Ellen Koskoff*

Zarzuela: Spanish Operetta, American Stage   *Janet L. Sturman*

Bluegrass Odyssey: A Documentary in Pictures and Words, 1966–86
    Carl Fleischhauer and Neil V. Rosenberg

That Old-Time Rock & Roll: A Chronicle of an Era, 1954–63   *Richard Aquila*

Labor's Troubadour   *Joe Glazer*

American Opera   *Elise K. Kirk*

Don't Get above Your Raisin': Country Music and the Southern
    Working Class   *Bill C. Malone*

John Alden Carpenter: A Chicago Composer   *Howard Pollack*

Heartbeat of the People: Music and Dance of the Northern Pow-wow
    Tara Browner

My Lord, What a Morning: An Autobiography   *Marian Anderson*

Marian Anderson: A Singer's Journey   *Allan Keiler*

Charles Ives Remembered: An Oral History   *Vivian Perlis*

Henry Cowell, Bohemian   *Michael Hicks*

Rap Music and Street Consciousness   *Cheryl L. Keyes*

Louis Prima   *Garry Boulard*

Marian McPartland's Jazz World: All in Good Time   *Marian McPartland*

Robert Johnson: Lost and Found   *Barry Lee Pearson and Bill McCulloch*

Bound for America: Three British Composers   *Nicholas Temperley*

Lost Sounds: Blacks and the Birth of the Recording Industry, 1890–1919
    Tim Brooks

Burn, Baby! BURN! The Autobiography of Magnificent Montague
    Magnificent Montague with Bob Baker
Way Up North in Dixie: A Black Family's Claim to the Confederate Anthem
    Howard L. Sacks and Judith Rose Sacks
The Bluegrass Reader   *Edited by Thomas Goldsmith*
Colin McPhee: Composer in Two Worlds   *Carol J. Oja*
Robert Johnson, Mythmaking, and Contemporary American Culture
    Patricia R. Schroeder
Composing a World: Lou Harrison, Musical Wayfarer   *Leta E. Miller*
    and Fredric Lieberman
Fritz Reiner, Maestro and Martinet   *Kenneth Morgan*
That Toddlin' Town: Chicago's White Dance Bands and Orchestras,
    1900–1950   *Charles A. Sengstock Jr.*
Dewey and Elvis: The Life and Times of a Rock 'n' Roll Deejay   *Louis Cantor*
Come Hither to Go Yonder: Playing Bluegrass with Bill Monroe   *Bob Black*
Chicago Blues: Portraits and Stories   *David Whiteis*
The Incredible Band of John Philip Sousa   *Paul E. Bierley*
"Maximum Clarity" and Other Writings on Music   *Ben Johnston;*
    edited by Bob Gilmore
Staging Tradition: John Lair and Sarah Gertrude Knott   *Michael Ann Williams*
Homegrown Music: Discovering Bluegrass   *Stephanie P. Ledgin*
Tales of a Theatrical Guru   *Danny Newman*
The Music of Bill Monroe   *Neil V. Rosenberg and Charles K. Wolfe*
Pressing On: The Roni Stoneman Story   *Roni Stoneman, as told to Ellen Wright*
Together Let Us Sweetly Live   *Jonathan C. David, with photographs by*
    Richard Holloway
Live Fast, Love Hard: The Faron Young Story   *Diane Diekman*
Air Castle of the South: WSM Radio and the Making of Music City
    Craig P. Havighurst
Traveling Home: Sacred Harp Singing and American Pluralism   *Kiri Miller*
Where Did Our Love Go? The Rise and Fall of the Motown Sound
    Nelson George
Lonesome Cowgirls and Honky-Tonk Angels: The Women of Barn Dance
    Radio   *Kristine M. McCusker*
California Polyphony: Ethnic Voices, Musical Crossroads   *Mina Yang*
The Never-Ending Revival: Rounder Records and the Folk Alliance
    Michael F. Scully
Sing It Pretty: A Memoir   *Bess Lomax Hawes*
Working Girl Blues: The Life and Music of Hazel Dickens   *Hazel Dickens*
    and Bill C. Malone
Charles Ives Reconsidered   *Gayle Sherwood Magee*

John Caps is an award-winning writer and producer of documentaries. He served as producer, writer, and host for four seasons of the National Public Radio syndicated series *The Cinema Soundtrack*, featuring interviews with and music of film composers. He lives in Baltimore, Maryland.

The University of Illinois Press
is a founding member of the
Association of American University Presses.

_____

Designed by Jim Proefrock
Composed in 10.5/14 Bell
with Trade Gothic and Desigers display
at the University of Illinois Press
Manufactured by Thomson-Shore, Inc.

University of Illinois Press
1325 South Oak Street
Champaign, IL 61820-6903
www.press.uillinois.edu